INSIDE THE
MIND
OF THE GRAND PRIX DRIVER

Second edition

Other books by this author:

Memories of Ayrton

Juan Pablo Montoya

Michael Schumacher
The greatest of all?

Ayrton Senna
As time goes by

Murray Walker
The last word

Murray Walker
The very last word

The Motorsport Art of Juan Carlos Ferrigno

Hitler's Grand Prix in England
Donington 1937 and 1938

INSIDE THE MIND

OF THE GRAND PRIX DRIVER

The psychology of the fastest men on earth: sex, danger and everything else

CHRISTOPHER HILTON

With expert commentary from

John Stevens (professional motor racing coach)
Bernie Shrosbree (manager, Benetton Human Performance Centre)
Andrew Walton (sports psychologist)

Haynes Publishing

First edition (hardback) published in October 2001
Second edition (paperback) published, with additional text, in October 2003

A catalogue record for this book is available from the British Library

ISBN 1 84425 017 2

Library of Congress control no 2003110424

Haynes North America Inc., 861 Lawrence Drive, Newbury Park, California 91320, USA.

Published by Haynes Publishing, Sparkford, Yeovil, Somerset BA22 7JJ, UK.
Tel: 01963 442030 Fax: 01963 440001
Int.tel: +44 1963 442030 Int.fax: +44 1963 440001
E-mail: sales@haynes.co.uk
Website: www.haynes.co.uk

Designed and typeset by Glad Stockdale
Printed and bound in Britain by J. H. Haynes & Co. Ltd., Sparkford

CONTENTS

Acknowledgements 6

Introduction 8

THE MAN

1. Why? 31
2. Live for ever 49
3. Decision: F1 67

THE PLACE

4. Both sides now 95
5. Gilded cage 125
6. The switch 149

THE MOMENT

7. Here today . . . 187
8. Breaking point 215
9. Not really a problem 233

THE PRICE

10. Darkness 277
11. The best way to travel 315
12. Timeline 339

Psychological analysis: The Right Track 359
Index 377

ACKNOWLEDGEMENTS

This paperback edition has been updated in two specific areas since the hardback appeared in 2001: the introduction and a new final chapter. The rest remains untouched, especially the musings of (then F1 driver) E. Irvine Esq.

I am especially indebted to the many drivers below who gave their time, and to three experts who offer insights into the psychological culture of Formula 1: John Stevens, a freelance motor racing coach; Bernie Shrosbree, manager of the Human Performance Centre at Benetton (not forgetting Wendy Chard for organising the interview); and Andrew Walton, a leading sports psychologist who set up Andrew Walton & Associates in 1981.

I formally thank Brian Hart for his experiences and expertise whenever I needed it; John Watson, Martin Donnelly, Ed Devlin, Karl Wendlinger, Johnny Herbert, Mika Salo, Stefan Johansson, Julian Bailey, Jonathan Palmer, the late Michele Alboreto (who gave the first interview for the book), Ralph Firman, Jarno Trulli, Ricardo Zonta, Heinz-Harald Frentzen, Bert and Allan McNish, Perry McCarthy, Mark Blundell, Tony Dodgins, Maurice Hamilton, Renaud de Laborderie, Eddie Irvine, James Thomas of Jaguar, Niki Lauda, Bobby Rahal, Agnes Carlier of Sauber, Nick Heidfeld, Kimi Räikkönen, Bill Sisley of Buckmore Park, Kai Ebel of RTL, Mario Andretti and his support team of Patty and Amy; Karen Shotbolt, PA to the Communications Director, Manchester United; John Surtees, David Coulthard, Virginie Papin of Prost, Ivan Capelli, the

Williams Media service, Philippe Streiff and Chantal; Jean Alesi; the Ferrari Press team, Rubens Barrichello and Nigel Wollheim; Antonio Pizzonia, and the Jaguar Communications Manager Jane Stewart; Richard West and Nigel Mihell of Richard West Associates; the Team Bentley PR, and David Brabham, Tom Kristensen, Dindo Capello, Guy Smith; David Hayhoe for lending tapes, searching out information and putting together the invaluable *Grand Prix Data Book* (Duke). Stan Piecha of *The Sun* newspaper, London, provided me with valuable words from Jenson Button and I owe a particular debt to Derick Allsop who was happy to talk about his interview with Michael Schumacher, allowed me to reproduce it, and helped in other valuable ways. The Schumacher interview was 'shared' with Wolfgang Reuter of *Focus* magazine in Germany and he, too, has allowed me to use the questions he posed. Rob Widdows produced a pass for the Goodwood Festival of Speed at short notice – invaluable, as it turned out.

For permission to quote, I'm grateful to: Renaud de Laborderie for Drapeau Rouge (Solar, Paris, 1992); Andrea Karall of Verlag Kremayr & Scheriau Orac for *To Hell and Back* by Nıkı Lauda; Mary Phelps of Uden Associates for an extract from the Equinox programme *Full Throttle*. Professor Mike Land of the School of Biological Sciences, University of Sussex, made a valuable contribution to that programme and was kind enough to send me many of his insights. Mark Burgess of *Karting* magazine, a mine of information on drivers' early years, was as helpful as ever.

INTRODUCTION

*Let's say it's a swimming pool full of sharks and you have
to find a way to survive in this swimming pool.
You must know how to defend yourself but that doesn't mean
you always have to be a shark.*
– Antonio Pizzonia

Three rooms, each quiet and each a contrast. The first: the
restaurant at the Grosvenor House Hotel, at lunch time.
Traffic ebbed and flowed down Park Lane outside the tall
windows but you couldn't hear it. The weight of the décor
seemed to insulate the place from everyday life. Other diners
seemed to whisper.

I'm sitting with Sir Jackie Stewart talking about where
Michael Schumacher ought to be placed in the pantheon of true
greatness. Stewart, so logical and reflective, has a simple creed –
*you can only be the best in your era, all further comparisons are
invalid* – but he deploys his knowledge to dissect what greatness
is, physically as well as mentally, and applies it to Schumacher.

Once upon a time the late David Benson, who covered Grand
Prix racing for the *Daily Express* for twenty years, described how
Stewart's mind worked. The *Express* had hired Stewart – then a
leading driver – to describe, after each Grand Prix, what
happened to him. Stewart had total recall and, despite the fact
that he'd just been in a hectic, dangerous and exhausting environment for close on two hours, could marshal his thoughts so

coherently that they required minimal editing before publication.

Stewart also told Benson that, instinctively and instantaneously, he could tell whether a sudden noise was life threatening or not. Suppose he was walking along the street and a car misfired. He wouldn't duck or turn round because he'd know it was a misfire, not gunfire.

Now, a couple of decades later, we're in the Grosvenor House.

A crack of sound rang out.

'Champagne cork,' he said evenly and kept on eating.

All unseen, a waitress had been struggling to open a bottle and the struggle excited the bubbles so much that the cork came out like a gunshot. How do I know? Because after I'd ducked I looked round.

Something else about that lunch. The menu was as extensive as you'd imagine and we needed some time climbing up and down it before we made our decision. I passed on a starter and Stewart did too. I said I'd have one of the elaborate sounding chicken dishes for a main course and he said he'd have that too – no, he said to the hovering waiter, I wonder if you could do it another way for me? He specified how, said he'd like a salad and specified how that should be. Of course, the waiter said. Water? Stewart inquired what kinds they had and chose one.

This was so normal that you're probably thinking so what? Stewart is dyslexic. I am betraying no confidences because this information has long been in the public domain and, across the years, he has done a tremendous amount to foster understanding of this severe reading disorder and banish any stigma associated with it.

He had ordered the meal without being able to read the menu, had done this so consummately that I was unaware of what was happening, *and got exactly the meal – and the water – he'd wanted*. No doubt many dyslexics learn such arts although whether they can execute them like that I don't know. I do know that if you ally that to the gunshot which never was, and ally that to the deeply penetrating dissection of Schumacher, you have someone who is not like most people.

A further example of the Stewart mind at work.

'The day Jochen [Rindt] was killed at Monza [in 1970] I was criticised for having gone out and driven again. Before I drove, I was with him in the medical centre. I knew he was dead. I was in floods of tears in the car – until the engine started. Then I could close that box and open the other.'[1]

They are not like you and me.

It's something we shall be returning to.

The second room: small, functional, tucked away at the back of a building big enough to be a hangar. An end-of-winter Maranello day held in sharp winter sunlight. The name Maranello has assumed a meaning of its own, so laden with folklore that it's tempting to forget this is a working town of 15,000 inhabitants not far from Bologna rather than simply a shrine to Ferrari, although Ferrari inevitably has a strong presence in terms of factories, gift shops, murals and the like, not to mention the Fiorano test track.

The 2003 car has just been launched in the hangar, which is beside the track. This is the way it goes: the international Press is divided into language groups and each installed in small rooms at the back of the building. The leading Ferrari personnel – from Jean Todt through Ross Brawn to Michael Schumacher and Rubens Barrichello – are rotated through these rooms giving a series of mini-Press Conferences. It's an equitable and practical way of meeting all the demands on them.

Schumacher, lean and poised in his driving overalls, gave a performance as consummate as Stewart's but completely different. He said everything which had to be said, responded to each question in a way which seemed positive but, when you came to transcribe the tape of it, was habitually defensive.

At one point I asked about his feelings that, in the coming season, he could literally overtake Juan Manuel Fangio's total of five World Championships. He said he didn't think about things like that. I pressed him. *You could soon be the most successful driver of all time and, in your most private moments, you don't think about it?* Our eyes met. He didn't blink. He modulated so adroitly into management-speak – team effort, collective credit for achievements and so on – that you were (almost) unaware of it.

Mind games: he has an immense fortune, his own five championships, a settled family life with wife and children and must be as secure as anybody on the planet, yet he still seems unwilling to depart from the script. He must have known that to claim he didn't think of beating Fangio was absurd, but he had moved into his Press Conference box and that was what was in the box.

Towards the end of the Press Conference a young lady with a camera crew said 'Michael, we have many clients in Germany. Could you give us your feelings on the new car in German?' He opened that box so fast that as she finished asking he was speaking in German. He spoke uninterrupted for – astonishingly – three seconds short of a full minute. He must have known that a minute was what they'd want because those are the sort of margins television deals in.

This is what he said: 'I am certainly very impressed, as I already said to the Italian Press. I am absolutely in love with this car. I was extremely surprised that you could alter last year's car to such an extent – I hope, obviously, for the better. I am also very 'nosy' about the car and interested to experience it. I would think it will become very intense, if you see how much the McLaren Mercedes has caught up in comparison to the others in winter testing. They have come strongly closer to us. Accordingly, it should be very interesting.'

Defensive, but that's not the point. It was the opening and closing of the boxes, and how fast that could be done.

In turn Rubens Barrichello came, physically and temperamentally so unlike Schumacher, all tic-tac gesturing, sunny smiles and a tumbling of words. This was the Barrichello who had, in 2000, accepted the ultimate challenge by joining Schumacher at Ferrari and who, long before, had said:

'When I signed for Ferrari, I took a big chance. I knew I'd have a very difficult task ahead. I knew I'd have pressure from Ferrari, pressure from the Press – the Italian Press especially – and pressure from the world. And on top of that, I knew I'd have the pressure of being compared with Michael. So why do it? For two reasons: because I wanted to pitch myself against the best, and because I knew Ferrari would build me a car in which I could win races.'[2]

Now Barrichello spoke of his feelings when, a few moments before, the new car had been unveiled. At that unveiling, while speeches were made, the car rotated silently on a platform.

'When the car was turning I couldn't stop looking at it and every "lap" there was a different thing that I was looking at on the car. It was emotional. I saw it yesterday for the first time but when it is turning you can see more.'

What do you feel about one lap qualifying?

'I love it! I think it's a fantastic idea. One reason is because the time that I love the most is qualifying. And one lap is very challenging. When I say that, I am already boiling inside. I feel like it's going to be a great time.'

You are mentally preparing yourself even now?

'Yes, yes. It's another way of thinking and you have to prepare for that.'

Are you as confident of a championship as you can be at the start of a season?

'Yes. I'm looking for a title.'

You're the first of Schumacher's partners that's pushed him.

'Yeah, in a way. I look at myself in the mirror and I see a happy person. If I've had a problem in the past, then I've overcome the problem. When I had my first two years at Ferrari there were things that I needed to improve and there were things that I improved because of Michael, by learning from him. He was even better at looking at things he needed for the car. No way am I afraid of my team-mate.'

Inevitably Barrichello was questioned about the infamous 2002 Austrian Grand Prix, when he was ordered to move aside and let Schumacher win.

'It's not written in my contract that I should have done that but it is written in my contract, and Michael's, that we have to obey what comes over the radio. So it's really stupid when you hear someone like [Jacques] Villeneuve saying he [Barrichello] should have read his contract – because it's not like that. Our contracts have the same clause so we just have to see life as it comes. I'm not worried at all. If Michael has 40 points again and I have zero the same thing will be done.'

And if Barrichello has 40 and Michael zero?

'Then it's another story. I'm a guy who plays for equal terms more than anything else. I like to be equal so we all have to talk on the same level – so, if Barrichello's 40 and he's zero then...'

An impression had been forming during this Press Conference that, as he'd hinted, Barrichello was not being blown away by the ultimate challenge. I said *you're really not frightened of him, are you* and we looked straight at each other. He didn't blink.

'No, I'm not. I'm very proud of Michael because I think he has pushed my career to the level it needed so I am looking on the positive side.'

Drivers have to think like this, or be second-rate. All are brave and ambitious; all believe they can, and will, conquer the world. The fact that every two weeks they are delivered evidence that they almost certainly won't, transmutes into an incentive and not a discouragement. Consider: I am writing these words in 2003 and in the five preceding years there have been only two World Champions, Schumacher and Mika Häkkinen. The rest didn't make it. And to make it, at some stage you will have to take on Schumacher, as team-mate or opponent, take him on in body and mind. It won't, let's say, be easy.

Schumacher, as it would seem, can move from box to box as completely as Stewart could. At the 2003 San Marino Grand Prix he drove a superbly controlled race and won, although his mother died the night before. He and Ralf had flown to Cologne after Saturday qualifying to see her in hospital, where she lay in a coma.

Both men were on the front row of the grid and, when the red lights went out, they *duelled* for the lead. Ralf, as controlled as his elder brother, eventually finished fourth.

The race done, Michael brought the Ferrari back to the *parc fermé* and sat in it for a long, private moment. His body language visibly altered as he moved boxes emotionally, from averaging 129mph for an hour and 28 minutes to grief.

The third room: a basement at Jack Barclay's in Barclay Square. They sell Bentleys upstairs, cars which resemble luxury ocean liners and seem at first glance to cost about as much. Immaculate salesmen watch. They can probably separate gawkers from buyers at a glance, and didn't approach me.

In the basement six men are sitting in groups of three: former Grand Prix drivers Mark Blundell, Johnny Herbert and David Brabham to one side, Tom Kristensen (who almost made it) Rinaldo (Dindo) Capello and Guy Smith to the other. They formed two teams who would contest the 2003 Le Mans 24 Hour race in Bentleys. Here was another box, and all six of them were in it. They had had to move from solitary and selfish single-seaters to become team players – a complete mental transition – and, this end-of-winter London day, they had decided to have some fun. Evidently there had been an attempt to get them to know their script. Selected highlights of what they did say:

Blundell: 'I feel a bit miffed because in dress rehearsal we were sitting in those seats nearest the car. These guys are pinching our seats so already it's a little bit competitive between the two teams, which I think is good in these early stages. We're trying to win it to give David a trophy (laughter).'

Herbert is making cheekie-chappie asides the whole time which convulse the other drivers.

Brabham: 'It's very important for me as a driver. My brother has won Le Mans and he reminds me that I haven't...'

Kristensen: 'I have been very close to Formula 1 a few times and obviously Formula 1 is the focus of what everybody gets – because they get it every fortnight. Le Mans is one race and for me it's the fastest long-distance race in the world. It only happens once a year. In 2000 I did some testing – the Michelin testing for Williams – and the Jaguar.'

What's the effort like in your mind to drive the Bentley compared to the Williams?

'A Formula 1 car is more physical on your body but when you finish a race in these cars you've gone ten or twelve times as far. During a sports car race, you have to regain your physical strength very, very quickly in order to come back and do another stint. Formula 1 is very short. This – a 24-hour race – gets to you like a torture in your mind. There is the constant overtaking of cars in slower categories and then there is the night and the rain. The best way is to work as a team. In Formula 1 everyone is out for themselves in their own right. Here at Le Mans the three drivers come as a team and they have to work well together. You have to think about the weakest link in every aspect because you need to give a lot, you need to open yourself and you need to be able to be honest. If you are not honest ...'

Herbert: 'Driving Le Mans hasn't done me any harm. In a Formula 1 race you basically go balls out and then it's finished, whereas here you have got to try and find a rhythm and they can pull you out of the car. Then you've got to hang around in the middle of the night before you get back in. I have to say I slept at Le Mans last year, but all the other years I've driven there I never have. I hadn't been able to switch off.'

Was that a conscious thing that you could switch off?

'It must have been. Probably that I'm getting older as well (grin). As you get older I think that does get easier.'

How do you compare this with Formula 1?

Brabham: 'Physically a Formula 1 car is more than this Bentley for sure, because it generates a lot more downforce but it's still a race car and you're still a racing driver so it doesn't matter what you drive: you still have to know and understand what you're driving and get the best out of it as well as the best out of yourself.

'From a driving point of view it's a different discipline. You have to push very hard but it's a 24-hour race so you've got that in your mind as well. The interesting thing is that in Formula 1 it's only you and your car. You have a team-mate but you are still very much on your own. You do your own thing. This is the exact opposite. You're working with two other drivers who have two different driving styles and for us to come to an agreement on how the car should be set up is an interesting experience.'

Even more interesting because by definition racers are selfish people.

'Yes, we are, for sure we are, but when you're with two team-mates that becomes a joint effort. The three of us and the three drivers in the other car have the same goal, which is to win Le Mans. Selfishly I want to win it for myself and they will too, but if I do win it that means my two team-mates win it as well – and I'd be just as happy for them as I would be for myself.'

How delicate is the team structure?

'Obviously with this type of organisation and this type of racing, communication is the biggest factor. No-one hides anything, whereas in Formula 1 it's a mad dog attitude.'

Why do you keep on doing it?

'You have to ask yourself why are we here? Why do we have this life? Why do we do things? Who are we? How to we respond to things? The way I see it is that you are here to experience who you are – who *you* are – and every thought, every word, every emotion, everything that you do is a feeling of self-expression. Being a racing driver and being involved in this business gives me, as a human being, something I love. I have a real passion for it. I am also fortunate that I am in a position to do something I love and I am very aware of that, but it's just the pure experience racing gives me. That's why I do it. That's the same in Formula 1, Formula 3000, Le Mans, racing in America – same self-expression but through slightly different mediums.'

Blundell: 'Sports car racing in general and Le Mans in particular is slightly different because you've got that camaraderie. It's a different feel. The pressure is equated between several people as opposed to just one, so you have to make a mental adjustment from being completely selfish. That's part of the attraction: getting six drivers who are level-headed.

'The buzz is the same, you are still a driver on your own, but if you crash you've two guys in the motorhome who won't be winning Le Mans either. That makes it all more difficult and I've been on the receiving end of that myself. That's one of the hardest parts.

'Sure there are going to be weaknesses and strengths but you find those out as you go along. From that you get a pecking order of what does what and who does what. You won't be getting people pulling strokes to try and get pole. We are all long enough in the tooth and we know each other. At the end of the day whatever the scenario is, whoever feels most confident or is getting the job done, really should be the one to go and get pole. We will all be able to live with that in a way which would be extremely difficult in single-seaters but it's a completely different mind-set.'

The events in the three rooms all happened within a short time of each other but that was coincidence. I've described what happened there as an introduction to the variety and complexity of the racing driver's mind. It is what this book is about.

One time, I was sitting in Monaco with Karl Wendlinger, still the lean, articulate, serious man he was when he drove Grand Prix cars. We're at a pavement café decorated by spring sunshine. It is in the new part of the Principality at the back of the Palace, far from the harbour-side chicane where, on 12 May

1994, he crashed so heavily that his life was endangered. The impact sent him into a coma with serious head injuries. Two weeks before, Roland Ratzenberger and Ayrton Senna had been killed at Imola and now the whole terrible trauma was torn open again. It was almost as if some malevolent spirit was visiting and revisiting its wrath upon Formula 1.

Wendlinger recovered, of course, and this is what he says about performance.

'I've read a lot of books about the brain, about energies. I think if your brain is strong enough and your concentration is good enough you do the lap time first in your brain and then in your car and in your body. This is something the good drivers can do but only Ayrton Senna made perfect.'

Wendlinger did some testing at Barcelona in the spring of 1995 then, months later, his team, Sauber, wanted him to test at Mugello. 'Because I'd only done a little driving I had time to prepare my body, to do training. I did a lot of concentration exercises. Then I arrived in Mugello. It was a two and a half day test and, the evening before, I thought "OK, one minute 30.4 would be a good lap time." I concentrated, I closed my eyes and as I crossed the line into the lap I started my stopwatch. I did a whole lap in my brain and looked. The stopwatch said 1:30.4. The next day on the track I did 1:30.4.

'Then I said to myself "it was too easy, tomorrow you have to do 1:29.3." The best lap that Heinz-Harald [Frentzen, Wendlinger's team-mate] did in Mugello all year was 1:29.0 and because I had done so little driving I thought 1:29.3 was competitive. I sat in the hotel again, closed my eyes and started the watch. I "drove" the lap and looked. 1:29.3. Next day I did 1:29.3. You know the best thing was – and this fascinates me about what you can do with your brain – I only did the 1:29.3

because I made a mistake and lost three-tenths. If I hadn't made that mistake I would have done 1:29.0 – but the evening before I had fixed in my brain 1:29.3 and not zero, and that's what happened. If I had fixed 1:29.0 maybe I wouldn't have made the mistake and I'd have done the time easily.

'In these weeks and months, when I had so little testing, I did something every day – twice, sometimes three times – with a friend. It was not quite like karate, not quite like Tae Kwon-Do, something similar but different. He said "with this, you get so much strength and energy in your brain that you can do everything." This was the reason I was so strong in my head. After Mugello, there was no mystery: you can do it. But how you prepare your brain and yourself to do this all the time, that I still don't know.'

David Coulthard does these mental laps too: 'I don't think that's unusual. Obviously it is not possible for races because of all the other factors but I do it in practice and qualifying.' He constructs the equivalent of a mental picture and sets off driving the lap he wants to drive in reality. The mental laps are generally within a tenth of a second of the real thing.

Coulthard was asked about it a couple of hours before qualifying for the 2001 San Marino Grand Prix. He was also asked if he'd prepared his qualifying lap and he replied that this was tricky because the track had been wet and was drying, which would impair a precise visualisation.

He took pole with the fastest lap ever driven round Imola.

Nor is this confined to driving. Senna used to run round a 400-metre track in Sao Paulo to keep fit. In the course of 40 laps he could do 33 or 34 to within one second of the same time, something which astonished his physiotherapist Nuno Cobra.

It seems to suggest that, in the small room at Maranello,

Schumacher had a mental image of sixty seconds for television and that was why he was only three seconds short.

All people are interesting, but the Formula 1 driver is rarefied, if only because there are so few of them: between 20 and 22 at any given moment. The special circumstances of the driver's life compel him to think in unusual ways. He lives not just with danger and the fabled fame and fortune but competitive ruthlessness, technical complexities and a merciless examination of who he really is. In his place of work there is little natural justice. Drives are not allocated simply on merit. Keeping a drive is not always based on ability. Losing a drive may happen because of politics, commerce or human intrigue. The efforts of a whole team who have flown to Australia, worked through the night to repair one of their cars and now watch it leading the race may be rendered useless because a tiny component fails.

We shall hear the (further) thoughts of Schumacher and Eddie Irvine and many others, past and present, who inhabited the front of the grid – but also those trying to make it, those in trouble and those who failed. Each has a place in this book. Some made millions, others earned a good living and at least one owed damn near a million.

A foretaste of the authentic Schumacher. 'I'm not perfect, not at all. There are areas where I may sometimes lean back a little. It comes to my attention and I raise myself again. But there are certain important things and disciplines which are simply natural. You do it without thinking. It's part of the game. There are other things, like training, where maybe I take a day off. It does not happen very often, but here and there it does and I feel bad afterwards, which is good because it keeps me doing it.'

A foretaste of the authentic Irvine, the words spoken when he was still in Formula 1 and never speaking to anybody's script but his own. 'Everything I hate is physical. I'm not into the physical. The only physical pleasure I like is sex. I don't like running, I don't like canoeing, I don't like bicycle riding, I don't like any physical exertion at all. Yes, sex is the only one and that is mental because it's in the head, isn't it?' Irvine, speaking to me in a chauffeur-driven limousine with a New York model at his elbow, has his own jet, his own housing estate spread across Europe, the biggest yacht at Monaco and an endearing way of seducing women. He'd also like a flat stomach.

In 1995, driving a Jordan-Peugeot, Irvine had a horrific pit-lane fire during the Belgian Grand Prix. Michel Quero, a Peugeot engineer, says that 'a couple of minutes after the fire I bumped into Eddie behind the pits. He was laughing his head off.'

Martin Donnelly, like Irvine an Ulsterman, has at times been less sanguine.

'One of the doctors came to my bedroom that night and said "Martin, I looked after the West Ham football team, they are professional football players, and I am telling you now in my official capacity that you and Grand Prix racing won't happen. It's finished." Floods of tears came down my face.'

Julian Bailey's Formula 1 career lasted seven races and produced a single point. 'I was a working class kid and aware of it. Johnny Herbert's a different guy because he comes from the same background but I don't think he cares. I did care. That's my problem. I thought about it too much and I did feel that sometimes I didn't belong in that razzmatazz multi-million dollar scene because I'd actually come from a council house in Woolwich.'

Sometimes their experiences are savage. 'I've gone back into the garage and all the team were there,' Perry McCarthy says of his nightmare with the Andrea Moda team in 1992. 'I was pushing everyone around. I wanted a fight. [Roberto] Moreno walked past. I body-checked him out of the way. I was screaming at everybody and I just wanted one person to raise a finger ...'

Sometimes the experiences are alarming, as when Michele Alboreto feuded with Ayrton Senna. Alboreto told Senna, 'you did that in Hockenheim, I do this in Zeltweg, so stay away from me. Until you say sorry for Hockenheim, every time I see you I push you in the grass.' Senna went, 'sooner or later somebody will be killed.' Alboreto said, 'yes, but maybe it will not be me.'

John Watson has moved into a certain gentility as middle age embraces him. We are sitting in his well-appointed house out-side Oxford, the kind that upwardly mobile executives (as well as racing drivers) pass through on their way to bankruptcy or millions. He is discussing Coulthard who, after surviving a plane crash in which the pilot died, drove in qualifying for the Spanish Grand Prix three days later.

'There would have been a cool detachment that David found himself in. It wouldn't have been conscious. He'd have stepped out of that plane and thought *my* God. He may well have seen the pilot but, immediately, that mechanism which I describe as cool detachment would have been triggered. You are capable of dealing with a situation without the kind of emotional breakdown any "normal" person would have.

'I think David just pushed the button he would have done if stepping out of an accident in a racing car. It was just another accident: "don't analyse it, don't intellectualise it, don't dwell on it. This was an accident I survived. Now, when do I get back in the car?" I did a radio interview about David and was asked "will he lose his nerve?" I said "no he will not. For him, it was another day at the office."'

The 'office' is a very strange place: part hunting ground, part monastery, part herbarium. It's an operating theatre, an ecosystem of egos, a stock exchange, an operational centre for upwardly mobile crumpet, an asylum, a sanctuary and – breathe deeply – it is on television, which makes it all really happening. Dr Wolfgang Reitzle, Vice President and Chief Technology Officer of Ford Motor Company, ploughs a furrow through the middle of all this when he says, 'in Formula 1 you only win when you have almost a kind of military discipline'.

How does this fit upon, say, Eddie Irvine Esq? This is curious, because it seems that Irvine might have taken a decision way back that he was not going to compromise on how he wanted to live his life: he would meet F1 on his terms. While others spent hours poring over computer printouts in motor homes he would be out partying. This is what he said.

'Always you have to make compromises, which is difficult because I'm not great at that. But in my work I have to do it my way, which means enjoying life as well. There's no point in being a Formula 1 racing driver and earning the money we earn and being miserable: you're missing out on life. I want to be sitting at 80, 90, 100 years old and have no regrets that I didn't do more when I was younger. I lead a much better life now than I did five years ago. When I was 17, 18, I hardly went out because I didn't have the money and all my efforts were going towards Formula 1. But it got me there and maybe if I'd started having this sort of lifestyle earlier I wouldn't have got to where I have. I guess this is my story and I'm pretty happy with it.

'I've walked a very narrow tightrope. One day I'll fall off for sure but at the minute I'm still on the rope.'

How does this fit upon, say, Kimi Räikkönen? Speaking about National Service he says, in the softest voice you have ever heard, 'I never liked the Army because the people are telling what you need to do. I want to do what I like.' He was at Sauber when he said this, and had not yet driven his first Grand Prix. He seemed waif-like and vulnerable, his face that of adolescence, his whole being *quiet*. Yet within the lifetime of this book, hardback to paperback, he had moved on to McLaren and, as I write these words, is leading the World Championship. He is *still* quiet. There are strengths in silence, and this is what he has.

Each group of humans evolves into a society, to use that word loosely. Large groups form nations. Small groups form, let's say, your local caged bird league. There is a need for structure, hierarchy and regulation. Motor racing, and specifically Grand Prix racing – which began in 1906 – reflects this. Its hierarchy revolves round the FIA, the governing body which handles regulation, and FOCA, Bernie Ecclestone's organisation, which understands Formula 1 money.

The driver operates within this society. He is unusual among sports people because for him technology plays such a decisive role. Good drivers do not win in bad cars. He has to master something other than himself and every instant of every lap he is doing that. Pole position round the uneven, narrow streets of Monaco and its 13 corners requires him to average 150kmh (93mph). The mind that is able to do this richly repays investigation.

This is not a neat book, as even these first few pages have shown. It features people from different nations, cultures, backgrounds – they have everything in common and almost nothing. It strays into sensitive areas and I pay tribute to many drivers for their candour. Interestingly, virtually to a man, they were initially dismissive of their own mental capabilities. When I explained that I wanted to explore their minds they said, 'well, this won't take long!' But it did …

I've tried to put this exploration into its proper context by enlisting three men who each have a particular knowledge of how such deeply-focused sportsmen operate. Two give their overviews in 'The right track', at the end of the book. Here John Stevens sets out an initial framework. Not many motorsport followers will have heard of Stevens. It's not just that he's soft-spoken and, in conversation, almost diffident – it's that, although he has coached Grand Prix (and countless other) drivers by showing them how to improve their technique, they insist on absolute secrecy. He emphasises that his teaching doesn't save careers or win races. 'The driver does that using his talent, his ability, his concentration. All I've done is show him different methods of driving.'

He accepts that Grand Prix drivers are 'probably surprised with, shall we say, a middle-aged gentleman getting in a car with them,' which itself is perplexing because in any other sport the coach is a valued and public figure. Tiger Woods, perhaps the greatest golfer ever, consults his coach every day. Tim Henman played Wimbledon in 2001 without a coach – a major sports story – then went looking for one. And so it goes, while Stevens labours within the pathological secrecy of Formula 1.

Stevens insists that drivers are not different, as they may sometimes appear from their behaviour – 'a car or bike racer is just a sportsman like anybody else. One of the problems is that motor racing, because of its nature, has an awful lot of hype in it and some drivers get carried away by their own publicity. But it comes down to one man doing his best in a car, just as in athletics it comes down to one man holding a javelin or whatever. OK, in motor racing you've a very complicated machine, but drivers are actually built up to be different from everybody else.'

What drives the Grand Prix driver?

'It can't be the speed because you get used to that in no time! It's the physical and mental challenge of taking a car at high speed round a circuit – and trying to take it round faster than anybody else. Incidentally, if I couldn't drive the car reasonably quickly the Grand Prix drivers could say to me, and quite rightly, "it's all right at your speed, John, but at mine it wouldn't work."'

I mention Niki Lauda's heavy crash in qualifying at Hockenheim in 1982, when I was new to the sport and thought he was running away from the car when in fact he was running towards the pits to get the spare.

'If you're trying to analyse courage, it's forcing or motivating yourself to do something where your life is at risk and you don't want to do it. If you do want to do it, if you enjoy doing it, that's a very different thing. If I'm sitting at home watching someone climb a mountain on television it frightens the life out of me. I couldn't do that, I wouldn't have the courage. But in a racing car it never bothers me. If I see somebody injured, OK, I feel sympathy for them, but apart from that I wouldn't even think about it.

'I was asked to do psychological tests with a group of other racing drivers and I only agreed to because I was promised I'd hear the results. It was a proper questionnaire. Six months later I was told "OK, I'll tell you one thing. We found that racing drivers are more aggressive than ordinary people but you were twice as aggressive as the normal racing driver!" It didn't surprise me. I remember a boxer. Out of the ring – fine. Put him in the ring and he became a madman, kill anybody. That's it. You switch on and switch off. My forte was driving racing cars, I was aggressive and I was known to be aggressive.

'I enjoy racing cars and bikes, I've had big accidents and been knocked around. It never troubled me in the slightest. For the first ten minutes after the accident you think what am I doing here? Half an hour later you've forgotten all about it. If you're not badly injured you could even be back in the car or on the bike again. I am sure Grand Prix drivers feel that way too.'

You have coached drivers on their way to Grand Prix racing and in it.

'They are very sceptical to start with and you can't blame them – race driving is very much an ego trip – but once we've started it's no problem because they can see the benefits. One very famous driver said "I like going out with you because you slap my wrist when I do something wrong." That wouldn't happen to him otherwise. Nobody in the racing team would tell him – they don't know!'

Stevens invites the driver to take him round in an ordinary saloon car at whatever speed he wants while Stevens sits and watches. The driver is asked to position the saloon as he would his Grand Prix car: the approach, the lines through the corner. After three or four laps the driver is asked to go faster – 'I want to watch that because very often the lines change. For instance, they may start turning in too early. The faster you drive the better your lines have to be.' They come in and Stevens explains that a Grand Prix car is designed on 'scientific principles which are utterly inflexible,' which means there's only one way to maximise its performance. Any variation in the driver's actions must lead to a variation in the result with the car.

'A driver looks at me and I can see it in his eyes: well, how does this fellow know he's got it right? I say "when you have got it right the car will tell you."'

They go back onto the circuit but with Stevens driving. He drives exactly the way he was being driven before, they discuss what's happening with the car and then Stevens shows the driver a different way to do it. 'I never say a better way, only different. You've got to know the lines, but you've got to know the technique to make the car work on the lines. We draw a comparison and there is a moment of acceptance. They don't actually say "this is making sense" and I've only ever had one driver refuse to do it.'

Stevens does not give precise figures for the improvements he can make – he's not dealing in exactitude – but instead illustrates the driver's mindset.

'I had an interesting situation a couple of years ago with a Grand Prix driver. We went round in a front-wheel-drive Mondeo, came in and he said to me "I didn't know that Ford built a rear-wheel-drive Mondeo." We had a discussion, he said "I'll prove to you that a front-wheel-drive car will not handle like that" and crawled under the car to have a look.'

How did he cope with being wrong?

'He didn't say anything.'

What is going on in the driver's mind to insist on secrecy?

'I don't think it's only their minds, it's the situation they are in, it's the ego trip – and it's not just the drivers who react like this but team owners too, because they may be worried that the sponsors could react unfavourably. Drivers don't say thank you at the end, I don't know why, and I never hear from some of them again.'

NOTES

1. *Daily Telegraph*, 15 March 2003.
2. *F1 Racing*, July 2002.

THE MAN

Chapter 1

WHY?

'God knows what else was being smoked, taken, abused, used. The beer was an inch deep on the floor. It was the end of term, everybody got pissed, nobody gave a toss. There was no British press corps there, no paparazzi – that's the difference.'
– John Watson

If you ask a driver 'Why?' he tends to look puzzled. He does not understand how anybody could not be, or want to be, a driver. If he could turn the question round it would be 'why don't you do this?'

The driver is a solitary hunter. He is always moving on the edge of extinction, constantly in danger because all manner of other solitary hunters are stalking him as he stalks them. That part he understands very well, perhaps intuitively and probably from childhood when he joined the hunt.

John Watson, who came close to the World Championship in 1982, puts this simply. 'I remember once I'd made a sweet pass on Stefan Johansson but he called it a hard move. That was his interpretation. I do remember making hard passes, really putting the other driver under extreme pressure. The reason was very deliberate: I wanted to dumb you down, I wanted to almost emasculate you, I wanted to beat you, I wanted to make you whimper. I wanted you not to come back. I'm sending you a message: you're not in the equation any more. The job of overtaking is not about the physical, it's about the mental, and understanding this and putting it into effect – that's what Ayrton Senna did.'

Senna was a hunter.

'Absolutely. It is wonderful. It's the greatest feeling in your life, believe me. Better than sex? It's a different feeling.'

The driver is a highly motivated person, a self-starter – these days before the age of eight – and has known nothing but this. To him it is not a strange, shadowy place fuelled by largely primitive impulses; it is not really drawn between survival or conquest, although invariably the driver thinks of it in this way. No. To him it is life.

The German television channel *RTL* were covering the Manchester United v Bayern Munich European Cup final in Barcelona in 1999 on the Wednesday before the Spanish Grand Prix. *RTL* also cover Formula 1 and their motor racing commentator, Kai Ebel, says 'we invited some guests to the football match – Frentzen, Coulthard and Häkkinen joined us. Although they were like friends, Coulthard got very emotional during the match and Frentzen did too. Mika: nothing. You had all this noise from the crowd, all this excitement and Mika didn't react at all. Afterwards I said "Mika, what happened, what was wrong?" and he replied "well, I am focused on Sunday's race." We were days away from that and he was already focused on it.'[1]

Häkkinen had isolated himself from the game, not to mention the noise the 90,245 spectators were making, and was somewhere around Catalunya's 4.7 kilometres (2.9 miles).

The induction starts early.

'I have always been hyper-competitive, partly because that's how my dad brought me up,' Jacques Villeneuve will say of

Gilles. 'Nothing was ever perfect with him. I don't have any memories of this – it's what I've been told. It was very hard for me because I was never good enough as a kid and, after he died my life actually became easier. That's when I relaxed a bit and that's when I grew up and became who I am. I started racing on skis when I was eight, so I've always been in a very competitive environment, pushing to the limit.'[2]

The child learns swiftly about the hunt. His friends are motor racing people; he speaks their language; the places he knows are garages, workshops, factories and circuits; almost as familiar as home is the motorway café after midnight, the race over, the car or kart outside on the trailer.

Allan McNish began in karting. Living in Scotland meant long journeys to and from races, his parents driving the van. 'You're sleeping on a Sunday night coming back from a meeting near Yeovil, for example, up to Dumfries and I had to be at school at 9am on the Monday. I wasn't going to sit up until two in the morning. I had to sleep, and I had to do my homework. It was a family thing but I wanted to go to the races and I wanted to win.'

Was winning the most important thing?

'The losing was horrible. And there can only be one winner. It's funny because you go there and you build up your hopes of being successful at every race, it builds and builds and it reaches a crescendo.'

Is the winning part of your nature?

'I do think so. You ask sportsmen what is the common thread and the answer will almost certainly be that they started something as a hobby and found they were good at it. Maybe they had a push from their parents, which is probably necessary when they're going out with girls or whatever. It's a profession that's born out of a hobby and it's something that you'd probably do for the love of it even if it wasn't a profession.

'It's not necessarily the competing, it's the winning. That's what makes you go out and run through the woods at 9.30 on a Sunday morning when it's raining like hell – to get yourself a little bit fitter. It's in my character and I think there is a difference in nationalities with this. You need that last, extra desire. I believe we can do whatever we want with ourselves. We can be a bodybuilder, we can train to be a racing driver, we can practise, practise, practise. Suppose it was mathematics. We might not be the best at it but we can get a lot, lot better. It depends how much you want it.

'France has produced one World Champion [Prost] but smaller countries like Finland and Scotland have more because the whole in-bred instinct over the years is that you've got to fight a wee bit harder for what you can get, and when you do get a knock you get back up and you keep on. There are certain people you come up against and you know if you can just get close to them they'll make a mistake. You'll break them psychologically. That will win you races more than talent.'

The losing remains terrible at all levels. Jarno Trulli began with Minardi in 1997 and came to Jordan via two and a half seasons at Prost.

If you have a bad race, how long does it take to get over it mentally?

'By the time of the next race I am back to normal. When I make mistakes or when something bad happens in a race it takes a couple of days. I reflect on it, try to understand, learn from it. I feel it very strongly. I am really disappointed. I'm in a bad mood. That doesn't mean that I am not motivated: I'm just thinking. The best thing will be a single race every day because every race I forget everything else, I forget the disappointments, and I am always positive for the next race. It's just like a revenge.'

It is entirely possible to operate within the hunting ground until middle age and know little of the curious place which the rest of humanity calls the real world. Every sport is self-sustaining and slightly unreal. That exacts a price. John Watson cites tennis as another sport where, to reach the pinnacle, participants require such a narrow focus that their normal social development is on hold. Quoting one Wimbledon champion he says: 'His life was focused solely on tennis. All he could do was play tennis. When he stopped playing tennis he suddenly became an adolescent.'

Maintaining a balance can be difficult, but not impossible. Jenson Button, as Watson points out, 'is someone who does allow himself to, let's say, enjoy life. He's a party animal, he doesn't mind having a few beers, dancing, whatever. He has a God-given natural ability which is outstanding but, at the same time, is careful not to expose his life – like some dumb football player might – to excesses. He's bright enough not to forsake the things that he needs to grow into a balanced human being.'

If you get this wrong you're looking back asking yourself whatever happened to those years between 20 and 25.

'It's when the driver gets to 29 and 30. His career is ending and suddenly he thinks "what life experiences have I apart from going round and round?"

'Let me relate this to, say, the 1970s and the end of the season at Watkins Glen.[3] I think the place everyone went to for the Sunday night party was called Seneca Lodge. Most of the guys would go down. All the mechanics were there pissed out of their brains. God knows what else was being smoked, taken, abused, used. The beer was like an inch deep on the floor. I remember seeing Carlos Pace[4] in there one night. Carlos couldn't remember his name, he couldn't even speak his name. James Hunt would be in there, everybody would be there. It was the end of term, nobody gave a toss. No British press corps there, no paparazzi there – that's the difference. Every sportsperson at the top of their profession is now living in a goldfish bowl. If they fart, burp, whatever, they are banged to rights.

'If you're a highly paid sportsperson in a profession like motor racing and you're seen to fall down drunk it's almost an international incident, so drivers are bandaged and isolated. They do get pissed. You go to the Log Cabin[5] at Suzuka in Japan, which traditionally has been the last Grand Prix of the year – there was always a Formula 1 party at the end of the year. Normally you'd see Michael [Schumacher] in there, Mika in there, but they preclude the media.'

At Suzuka in 1999, in the Log Cabin or thereabouts, Schumacher evidently celebrated the end of the season as a man might, with a glass or two. The media, faking politically correct shock-horror, took this up to the point where Luca di Montezemolo, Ferrari's President, felt obliged to comment. 'I'd rather,' he said, 'have a Schumacher who is human enough to get drunk once a year than not have a Schumacher at all.'

Formula 1 is not monastic but it does guard a measure of secrecy. At any Grand Prix there'll be around 100 journalists who are regulars and a further 100 from the local press. The spread of photographers will be 60 plus 30. Cumulatively their output is prodigious and most of it centres on the personalities, specifically the drivers. Irvine is much more interesting than traction control, his women more sensuous than any bodywork.

For top drivers, money will become significant but that comes later, and only a very few get to see the multi-millions. Ron Dennis offered a profundity about this. He said that if there was no money F1 drivers would race just the same.

Bobby Rahal, the American who drove in two Grands Prix in 1978 and was a leading IndyCar driver, before briefly running the Jaguar team, believes that drivers' mentalities are essentially the same although 'today there is a lot more money than there was decades ago, and that maybe changes people's attitude, plus it's considerably safer.'

But wouldn't they still be doing it without the money?

'Well, they say they would! I think if you are a real racer you're not doing it for the money. All the money in the world can't convince you to get in a racecar. To me money is nothing more than a yardstick, a ruler, as to your value.

'What happens in a racecar is universal. The cars may be different, the capabilities may be a little bit different, but certainly the forces are the same and so is what goes on in a driver's mind, how he feels about what he is doing. They remain the same. Always will.'

It is the chase which holds the solitary hunter. Johnny Herbert almost lost a foot in a Formula 3000 crash at Brands Hatch before his Grand Prix career began. When his mother pointed this out to him in hospital, he said in a matter-of-fact way that he didn't need feet because stumps would do nicely to press the pedals on the racing cars he would be driving again.

Actually, it wasn't quite like that.

'I always used to say I'd drive with stumps, but of course I wouldn't have had the sensitivity and the feel. I wasn't bluffing my mother – to joke about things was the only way I could survive. It was my way of being able to get over the problem.

'I laughed about everything. From what I can gather, before the accident I was known as miserable and stuck up. It was partly my shyness. I never used to speak to that many people in the paddock. I was lucky in that I had my karting and Formula 3 and everything else so I have been able to slowly emerge but if I go back to when I was young I was shy as hell. Karting was good for me because it got me to come out.'

Even so, without the accident at Brands Hatch, Herbert estimates that 'I think I would have been selfish and self-contained.'

Do you get frightened?

'... There is something but I can't remember what ... It's probably a silly thing like playing football, falling over and breaking my arm. I can't do very much' – because of the feet – 'so it can't be that. What is it ...? It's when I'm on my bike. I remember that when I was about six I had a bike with really sharp brakes and I went over the handlebars ... Yes, and that's the only thing. It's something that's stuck.'

You're not telling me that you survived the crash at Brands, you survived a crash in your last Grand Prix and you're frightened of push bikes ...?

'I'd think more about flipping over the top of the push bike than I'd do driving a car. It must be true because if it wasn't I'd be frightened of speed – and I'm not.'

Whatever drives such a man, it clearly is not pay. Michael Schumacher insists that although he's been racing since he was four 'money has never been my main motivation.' Senna once said that at McLaren he became embroiled in contract re-negotiations with Ron Dennis and – both determined men ('strong willed,' Dennis told me) with a consuming grasp of detail – they went on and on and on into an impasse. It became a principle of finding a way forward and they agreed to settle the matter on the toss of a coin. Senna said he called wrong and it cost him $1.5 million over three years. This did not unduly concern him because his family was rich and he was well-paid anyway. What mattered was that he was paid more than any other driver; that in the F1 market place he was evaluated as the best. If you paid Nigel Mansell $100,000 Senna wanted at least $100,001. If you paid Mansell $1,000,000 Senna wanted at least $1,000,001. Senna offered to drive for Williams, then employing Mansell, for nothing because in 1992 they had a Championship-winning car that he coveted mightily.

Senna would have found life difficult without the wealth but intolerable without the racing.

Each driver must find his own balance, of course. As Watson says, 'Eddie Irvine gets castigated at times for being almost misogynist – a male chauvinist pig! Thank God the media has got an Eddie Irvine because they love him. He's the only human being in the paddock who will come out and say it as it is. And his parents are lovely as well. They are just normal, Eddie is just normal. I know his parents through coming to races and I know their son is not the person in that film that was made of him last year[6]. That is the "professional" Eddie Irvine, or playboy, or whatever. He is a normal guy who is very kind. I think he is quite shy but he's evolved mechanisms to project something else and protect himself.

'In a way he is the most popular driver in Formula 1, in certain areas of the UK media, especially in the tabloid end, because the audience that Eddie is appealing to is a mass audience: not an intellectual one, or semi-intellectual, or classically educated. Eddie is representing a majority of the views of the young male population.

'In Japan in 1999 [the Championship-deciding race] I saw him briefly in that sort of cattle market thing when they stand and do their interviews. For a guy who'd lost a World Championship it was just as if a pressure was lifted. He went into Tokyo that night and Tokyo is Eddie's city. It's the city that he knows best and probably loves best. He drove in Japan for three years. Went down to Rupungi[7] with his manager and they had the party of all parties. It wasn't a celebration, it wasn't a wake, it was a party I think of pure relief. And on Monday morning I was sitting having breakfast and he came down. I saw in him a man who was now free of all his own pressure but there was something much more: he was free of the responsibility not just of a team but of a nation – Italy.

'That's partly the same reason why Michael Schumacher burst into tears in Monza. He was experiencing the relief of winning a Grand Prix in a Ferrari – the Italian Grand Prix – and he'd put the momentum back into his 2000 Championship attempt. Even he uses mechanisms to screen some of the pressures, but as a result of a combination of the accident with the marshal [killed by crash debris], the relief of winning and the passions of Monza, the guy broke down. He is no less human than you or I, but put him into the context of a Grand Prix, put him in the paddock in a racing car and the switch is flicked: he's super professional, he's cold, he's calculating.'

I tell Irvine that Watson felt he looked like a man who had shed a burden. 'I don't think I was relieved, I was pissed off. Pissed off that I hadn't won it.' Not a shred of self-pity. 'You either win it or you don't.'

Are you really able to look at it that way? Maybe you'll never win it.

'Maybe I never will. You just never know. As long as you've

got the will that's all you need in Formula 1. Fitness is not an issue. It's the will that's the issue.'

Were you born with that?

'I'd have never thought I was competitive as a kid, but I was. Yep. In everything, yep, yep. I've never lost a game of Monopoly in my life.'

This willpower compresses into self-belief. Perry McCarthy is famous for giving a virtuoso and terrifying demonstration of the point with Andrea Moda in 1992. 'Belief is the fundamental thing. If you were to turn round at whatever age and say "I'm going to be a professional racing driver" the odds against are pretty long. If you turn round and say "I am going to be a Formula 1 racing driver" then, as they did in my case, most people just burst out laughing. They laugh firstly out of ignorance because they don't know what it takes, and if they did they would laugh even harder.

'Grand Prix motor racing is perhaps the most elite sport, with only 22 drivers or so at the very top. Sure there are very talented drivers in other formulas but if you want to go after being World Champion it's Formula 1 and the places are highly rationed.'

Did you set out specifically to reach Formula 1?

'It was there. I would never have come into motor racing without that goal. When I was younger I always knew that I had the mentality of switching on and saying "that's it" once I'd found what I wanted. I have an On and an Off switch and once it switches On that's it. Push-push-push. I will not take no for an answer.'

Have you ever had self doubts?

'There have been things that have happened to me across my career that have supported my claim that I am probably one of the very fastest. The problem is I couldn't sustain that challenge because of lack of money. You need all these ingredients to come together and you need them to constantly come together. Look at Jenson Button. It's been an absolute dream so far [in 2000] but he is also an exceptionally talented driver. And he's got an innate confidence. And he's been shielded from the outside world to a large degree because it's all happened so quickly. So that confidence, rather than being knocked or tested, is actually re-supported by all the things that are happening to him and for him. When you've got the older drivers – myself, Damon, Blundell and so forth – we've all had very big knocks along the way and probably I'm well known for taking more knocks than anybody and still keeping going.'

From this, I assume that McCarthy has not entertained self-doubts.

'Sometimes there might be a moment on track when a driver who's trying to convince a team to hire him is thinking "should I take this chance, because if I mess up it's my last chance?" even though you know you have the ability to do it. I have never operated like that. It's always been go for broke. The crash helmet goes on, the visor goes down and I believe that I will take my final and last chance by having been incredibly quick against the odds, whether it's in that final race or in that final test.'

Is that wise?

'It's just how I am. I have always said that if I was going to make it I was going to make it on my terms. I was once quoted in *Autosport*, large, as saying "I'm not going to have a frontal lobotomy to be a Grand Prix driver." That meant I didn't want to have a different personality or be the quiet guy or do this or do that or toe the line and not argue with anyone. The problem is, it's very difficult for me not to argue because, you know, I am a man who's been through an awful lot, and has got out of a lot, and has made a lot of things happen. If I've got someone telling me to do some things and I have no respect for that person I'm not going to sit there like a good little boy. I'll mouth off and that's probably not done me any favours.

'I've always said, however, that my temper is part of my passion and my passion is what makes me fast. Now if I start modifying myself, if I become terribly corporate, calmer, quieter, then that fire's been put out and perhaps there's not that anger and that absolute need to be fastest. When somebody goes quicker than me, although I am probably well known as a bloke who makes a joke and smiles and has a laugh and congratulates everybody – which I believe is correct – it hurts me badly. I will be back out in the car trying to go even faster because my currency is to be seen to be one of the fastest.'

There are many in Formula 1 who think this is how a driver should react. With aggression. Alan Jones is remembered fondly, except perhaps by the American driver Eddie Cheever because, at Zolder in deepest Belgium, Cheever did something on track which displeased Mr. Jones. Mr. Jones, overall top folded down to the waist, the arms trailing along behind, advanced down the pit lane, seized Cheever – a big man – lifted him off the ground and communicated verbally with him. The dialogue was not by Shakespeare …

Sir Frank Williams says Jones 'spoilt' the team in the sense that he didn't complain, didn't make a nuisance of himself, didn't throw tantrums but got in whatever car they gave him and drove the balls off it. Williams liked that. This same Jones, when asked if he would like to bury the hatchet with a team-mate after some bitter feuding, replied yes, he would like to, right between the shoulder blades. This same Jones – a chunk of a man – was checking out of the Renaissance Centre Hotel in Detroit one year after the USA-East Grand Prix. 'Know what I've been doing?' he mused. 'Putting porn pictures in the Gideon's Bible in my room ...'

It was Jones's balance. At the furthest remove from this strange anecdote, McCarthy describes the strategies of struggle when, suddenly, you are offered a chance. 'You get in the car, you grip the steering wheel – this is way against Jackie Stewart's philosophy and everything else[8] – but you grip the wheel and tell yourself "we are going even deeper into this corner, we are keeping the foot flat as I turn in." Sometimes I have gone into a corner when it's pure desperation, and I've not been sure if the car's going to come back out the other side. It's because I've got no time. I've no more than ten or fifteen laps to put a fast lap in – that's the team's assessment of me, that's the total they've given me. You get to a point where what are you going to do, come in and say "well, this wasn't right, that wasn't right, the other wasn't good enough for me?" No. It's now. That's the deal.'

The problem is that Stewart's got three World Championships and you haven't.

'That's quite true and there were things that were working for Jackie or that perhaps he'd made work for him – and we are talking about different eras, of course – but I am saying he was able to go about it as he did, he was able to affect the team with the way he worked.'

But also his mind worked that way. If it came to the 15-lap test, I think he would have handled it in a completely different way. He would have brought his Scottish logic to bear and he'd have convinced them the car wasn't right and they'd have given him a second test.

'I don't know. It's certainly made me pretty different from

most people, and that might be an attribute. Anyway, that's what's going to happen and I make it happen. Might be in business, might be on the track. I think of all drivers as pie charts. That can be determination, sheer natural talent, technical understanding, PR, personality, whatever. You can have massive reserves of natural talent but it's the hunger, it's the need, that's the dividing factor.'

Is that what you reckon would be the biggest segment on the pie chart?

'I personally cannot understand how it wouldn't be. Drivers are faced with consistent insecurity. They're out of a job almost every single year – OK some have two-year contracts, but you take the point. There is not a pension fund built in. So where am I? What's my currency? What's my stock value? Beat your team-mate, do something special, get noticed. That's what the deal's about.'

The notion of surviving in the outside world is something Allan McNish had to try, and it demonstrated to him how wonderful being a racing driver is. We were talking towards the end of 2000 and McNish was test driver for the Toyota Formula 1 team due to go into Grand Prix racing in 2002.

'In the years from 1992 to 1995, if a Minardi or someone of that ilk on the grid had come along and said "OK we want you to race for us in Formula 1" I'd probably have said yes. Then after the year at Porsche [in sportscars] I changed my attitude. I said to myself "there are other things outside of Formula 1 and outside of just being on the grid." Porsche was a serious commitment too. We won Le Mans and to stand there on the podium was like a hit on the head: it's more important to win races than just be in Formula 1. I need to race to win. I don't need to race to race. Do I enjoy driving a car? Yes. Do I enjoy working with teams? Yes. But what do I enjoy most? Winning. And that's why I changed my attitude a wee bit. I realised that the thing which made me tick was the winning. That win at Le Mans revitalised me.[9] The pressure was phenomenal: 70,000 or so Brits there ...

'What was always in the back of our mind was that the car was built purely to win the race. The day after Le Mans was the fiftieth anniversary of Porsche and that year was the hundredth anniversary of Michelin, the tyre sponsors. The whole board were there – flew in on the Saturday morning, flew out on the Sunday night. They had 1,000 guests so, if we hadn't won, it would have been a big let-down and that made for pressure for everybody.

'And when it was over I realised I needed to win races – to be involved in races and win them – to be happy. I realised that the last few years before, I hadn't been happy. It had been a grind. It wasn't necessarily that I thought about quitting, because the real world outside motor racing wasn't that exciting in comparison. Having to work for a living is quite a hard thing to do.

'In motor racing, we live in a very closeted environment and, in general, it doesn't give a fair idea of what working for a living is about. My father had a hip operation in 1996 and I went up to the garage and basically I sat there for three or four weeks while he was in hospital, and I couldn't believe it. You have to get up early in the morning, you have to work from eight o'clock until eight o'clock at night, you've got problems all the time, you've got the responsibility of having 20 people working for you and their wages every month, and other people's problems are suddenly your problem. All these things made me realise that the world outside is a hard place.

'We are very lucky – really, really lucky – to be involved in something that's worldwide and gives you the ability to travel and see different lifestyles. I wouldn't change it. It's a drug. I can see why drivers find it difficult when they stop racing. There's nowhere else to go. You don't usually have another trade because you left school racing karts and were basically a professional karting driver. What you know is what you have always known, the racing.'

So that's part of the motivation. The actual act of driving provides some of the answer too. As John Watson attests, you become a kind of animal in the car.

'Either you make it or I make it but we ain't both going to make it, so it's a form of crude survival. We go back to our primeval state, if you like. Through evolution we are what we are today. If we could transpose ourselves back across however many thousands of years and go back to life as it was when it first began, it was a question of you survive or you don't. Take pets. Those thousands of years ago they were wild animals and we have domesticated them but on occasions you see them react in that primeval way. They will almost attack you: the survival mechanism is suddenly still there. And I think we human beings have got it.'

The interesting thing is that in a racing car you behave like that but the moment you get out of the car you become John Watson again.

'That's what people generally find hard to understand but it is something you can do when you understand how to access it. In the same way I learned in a very crude manner how to control overtaking situations. I did it with my team-mate, I did it with other people and I discovered that overtaking is about a mental thing. If I can beat you mentally I can beat you physically and you've had it.'

That's Why.

NOTES

1. Manchester United won 2–1 with both their goals coming in the last minute. It gave them the treble of the English Premiership, the FA Cup and the European Cup.

2. Quoted in the March 2001 issue of *F1 Racing*.

3. Watkins Glen, situated in Upstate New York, hosted 20 Grands Prix between 1961 and 1980. It was usually at or near the end of the season.

4. Carlos Pace (Brazil) drove in 72 Grands Prix between 1972 and 1977.

5. Suzuka is an unusual circuit surrounded by a vast themed parkland – part funfair, part exhibition stands, part gardens. Within this is an hotel and the Log Cabin is a bar nearby.

6. A programme shown on British television called *Eddie Irvine: The Inside Track* © Formula One Administration Ltd.

7. Rupungi is a night club area of Tokyo.

8. Stewart has described how before a race he imagined himself to be a balloon slowly deflating. He mentally dissipated the gathering tension. He has also described how you can learn to see the corner rushing at you in slow motion, so that it happens frame by frame.

9. At Le Mans in 1998, the Porsche of McNish/Laurent Aiello/Stéphane Ortelli beat the Porsche of Jörg Müller/Uwe Alzen/Bob Wollek by a lap.

Chapter 2

LIVE FOR EVER

'Some of my experiences with parents are the worst I have ever had in motorsport. The language, abuse and plain thuggishness I have seen from both mothers and fathers really are the worst. That is the sad side. Luckily it is a small element although it is vocal. It can make it very unpleasant.'

– John Surtees

It's logical to begin this chapter with another question, 'When?' Bill Sisley, who runs Buckmore Park, a karting circuit in Kent, has seen generations of youngsters come and go, including Johnny Herbert. He sets out the context of the beginning. 'You cannot get a competition licence until you are eight, although you can practise when you're seven. I've probably seen a couple of six-year-olds recently too. I feel, however, that they are not ready mentally until they are at least eight. It used to be 11 for the licence – when Johnny Herbert was here – and what's happened is that drivers like Jenson Button and Kimi Räikkönen are getting there three years earlier. Those three years are crucial. At eight it can already be more a career than a sport. They show up with dads who have money and a motorhome. By 13 they understand data logging, which in the old days they weren't doing until they'd reached Formula 3 in cars. They mature very quickly and, by 13, might be living in Italy' – karting is very big there.

'Young sportsmen,' Herbert says, 'are completely different to what I remember. They're more grown up. They can take a lot more very much earlier on, like Räikkönen. In certain respects he's had less experience than Jenson although most of them were doing race after race in karting. Ralf Schumacher did, Michael did, Häkkinen did, Alesi I think did. A majority who got into Formula 1 did.'

McNish describes the young generation of karters as 'much more attuned to presenting themselves than I was when I raced karts. There was no TV for karting at the time, no radio coverage, no media coverage – so to think like that wasn't necessary. Now it is.'

John Surtees, the only man to win World Championships on two wheels and four (500cc four times between 1956 and 1960, Formula 1 with Ferrari in 1964), has now gone karting with his 10-year-old son Henry.

Did he take it up at your instigation?

'No, a good friend had a little function – some people going down to Buckmore – and he said "let Henry come along." Henry went along and my daughter Edwina went as well and they loved it. My wife turned round and said "not both of them!" and Edwina got the short straw. She went over to ponies.'

... which is even more dangerous.

'Well, I think so. Anyway, Henry said "I want to go karting" so that started me on something which – oh, dear – is an ever-increasing involvement.'

Were you surprised by how professional it is?

'I have been surprised by a number of things. The best part about it is finding these little people who are all emotionally involved. What is so important, of course, in life is that people get emotionally involved in something. Too many kids these days are without any direction and just wander from disaster to disaster. By contrast we went out to a major British circuit and they turned away ten competitors because there was an over-subscription. There were 60 karts and every dad or mum, if they're running a season, must have been talking of a minimum of £10,000 and normally about £20,000.'

How do the youngsters take it mentally?

'The youngsters are ... youngsters. They can be affected by all the pressures but generally they show themselves as immensely competitive, and the way they adapt and are able to cope with these karts is something to see. You're a youngster, eight years of age, and suddenly you've got a kart which will do 55 to nearly 60 miles an hour and you're sitting with your bottom an inch off the ground. It feels very fast, particularly for someone of eight. Henry is ten and he's been doing it for just over a year. They show an immense amount of skill, a natural ability to work with a piece of machinery. Even if they don't become racing drivers further on – and frankly there's not room for all of them – with a bit of luck it will inspire them to be involved in engineering and technology from the point of view of creating a relationship with a piece of machinery, or in turn it will at least make them better drivers.'

Do you have slight misgivings about putting an eight- or nine-year-old in a situation where they are going to have to grow up both physically and mentally before their time?

'I don't know if that is the case. The important thing centres round the mothers and fathers, and this is some of the worst aspects of karting. If you try and make sure there is a balance, so that the kids of eight don't forget their teddy bears and can still be eight-year-olds but switch on and have a degree of maturity when they sit in their kart, then that's OK. It mustn't be rammed into their heads all the time that they've got to go out and be successful, knock this or that person off the track, and "you're going to be a Formula 1 driver." That is wrong. Unfortunately there is a small core who push their kids too hard. They are trying to live out an experience: perhaps they never had the opportunity, perhaps they are failed racing drivers, perhaps they are just dreamers.

'Some of my experiences with parents are the worst I have ever had in motorsport. The language, abuse and plain thuggishness I have seen from both mothers and fathers really are the worst. That is the sad side. Luckily it is a small element although it is vocal. It can make it very unpleasant. For a while Henry – perhaps because of his name – got very targeted by two or three families. They threatened him and did all sorts of things. It had a real effect, it nearly switched him off. It's not that different to what you see sometimes at a school football match with the parents on the touch-line screaming and shouting and getting abusive. Luckily motorsport generally is cleaner and tidier, but you still have some of the football thug element there, however partially. That is the danger to the youngsters.'

Henry, at nine, could have been damaged by that.

'Well, we've certainly had to go through a situation which was almost like where a lad can be damaged by bullying at school, a few months where we had to be very careful with Henry and in fact I pulled him out of racing and just let him test. On the other hand, when you talk to and see these lads getting it all right and putting it all together, you say "if they are showing that amount of ability why should you deny them the opportunity of actually doing it?" If it's not there, and they are frightening themselves, they shouldn't be there and some of the kids perhaps shouldn't do it.

'To keep the balance is very important. If I start seeing Henry turning into someone who is 90% a racing driver in his thoughts I'll stop him because I don't want him to grow up too quickly. I want him to show a certain maturity, I want him to relate to that piece of machinery and switch on when he's doing it, switch off when he's not. It's like a Formula 1 race. You have certain drivers who sit there in their cars and they are out-and-out 100% Formula 1 drivers. When they are away from it they switch off and can be family people. It is important that the kids are likewise. And the kids get pressure over it, even at school, because other kids can be a bit jealous. It's not easy.'

You came into motorsport via your dad …

'I had a £6 motor bike which I had to put together in the corner and in order to see whether it went or not dad said "you'd better try and ride it." I rode it round the outside of the cinder track at Brands Hatch.'

Your son is in a sense following on.

'In a broad sense. Nowadays I am only involved in the historic side, consultancy with people driving the old Grand Prix cars, doing a bit with the motor cycles, so it's still part of my life but my children never saw me racing because I had them late. I never spoke about racing to Henry but he took a bit of an interest – technology is one of his best subjects, fiddling and creating and making things – and then he was introduced to a kart and he wanted a kart. What he will or won't do, who knows? All I want him to do is enjoy it. I said "if you'd prefer to concentrate on rugby" – he's very keen on that – "we'll do it tomorrow. I will support you, but only while you have your heart in it." He's only ten!'

To be a racing driver you need a certain mental approach. Can you inherit that?

'I think there is something in that, a degree of growing up in an environment of racing. To start with, racing drivers as such will all be competitive people so if you grow up in a family which has a little bit of a competitive line running through it you will naturally get involved in competitive things. That'll be sports of different sorts and I think it is an attitude of mind. You will find that when a racing driver stops, he doesn't stop being competitive – he will compete in other things.'

When you were driving the pre-war Mercedes at Donington a couple of years ago, you were competing with the past.

'You are competing with the past and relating to the past. You're sitting there saying "right, well I'm with Seaman" or "I'm driving Caracciola's car or Rosemeyer's car."[1] I relate to machinery, and I think in his own way Henry does too. He is an extremely smooth little driver, not all arms and legs. He bubbles. When he comes in and he's done quite a good job, whether it's practice or a race, you can see it.'

Interestingly, Bill Sisley insists that the standard of competitiveness in karting has not altered over the last 20 years. 'The change is that the top end – Formula 1 – has realised the value of karting.'

Let's apply that to Jarno Trulli, the Italian driver who karted for 12 years and, as the Jordan team proclaims, 'is the only Formula 1 driver to have won everything there is to win in karting.' Trulli insists that 'it was very important for me to get my grounding in karting. I used to go to karting events from the age of three. My father drove as a hobby and I'd go along with my mother to support him.' Trulli started watching Formula 1 aged four. 'Then one day when I was about seven there was a new category for young people called mini-kart and my dad asked me if I wanted a go. Once I was in the kart that was it. I didn't want to get out again, although I never dreamed where it would lead me.'

There are two points here. The first confirms the conclusion reached in the previous chapter. For anyone like Trulli, the desire to earn fortunes was not a consideration. How could it be for a seven-year-old? The second is that the initial sensation of karting – speed, control, risk, impossible cornering, noise – is intoxicating, fulfilling and, ultimately, addictive. It gives the youngster a new dimension and may well shape the rest of his life. When he starts serious racing (Trulli took his first major title at 13) the intoxication deepens into the hunt and the hunters. You cannot watch a pack of karts snarling and snapping into a corner and mistake that.

This is a significant change from The Good Old Days because the mind of the driver is being sharpened so early. I approached John Watson with this.

Do you think genuine friendship is possible in Formula 1?

'There is friendship but it changed from around the 1970s when, let's say, if there'd been a Malaysian Grand Prix on the back of a Japanese Grand Prix on the back of a US Grand Prix [as there was in 2000: Indianapolis 24 September, Suzuka 8 October, Sepang 22 October] I promise you that drivers from different teams would have gone off between those races windsurfing, scuba diving, waterski-ing, had dinner together.

'In the 1970s Ronnie Peterson was a friend, Mario Andretti became a friend, Gunnar Nilsson too. Niki was a friend when he was a team-mate although afterwards he became isolated in the Ferrari thing. James Hunt was a friend to some degree. You'd do things together, go to the shopping mall, go to the movies, go and have dinner, go to a "tittie" club, a disco, whatever, and you'd do it as mates in the way that kids in Formula 3 today might do when they go to Macau.[2] They'll go to the tittie bars, have a few beers, be drunk as lords, fall out of the place, and spew all over the pavement. The growing up process is occurring at 18, 19 and 20 whereas we were doing it in our late 20s and early 30s.

'I think this has been an evolutionary thing and, although I've said the 1970s, perhaps the bigger change occurred when people like Nelson Piquet, Elio de Angelis and Riccardo Patrese reached Formula 1. They'd come up through karting. The advent and growth of karting as a profession was a significant change. You'd see youngsters coming from it to single-seater racing with serious attitude. That began in the late 1970s. Don't forget that Alain Prost came up through karting.

'There was that point when it became a very clear feeder into the junior formulae and people were being taken through those formulae very quickly: Piquet got taken out of Formula 3 and straight into Formula 1, same with Senna – so it became very apparent that the karting experience was where the talent was really being fostered as opposed to the traditional route of FF1600, then Formula 3, then Formula 3000.

'Suddenly here were, and are, very bright lights shining very early in a career. They're young, they're probably not too expensive to hire and they've got longer term potential. Like everything, the pressure in karting has increased. These little soldiers are coming out, and they are little soldiers – hard as nails.'

Allan McNish 'started because my next door neighbour lived on a farm and he had a kart you could drive around the fields on, a little Honda lawnmower engine and a square tube frame. I had a wee go on that and quite liked it. We went to a kart race, I had a go in one and it developed from there.' He was competing at

11. 'I got pretty good in the kart locally and nationally and then ultimately internationally.' If McNish's 'it' moment is more muted than Trulli's that may reflect their personalities and their nationalities: any Italian 'it' will be volcanic.

For glimpses of the young hunters in action I'm indebted to *Karting* magazine and their coverage of the CIK Junior Cup at Le Mans (equivalent of the World Championships for U-16s) in 1985.

Section A: 'Although McNish was on pole, Schumacher shot straight into the lead never to be headed. Allan threatened occasionally but never looked likely to get past.'

Pre-final: 'The first corner saw a six-kart pile-up, due in the main to the very fast starts. Muller led with Beggio, Schumacher, McNish and the rest chasing hard.'

Final: 'Schumacher was away followed by Muller, Beggio, Gilardi and McNish and Orsini and for the next five laps or so the leaders chopped and changed.'

Junior pre-final: 'By lap seven McNish was all over Schumacher and then got past but was unable to shake off the very determined German who kept up the pressure.'

There's a photograph of the podium, the Italian Andrea Gilardi on the top rung, Schumacher – hands on hips, face not masking disappointment – on the second and McNish, looking boyish and slight, on the third. Who can tell which way a career will go? Where is Gilardi? Who could know that Schumacher would be regarded as one of the greatest drivers and McNish (at the time of writing) had yet to contest a Grand Prix?

The 'When?' is important, but not as important as what follows it.

Here is one last vignette, from the 100cc European Championships in Gothenburg in 1986: 'McNish in second place was obviously struggling to hold off Schumacher and eventually succumbed to a nice out-braking move on the hairpin. Schumacher pulled out a few lengths but couldn't quite get away.'

McNish says the karting was 'a hobby, a serious hobby, and it took me to the World Championships. It is also a family sport. You've got to have the back-up of your parents because if you don't you can't get there in the first place.'

Does this desire to win come to apply to other things?

'Yes. I have really had to learn not to create competition in everything I do, because you can become quite a bitter and twisted old person. You can't bring it into your social life. OK, when I play sport I don't want to do it badly, I don't want to look stupid and I want to win – but I really try and keep it all for the track.'

Is that difficult?

'Sometimes it is. I find it quite hard because you have to be very ruthless to win in motorsport. It's a factor, a must. You have to be very ruthless because if you aren't you'll finish second and if you're finishing second the whole thing will go past you. You can't let that happen. You have to be very hard with the opposition and you have to be very hard with your own self because you have to perform 100% every single time you get in the car, the kart or whatever. That side of it, the competitive instinct, is in your nature. Some people are just not competitive. They aren't a lesser person, not at all, they're just not competitive. Some people are ...'

... hunters.

Is this what separates you from other people?

'Any sportsman is a little bit separate because we're doing something we love. I don't think you find many drivers, athletes, football players who at the age of 12 or 13 – whenever they start – do it for any other reason. They don't do it because they think "in 15 years I am going to be successful in Formula 1, I am going to be earning this much money and have this sort of lifestyle." It is not about that. It starts as a hobby that they become very good at and then it becomes a profession.'

The crucial difference with motorsport and the rest is that you need the kart to play, whereas you and I could go out with a football – or even use a tennis ball – and have a 'game' of football.

'Initially karts are provided by somebody else, usually the parents, and I was lucky in that respect. My first kart, all the spares, plus the overalls, tyres and everything else cost £300 and, even accepting the change in the value of money, it was still quite cheap compared to now.'

Either way, it's plenty to a lot of people in the back streets of Glasgow.

'At a high level, and especially now, karting is definitely not cheap. There is no question about that. The average cost absolutely terrifies me. A youngster will be spending the sort of money they'd spend on a Formula 3 season.'

Did you want to start or was it your parents giving you the chance that made you start?

'I had a motocross bike, and I did a couple of races on that. I was very small as a kid and I had to get a bigger bike to be able to race. I'd say that the whole thing was because my father hadn't been in a position to do it himself in his time. He'd liked it and he used to do some motocross when he was younger but he couldn't really afford to take it any further so he was giving me the opportunity he didn't have. Obviously there was interest very quickly from myself.'

Plus he had a garage.

'Plus he had a garage ... and his best friend sold motor bikes. The whole scene sort of interacts. As I say, I was then too small to ride the bike and I had to get a bigger one. My feet were still six inches off the ground and it was just dangerous. I was probably a bit dangerous anyway, never mind on a big bike.'

You don't care at that age.

'No, you don't and I enjoyed doing it, no question.'

McNish's father Bert explains that Allan did six motocross races and won the sixth but, because of his age, would have had to move up into a more senior category the following season and took to karting instead. Bert accepts that it was he who introduced Allan to motocross but it was done with no ulterior motive like hooking him into a career.

So virtually anyone with the cash can get started in motor racing. All they have to be is determined enough. Here are two men from completely different backgrounds, Julian Bailey and Jonathan Palmer.

Bailey was from a council house in Woolwich.

What did your dad do?

'He was a lorry driver.'

Quick?

'I don't know! When I was 12 we moved to Spain. He wanted to get out of the situation we were living in and so we went over there. He bought a supermarket and he ran it. I grew up there, in Majorca, and I started karting because I'd always liked karts and bikes and things like that. Then I came back to England and started Formula Ford.

'I had a big problem when I came back to England at 17 because I had the vocabulary of a 12-year-old in English. I spoke better Spanish than I did English, which was a problem because when I came to write a letter I wanted to put Spanish words in as well. What I used to do was copy other people's letters, changing them round to suit me, chop bits out and use them. I think I spelt "sincerely" wrong for about three years, then I saw how somebody else had spelt it. There were lots of things like that.'

Jonathan Palmer was a product of a middle class environment.

There was a moment when you had to choose, because you could have been a doctor.

'It wasn't really very complicated: if you give the average motorsport-crazed 24-year-old a choice of going into motor racing full-time or continue with his medical career, very few would make a different choice. They'd pick the motor racing while they were young enough to give it a go.'

And if it doesn't work out you've got the fall-back position.

'Yes, but at that age you don't particularly bother about fall-back positions, do you? I didn't. You're going to live for ever, you're going to be successful in whatever you do, and the notion of having a fall didn't even occur to me. I suppose the medical career was the sensible, methodical route having come from a sensible, methodical family. My father was a GP, mother was a nurse who ran a nursing home. I remember before deciding on A levels that, effectively, I was going to do medicine or engineering.

'I loved cars as a child, I was passionate about cars. I built go-karts and crashed motor bikes and cars around the paddock at home and everyone who knew me knew that I was just infatuated with cars and driving and going fast. But when it came to what I am going to do with my life, because of my professional family, there wasn't huge pressure but it was rather assumed by all, I suppose, that I'd go into a profession. I was probably a) sensible enough and b) aware of the fact that I knew nothing about the competing end of motorsport.

'I watched scrambling on the TV, watched rallycross and after about 40 minutes I had to burst out and go and get on my own motorbike and thrash round. My Saturday afternoons would be punctuated with watching any motorsport, I'd get bored after a while and want to do it – but I hadn't grown up with a family that worked in the motor trade or who competed. My father never competed in anything in his life.

'Build go-karts? I don't remember him building a thing or tinkering with the car. His hobbies were photography and coin collecting. He wasn't a car fiddler. By the time I got to 12 or 13 I knew much more about cars than he did. He'd ask me what he should buy. I used to read *Motor* and *Autocar* and can remember to this day the 0–50 times of Lotus Cortinas so, in a way, it was a story in my life. I was pioneering a path within my family in the pursuit of my own ambition and interest. Medicine was a comfortable thing to do. I didn't know where to start to go off and be a racing driver.

'As a 16- to 18-year-old I knew nothing about engineering and thought I'd end up behind an office desk. I said to myself "that's not for me." I didn't like the idea of being part of a big company. In respect of weighing the two options, I suspected I'd go in for medicine and I knew too that my father – although he never said anything – would be dead chuffed if I opted for medicine; and I did. He'd studied at Guy's and I got into Guy's.

'It was the passive choice, in a way, and I don't think it was the wrong thing to do. Virtually all the drivers I saw in Formula Palmer Audi[3] – and most of them who were contemporaries of mine – had families who'd been around the motor trade and they'd grown up amidst karting, with father helping and that kind of thing. I would have been out of my depth getting into motor racing that way. But as soon as I started at medical school I knew I wanted to get in somehow. I bought this old Sprite and I did it all myself. I had no money from my family: they were always mortgaged to the eyeballs.

'I don't regret it at all, and I see this as a difference between many people around me and myself. If you make it in motor racing against a background of no-one in your immediate environment having ever done the sport or having any idea about it, that means you have the desire and the passion.

'I remember my days of racing the frog-eyed Sprite. Every race in that meant as much to me in my first year as an 18-year-old, with my 13-year-old brother as my mechanic, as the Grands Prix when I was with Tyrrell. In fact every race through my career was that way. I did a race at Thruxton on a Saturday, then went to Brands Hatch on the Sunday, and I can distinctly remember what happened. We used to prepare the car in a garage next to the house, as many do, and I had a row with my brother because we had a lot to do on the car, changing the long dif for Thruxton to a short one for Brands. It was pouring with rain on this November night and we were outside in the drive. My brother was taking too long changing the dif and I was getting annoyed – and, to think of it now, here he was, a kid brother. If I'd looked over the fence and seen a neighbour doing that – dad nowhere to be seen, 13-year-old brother under there with a spanner – I would have been terribly impressed at the level of endeavour and commitment.'

The journey from karting towards Formula 1 moves across junior formulae on an ascending scale, each harder to reach than the one before. This is the survival of the fittest, which accords nicely with the hunting analogy.

However the former French Grand Prix driver Philippe Streiff insists that the journey becomes easier. 'At the beginning, you are nothing. Nobody knows you and why should they? Then you get some results and you can find sponsors ...'

Streiff's journey involved karting, building his own car with insurance money from a claim, falling out with the most famous driving school in France, and winning a competition for promising talent. At 18 his parents insisted he go to university for four years studying engineering. He also reached French Formula 3, then progressed through Formula 3000. At this time, as it seemed, all France wanted a World Champion and companies like Renault and Elf were investing in that.

Young drivers tend to fall into two categories: those whose journey is smoothed by major sponsorship and those whose journey certainly isn't. Streiff is in the former – so are many helped by Marlboro, such as Häkkinen and McNish. Michael Schumacher was brought on by Mercedes. These drivers do not need to question their chosen career because it is unfolding nicely.

The majority, including Nigel Mansell, are in the latter category and the years between karting and Formula 1 represent a formidable struggle. Those who lack mental resilience fall away. Nor is surviving the struggle any guarantee of success.

Eric Bernard was a virtual contemporary of Streiff in the 1980s (although their Grand Prix careers did not overlap), and knew all about the struggle.

'It's difficult because of the money: it costs a lot. The problem in France in my era was that the only competitive team – backed by Marlboro, who had most money – was Oreca.[4] Unfortunately the team was "full" and there was no place for me so I decided to form my own Formula 3 team.'

To do this, you have to be absolutely certain that motor racing is your future.

'For me it was absolutely necessary to do something in Formula 3 for my career to continue. It didn't matter what obstacles I encountered.'

Footballers don't need to raise these sums. Imagine saying to a young footballer 'you have to raise £100,000 to play in a big club's third team' ...

'This is the problem of the car, if I can put it like that. You must have money to drive in these formulae of promotion, and the problem must be faced by all young drivers. In contrast, if you can't bring any money to football it's OK.'

Do you think the struggle is a measure of your desire?

'You don't have a choice. If you want a career you need a budget in order to find a team. Forming my own team might not have been the easiest way but it was my only possibility.'

Bernard progressed through Formula 3000 and reached Formula 1 in 1989. He thus takes his place among the other 618 who made it (from 1950 up to the end of 2000). Nobody can know how many thousands were eliminated but, certainly from the 1980s onwards, the lack of mental resilience would be decisive.

This brings us briefly to Senna, who existed in a category of his own. When he was in Formula 3 he tried to dictate conditions to Ron Dennis of the McLaren Formula 1 team (to Dennis's consternation and amazement) and explained to Alex Hawkridge of Toleman that he was uninterested in Formula 1 unless he could dominate it. Mental resilience is what Senna did have. Self doubt is what Ayrton Senna did not have. You know the rest of the story.

NOTES

1. Dick Seaman, Bernd Rosemeyer and Rudolf Caracciola were leading Grand Prix drivers in the mid to late 1930s. Seaman and Caracciola drove for Mercedes and Rosemeyer for Auto Union (Audi).

2. The Macau Grand Prix, a street race in the Portuguese colony across the way from Hong Kong, began in 1954 and, from 1983 when Senna won, became a celebrated and highly-rated Formula 3 race.

3. Formula Palmer Audi was a single-seater championship set up by Jonathan Palmer in 1998 to encourage young talent. The cars were all the same.

4. Oreca, run by Hughes de Chaunac and based near Paul Ricard, was virtually a French national institution and most leading French drivers were associated with it.

Chapter 3

DECISION: F1

'I went down to see Ken Tyrrell and he asked what the situation was. I said I had this sponsorship but also what I was going to do was sell my pub and give him three hundred grand. He said "no, I'm not taking that, I'm not taking your money." So I was sitting there and the bloke wouldn't take the three hundred grand off me.'
– Julian Bailey

The last step, into Formula 1, might seem a logical extension of what the driver has always wanted, what he has been preparing himself for, but even this is an examination of the man and how he thinks. There is so much to master. He understands the rules of the hunt: any weakness will be exploited and the young, the old, the lame, the slow and the inexperienced are immediately vulnerable. To survive, the driver needs rigid self-belief. This is how Ralf Schumacher expresses it.

Are there any other drivers you admire?

'No.'

What qualities do you dislike in others?

'Envy.'

What do you believe in?

'Before you can believe in anything you have to believe in yourself.'

Physically, the first time in a Formula 1 car does not, as it seems, take their breath away. Johnny Herbert débuted in a

Benetton before his accident in Formula 3000 and reflects on how things have changed. 'For the test with Benetton at Brands, when Boutsen was there, I never had a seat fitting, I used Teo Fabi's seat.[1] He was quite small but chunky. They put a load of pillows in the car and nowadays that would be just laughable. I sat in it, I went quick and I didn't really have a seat.'

Did you not have to think about driving an F1 car?

'I could do it straight away. It was mightily quick, I remember, because I was used to 165 horsepower and I'd jumped into something which had nine and a half [950] but the instinct was there. Paddock wasn't such a big thing, it was more braking for Druids, then you're down through Graham Hill bend.[2] It really was instinct and I never lost that.'

Jenson Button, speaking before the start of the 2001 season after an amazingly accomplished début with Williams in 2000[3], said: 'Formula 1 is not a sport where you win world titles by adopting "after you Claude" tactics. It is a fiercely competitive one where only the toughest survive. Some of Michael Schumacher's tactics have been widely criticised but as long as they are within the rules I don't see anything wrong. I don't see anything wrong with being aggressive on the track. I can see how it may upset followers who used to watch motor racing in cloth caps and tweed jackets, but the sport has changed so much in recent years.

'I think young sportsmen look at things differently these days. Obviously I would never consider doing anything which endangered someone's life or went well beyond the boundaries of Formula 1, but to be a winner you have to be able to mix it at 200mph and grab any chances providing they are within the rules.'

On Hill's crash with Schumacher in 1994[4] Button said: 'I

thought that was all right. He [Schumacher] won the title and that's the most important thing. I would have done the same in his position. It didn't look good but it worked. About the 1997 incident with Villeneuve[5] I can't say what I would have done had I been in Michael's position but the only thing that was wrong with what he did was that it didn't work. A lot was made of Michael's starts last season when he'd get off the grid and pull straight in front of other drivers. I have never believed that to be a bad thing because it is within the rules. There is so much at stake these days that you have to be more aggressive.'

To broaden this, here is an exchange with Eddie Irvine:

When you look in a mirror what do you see?

'Me. Me.'

Self-doubt?

'No. I'd like to be taller, I'd like to be stronger, I'd like to have a flat belly – lots of things I'd like but, all in all, I can't complain. Mentally I don't get nervous about things.'

Suppose you had to make a speech to the UN? Would you get butterflies?

'Oh yes, but that's not my game, making speeches. You know Jackie Stewart sends drivers away to practise making speeches so, OK, he gets loads of people that can make speeches in the same way and, you know, what does that do? They're all the same – so it's perfect. Great.'

Would you have mechanisms for getting over the butterflies?

'I would – I'd just avoid it …'

But if you had to?

'I'd do it, I'd do it. I'd do it but it wouldn't be an IMG[6] Jackie Stewart speech, there'd be mistakes, there'd be pauses – but that's me. I'd be a bit nervous thinking about it, yeah, yeah, yeah, yeah. I have the mentality of the circuit because that's my job and that's what I've been practising for years and that's what I'm good at. I've built a little knowledge up so I know what to do. Speeches? I don't know what to do and I don't want to learn what to do. Why? Because I just don't.'

John Watson remembers his own rather more deferential attitude as a newcomer. 'I had to pinch myself to think that here really was *the* Graham Hill on the same grid as me. I remember in my second Formula 2 race the front row was Jochen Rindt and Jackie Ickx. I thought "I'm going to wake up and find it's been a dream." Maybe as I got more grown up and more worldly that effect became less, but I never had the arrogance of a James Hunt. Incidentally, Niki didn't have arrogance, he had confidence.'

I'm not sure James had arrogance. I think what he had was a Public School ability to portray arrogance.

'In his early days James was the archetypal Public Schoolboy and, by virtue of that, the world was there at his feet. This is the whole foundation of the English class system. I was not a product of that. I had a very good home life, I had no interest in education whatsoever: it was nothing to do with driving racing cars. As a consequence of 30-odd years out of Ireland, I have learned more than I learned during my time at school. I am not an academic but I have learned by observation, by listening, and exploiting whatever natural intelligence I possess.'

That last sentence, taken as a thumbnail sketch of what the driver arriving in Formula 1 will need, is perfect.

We shall be hearing how Watson managed this process, particularly when he found himself pitted mentally against Lauda. At the other extreme sat Kimi Räikkönen, just a few weeks into 2001 when I met him at the Sauber launch in their Hinwil factory near Zurich. Agnes Carlier, handling Press

Relations for the team, ushered me into a room where Räikkönen sat preparing to do a succession of interviews. Aged just 21, he seemed impossibly young, fresh-faced and somehow vulnerable. With the Australian Grand Prix at Melbourne weeks away, it was almost alarming to think that he had only driven 23 car races. Ever. His curriculum vitae was a slight document: karting from 1991 to 1999 when he began in cars. Max Mosley, President of the FIA, even opposed his being granted a Superlicence on the grounds that, while there should always be exceptions to rules for good reason – and Mosley was not questioning Räikkönen's potential – he wondered aloud and in public if there was a good reason here. He was unhappy that so far Räikkönen had only taken part in 'promotional' formulae (Formula Renault, Formula Ford Zetec Euro Cup, Formula Renault 2000) rather than a series like Formula 3 which more closely reflected Formula 1. Mosley was heavily outvoted. At the time of the Sauber launch, Räikkönen had done 1,034 kilometres testing at Mugello and 549 at Jerez.

How are you preparing mentally, because it's a very big test?

'I don't know – it's nothing different than last year in Formula Renault [moving up to the 2000 series]. Of course I realise Formula 1 is a bigger world, everything is much bigger all round F1. It is going to be a big shock, the first race.' He speaks very softly, with a politeness of youth long vanished, and his words are tinged with gentle Finnish intonations.

What sort of a person are you?

'I don't take any pressure from things around me. I just work.'

Are you really able to do that?

'Yes, usually I am because it's unhealthy to take any pressures and stuff like that. Always you are handling the pressure all day and you don't get nervous or something like that if you are going to handle it.'

But the whole world will be watching.

'Yeah, but ... so?'

And in due course you'll be at Monaco and it could be raining ...

'Yeah but that's the life I don't know yet. I have been working the whole life for this moment of getting into Formula 1 and now when I'm here I don't worry, I am just looking forward.'

Do you wake up in the night and think about it?

'No, not really.'

I would.

'Yeah, yeah, yeah I understand that but no, no, I don't have any problems with it.'

Are you a calm person?

'Yes.'

Do you lose your temper, shout at people?

'No, I don't really. Sometimes, but ...'

OK, *when was the last time you lost your temper?*

'I don't remember, no, I don't remember.'

Does that mean it's some years ago?

'No, maybe it was last year or something, and it's not with many people – only maybe in the army in Finland when I got pissed off sometimes.'

The army is the one place you're not meant to do it.

'I know, I know, but I never liked that place.'

Why not?

'Because people are telling what you need to do and I am not used to it. I have always been like that. I want to do what I like and I don't like it if people are telling you what you need to do.'

In Formula 1 you must have no self-doubts about anything.

'Yes.'

Do you quietly have doubts, when you are by yourself?

'No, because it is just one part of the game.'

So you don't have any doubt at all?

'It is hard sometimes to do these things [like being asked questions incessantly] because it is not the very nicest thing in this sport. Sometimes you would like to stay in your own place and stay quiet.'

Do you get frightened?

'No.'

In life in general?

'No, because, if something happens, afterwards I am just usually thinking of what I have done. I am not that frightened. Some things, of course, but that's normal.'

What things?

'Er ... I don't know. It is hard. Usually when I start thinking about what could have happened – what if? Nothing else I can be sure about.'

Most people are frightened of the unknown – and you're travelling into the unknown.

'For me it is just a new experience.'

How do you think other drivers will regard you, because you could be a problem for them?

'Yeah.'

They don't know what you are going to do.

'Yeah, for sure but I also don't know what they're going to do!'

Apart from Heidfeld, your team-mate at Sauber, have you met any of the other drivers when you were testing?

'Not really. Well, Jenson Button, I know him a little bit because he was go-karting at the same time as me. I raced against him but I don't know him very well. All the other drivers are strangers. I don't think it matters and maybe sometimes it's better when you race against them ...'

Is there anything about driving the Formula 1 car you find difficult?

'No, not really although you have so many controls and so much telemetry and you have to learn all those things. You are learning all the time, more and more, when you are driving it. Yeah, of course the first time was difficult. Everything was new and I had so many problems with the steering but then you get used to it. That was the first day. The second day was easier – because the first day, the corners came so quickly. Then the second day when you jumped into the car it was like everything had slowed down. Your brain gets used to it. The first day it really is the corners coming so quick, you accelerate out of the corner and [expletive] the next corner is already there. It all happens so quick. Then you get used to it.'

A lot of drivers say they see things slowly.

'I found that ... on the second day.'

Is that an automatic mental process?

'It's just coming from ... I don't know where. It just happens.'

Jarno Trulli faced a similar sort of examination. What did he make of Räikkönen getting there so early in a career? 'I have a feel of the situation. Probably I had less chance than Kimi or Jenson because before my first race in Australia [in 1997 with Minardi] I did only 300 kilometres in a Formula 1 car, which is nothing, so I was really afraid. It was probably worse for me than for Jenson. It was somehow very dangerous' – during the Grand Prix weekend he was having to discover virtually everything.

'Now drivers are much more prepared for Formula 1

compared to ten years ago because even in Formula Renault and Formula 3 they already have electronics and telemetry. Then they get in a Formula 1 car and first of all they get a lot of kilometres so they gain much experience. I've seen Kimi running and running every test and it's very good because it's the only way to learn.

'The second point is that he came from a category of racing where the level is very high in terms of technology. The third point is that I have never found myself in a position where I've had the responsibility of stopping someone else's career when they've had the chance of their lives. It's too important. I know Kimi is young but give him a chance because you cannot decide for someone else.'

Chance is a word with various meanings. By chance is how Martin Donnelly found himself driving an Arrows in the 1989 French Grand Prix at the Paul Ricard circuit. That year he was in the Eddie Jordan Formula 3000 team partnering Jean Alesi.

Donnelly explains that 'Alesi was leading the championship and Derek Warwick [an Arrows driver] has an accident in a kart and EJ [Eddie Jordan] has gone "right!" For whatever reason and I don't know why, he pushed me forward. A fortnight before, the Goodyear tyre test had taken place at Silverstone and I'd done a good job in a Lotus.[7] Maybe EJ thought it was easier to push me into the Arrows drive. Alesi was contracted to EJ, as I was, the next race was the French Grand Prix, Alesi was leading the 3000 and surely he should have priority over Martin Donnelly? Anyway I got the drive. Michele Alboreto fell out with Tyrrell, Alesi got the Tyrrell drive, qualified brilliantly and finished in the points. If it had gone the other way and I'd gone to Tyrrell, who knows?'

As we have seen, Jonathan Palmer was separated from most young drivers because his family had no connection with motorsport and he had a career beckoning as a doctor. Palmer ruminates on that.

Racing is the most ruthless examination of all the sports I have come across. It's not about learning, say, to play tennis with a homemade racket, it's about a total commitment – mental, physical, financial – from the earliest moments. And it finds out the people who won't make that commitment.

'I'm not sure that motor racing is much different from many other sports in terms of the motivation to get to the top. I don't see why it should be.'

Because you need the car to play.

'It can work two ways. If my passion was tennis, it certainly would have been a lot easier to participate because I wouldn't have had to find the money, but it works the other way too, because if half the drivers in motor racing don't have a silver spoon they are pretty well fed with opportunities by parents and friends. For those people it can be easier than other sports: in tennis they can't buy themselves an advantage by having superior equipment. Any kid who wants to play football or tennis can go and do it. In motor racing those who are privileged have a much easier time when you consider how many youngsters would love to do it but don't have the money. There are very few like me – and I don't want to sound arrogant – who had the combination of a good education and a profession. Because of my character and upbringing, I had a better opportunity than most, given a blank sheet of paper but, having said that, I still had a worse opportunity than most other drivers.'

I think this is relevant. If the going gets really tough, as it can, and if you have an 'out' like becoming a doctor, it is doubly a commitment to stay in.

'I think you're probably right. I always had a very good alternative to being a doctor, and that alternative – motor racing – would have to be even more important to me than being as comfortable as a doctor. I suppose it's a reflection of my total commitment that this never really occurred to me. There was never any question of not continuing motor racing. Had I been brought up with a dad who encouraged me and pushed me, and I was being swept along with that, I wouldn't have had the level of unquestioning confidence in what I wanted to do.

'I have frequently been accused of being someone who is confident and arrogant in motor racing but, at the end of the day, I got myself there and you have to get things done. I remember, whether it was in Formula 3 or Formula 2, having rows with Ron Tauranac[8] about the set-up of cars. If I felt something was right I'd say it.'

This is an awfully fine line, stating your case but staying just the polite side of saying 'hey, you're not pushing me around'.

'I went through my motor racing career trying to get the best result which, when it came to co-ordinating with the team, meant pushing as hard as you could and getting them seriously cheesed off. It's that fine line you tread between pushing and shoving and not actually crossing it.

'Senna was obviously hugely talented, but he also came from a pretty wealthy family. A problem that I did have is that I was always working so hard because an awful lot of motor racing is selling yourself to teams. You are effectively a supplier who is trying to sell to the customer, and you always wait desperately for when they buy from you because you are selling your way up: selling to more sponsors and bigger teams through Formula 3, Formula 2 and Formula 1.

'I ended up with far too much deep-seated gratitude for the opportunity, rather than pursuing my right to have the drive, and frankly it should have been a lot better, whereas someone like Senna, who knew he was outstanding, said "I'm not going to drive it" or "yes, I'm going to drive it if it's got this, that and the other. These are the conditions." If you're outstanding to that degree the world changes. For most of us, we're always clinging on to any hope of getting a drive and then, when we've got ourselves one, trying to keep it.

'My first glimpse of getting into Formula 1 was before the British Grand Prix in 1981 when I was offered a drive by March, run by John McDonald. I was leading the F3 Championship but I turned down the drive then – and I was right to do that – because the March wasn't desperately competitive. I might have done a good job but it's very hard in a bad car to do a job good enough to make people think "wow, he's impressive."'

Was there a moment when you consciously thought 'I must go for Formula 1?'

'Yes. When I'd won the Formula 3 Championship. That was a fairy-tale year, 1981. I won my first Formula 3 race ever, won the first four consecutively, won the championship and I was very much the Jenson Button of the time.[9] I did test at Silverstone in the McLaren and, apart from being quick, I went out in the car to start with, came back and said "look, something's not right, I think it's a damper on the right rear." Sure enough there was and they thought "well …"

'Ron Dennis said "can you get your girlfriend to drive your car home, I want you to come back with me?" He drove me back to the factory, I met John Barnard and we all had a chat. It was looking pretty good. They were seriously considering me to drive next year in the team, but what scuppered it was that Niki Lauda came out of retirement. I have heard it said that if he hadn't, it could well have been me although I don't know. That was my first near-miss on Formula 1.'

It's important to describe these heady days because many, many drivers work hard at this last step, selling themselves feverishly, and a rarefied few suddenly find themselves in demand everywhere. Consider Palmer. The final Formula 3 race was at Thruxton on October 25. That week he was invited to test with Lotus at Paul Ricard, and did at the beginning of November (with three other young drivers, Eliseo Salazar, Dave Scott and Roberto Moreno). He moved to a three-day Williams test also at Ricard with Keke Rosberg and did a 'respectable' 1m 6.6s (in the Lotus he'd done a 1m 9.4s). He flew back to Britain and tested the McLaren.

This is the finest of judgements. Do you wait and hope a Formula 1 contract will materialise from somewhere and, by waiting, risk having no drive where you are – in this case a Formula 2 contract with Ron Tauranac guaranteeing employment and a good drive with the chance to re-emphasise your quality to the Formula 1 fraternity the following season? For Palmer it wasn't even that simple although he did have offers of testing contracts with McLaren and Williams and 'eventually I opted for Williams'.

After the McLaren test, 'Jackie Oliver phoned me up and said "are you interested in joining Arrows next year?" I said "great." He said "come up to the factory, I'd like you to meet Alan Rees."[10] I went up to Milton Keynes, looked round the factory and within a week I signed a three-year contract.'

No question of paying?

'No question of paying. I think the first year was 30 grand and the second year was 130 or 200 grand. I was an Arrows driver for 1982 except for one little thing in the contract, and that was a delete option. Basically the contract was valid but he had the right to confirm it in case there were any problems with sponsors before December 31. And December 31, bugger me, the phone goes. "Hello, Jonathan. It's Jackie Oliver. I'm very sorry but you know we've got problems with this sponsor, and they really want an Italian and so I'm afraid we can't go ahead on the contract." I found out that he had, I think, four people on the same contract: me, Brian Henton, Bruno Giacomelli, Marc Surer. Confidentiality was involved so you can't speak to anybody, no Press, di-da-di-da. So Arrows came and went. First thing I turned down the March. Second thing McLaren might have happened but Lauda came back. Third thing Arrows. Fourth thing I never got Williams.

'Anyway, Ron Tauranac was very keen and I tested with his Formula 2 car and he was eager I should drive it so I signed for Formula 2. The first year we had Bridgestone tyres and they weren't very good but within two or three races in Formula 2 another of these things happened where fate stepped in. Carlos Reutemann was partnering Rosberg in the Williams and after two or three races Reutemann threw in the towel. Frank Williams drove down to Thruxton for the Easter Monday Formula 2 race to talk to Ron about me driving the rest of the season. I remember looking up from the car at them chatting but a) Ron didn't want to lose me and b) it wasn't to be, anyway, and Derek Daly took over the Williams drive. To be fair, I hadn't started the season in stunning form. I made a mistake and crashed at Silverstone in the wet.'

It's bloody difficult to get into Formula 1, so there is a tempta-tion to get in regardless. But if you go in through the wrong door ...

'Oh very much. Once you get in the car, everyone's watching and they're not going to be very impressed unless you really do impress them. It's as if a question is being asked: are you simply part of the wallpaper? You will be unless you do something extraordinary – you'll be seen to be reasonable but nothing exceptional. In 1982 I remember testing with ATS[11] at Silverstone and driving this bloody great BMW turbo engine – it was quick! It was also porpoising so badly that going down towards Stowe corner you got to 150mph and it bucked and kicked and the front bounced. You couldn't see where you were going and you couldn't keep your feet on the pedals, and you had to really mash your foot down because you had to get through the next 20mph – at 170 it smoothed out again and the aerodynamics sorted themselves out. They only did that when you'd been through this transition.

'In 1983 I stayed with the Ralt and stayed with Williams testing. Ralt were on Michelin tyres and it was a totally different ball game: won half the races and won the championship. That was a great year. I thought "now I am Formula 2 champion I have to move to Formula 1." I was, I remember, so confident. [Palmer made his Grand Prix début at the 1983 European Grand Prix, driving a Williams – the team ran three cars.]

'I spoke to Tyrrell, actually, and as it turned out Tyrrell had signed Martin Brundle but he always denied that he had! I suppose he'd have to say that when I asked him. The other option was RAM[12] and eventually I went for RAM. I had to take a quarter of a million pounds to the team to get in what was undoubtedly the worst car on the grid, but I have a lot of time for John McDonald because he gave me the offer in '81 and he was keen to get me in the car.'

Was that the only offer you had?

'Really, yes, it was.'

You could not stay in Formula 2.

'Ron Tauranac wanted me to for another year but I couldn't.'

You'd have been making a statement: I'm not up to Formula 1.

'Absolutely, and no way. I had to move on. I had to find a quarter of a million quid to get into the RAM. I'd bits and pieces of sponsorship. I borrowed about £100,000 and raised £150,000. I got £25,000 from Peter de Savary.[13] He supported me. I got 25 grand from *Arai* helmets and 25 grand from a company owned by David Evans of Luton Football Club, whose son was in Formula 3. I was looking after him.

'Pirelli did 25. I was, however, £75,000 short. I went to a guy called Peter Millward who was a partner in a company I'd learnt to fly helicopters with. I said "if you can lend me £75,000 to close my deal and get me into Formula 1, I'll pay you back double if I make it big when I get there."' In the first RAM year, however, Palmer said to Millward that 'of any money I make, I'll take the first £30,000 to live on and after that I'll split it. To his credit he said "yeah, OK, I'll do that." It was fantastic of him because it was a big risk and I was so grateful.'

Palmer had taken the final step.

As it turned out, he had raised £250,000 for the privilege of getting in a car which in 1984 failed seven times, allowed his best qualifying to be no higher than 21st and secured him not a single point. That 'deal' must seem like madness to virtually anyone beyond motor racing. Only people who are very sure of themselves, and are capable of raising that amount of money, can even contemplate such a risk. Julian Bailey went beyond even this. He and his brother co-owned a very pleasant pub along the main street of a Hertfordshire village called St. Margarets.

'It was a good pub. I won a 3000 race at Brands Hatch and Ken Tyrrell was there in John Webb's box. John Webb was always a good supporter of mine, helped me in lots of ways.[14] I was a salesman at the time selling anything to anybody and Brands was a customer. I remember once I heard that they were ordering 24 tables and 500 chairs. I'd find out where they were going to buy them from, go in, do a cheaper deal and take some commission. They would place any order through me as long as it was the same price or a bit cheaper and I did a lot of business with Brands.

'That helped fund my racing rather than just getting sponsorship and John writing a cheque out for me. He actually made me work for it and was very good to me. Also that day he helped promote me to Ken when I won the 3000 race. Ken was on the look-out for someone he thought was half reasonable and had money. That day at Brands I became the first British driver to win a 3000 race and obviously it stuck in Ken's mind.[15]

'I didn't know what to do at the season's end, whether 3000 again. I spoke to Ken in the February and said "I'll tell you what, if you give me the drive I'll give you £500,000 for it" and he said "I don't believe you. No British driver's got £500,000!" I said "I'll come down and give it to you if you like." He said "OK, why don't you come down on Saturday and we'll have a chat." So I went down with Cavendish Finance who were my sponsors at the time – they were prepared to put in £150,000 and the rest was going to be down to me. I had another sponsor who said "if you do get into Formula 1, I'll put £50,000 in" so that was £200,000.

'My brother and I owned the pub which was worth about £500,000 but we owed about £200,000 on it so I thought "what we'll do is sell the pub." My brother agreed to that and, although we both ran it, he was mainly doing that because I was racing. I went down to see Ken Tyrrell and he asked what the situation was. I said I had this sponsorship but also I was going to sell my pub and give him 300 grand. He said "no, I'm not taking that, I'm not taking your money." I asked "why not?" He said "you keep your money and find a sponsor for the whole cost or you don't get the drive." I was sitting there and the bloke wouldn't take the 300 grand off me. He didn't want to be responsible for me losing my money.'

How did you react to that?

'I realised that Ken was different from most people, a different type of operator – he wasn't greedy, wasn't grabbing. He was a man of integrity. I said "OK, we won't sell the pub." Then I went to Cavendish and said "OK, I'll sell the pub, give you the money and you give it back to me" – Ken thought all the money was coming from Cavendish and he was happy with that. He said "OK, that's it." He didn't know that we subsequently sold the pub.'

Did you have any doubts about doing that?

'No, because you don't get many chances to go into Formula 1 and it was either that or another year of 3000 and then maybe disappear, as so many people do. I was on a high, I had to hit it at the right time.'

What about your brother?

'He was quite happy because it was a bit of a dream I'd get

to Formula 1 and you could hope I'd earn enough to give him his share back.'

Far from having Palmer's £250,000 or Bailey's £500,000, Perry McCarthy had to borrow the air fare to get to his first Grand Prix with the tiny Andrea Moda team in 1992.

'I was then 31 so it was actually quite late in Formula 1 terms. The chance? It was everything. We were on the way to losing the house, we had no money, I'd been knocking on industrial estate doors all the way through my career, we'd had massive ups and downs, some very big accidents, I'd been hurt, I'd got better la-di-da, and now against every single odds going here I was in Grands Prix. There'd been nothing for me that year – I couldn't have even got into Formula 3000 – and suddenly I'm in Grands Prix, which is where I wanted to be. I had a fight over getting a Superlicence but I kept saying "no, no, no, I want it, I want it, I want it" and people believed in me. They said "this guy's got to have a chance." It was like a dog with an old bone and I think that the Brits love an underdog anyway.'

So you had no money at all?

'Nothing. I had to borrow £800 from my cousin to get out to the first Grand Prix [Brazil].'

They obviously couldn't ask you for money.

'No, they couldn't, because I didn't have any but they took me on because the people who'd been advising them said "this is going to be a difficult situation and you want a guy in there who is never ever going to quit."'

They were not offering you any money.

'No, they weren't. I didn't get any money and I had to find my own expenses.'

Expenses can be …

'It doesn't matter. I was in. I'd worry about the expenses later. I would get anywhere I needed to be. I'd con my way onto an airline, into an hotel room, whatever it took, but I would be in Formula 1. Expenses? I didn't even think about that problem. I'd already come through far worse and the grounding I'd had by then was to know how to be able to do everything against the odds. Expenses? A cinch. I'll tell you what it takes, and it comes as a question: how much do you want this?'

And if you don't want it that much you're automatically eliminated.

'What you have here, I think, as much as the love of driving and the love of going quick, is a need to go further down into the drivers' psychology, and there it's always the same. "I'm a star, right? I am the one, right? I want attention, right? I want to be recognised as the fastest, right?" And when I get out of the car back in the pits when I've just gone fastest I'm smiling and I'm happy because *that says* I am right. It's always the same. That says all the way through my career, no matter what I have had to put up against, I am right.'

Is that the whole thing?

'Yes … I think it is. I do love getting it right, getting the car's drift right, which again says I'm right. You've got the apex just exactly where you wanted it to be, you've controlled the drift out exactly, you've kept your foot down, there's no way you ought to be able to stay flat and you have just stayed flat. There is something in this which makes you turn round and say [ALMOST SHOUTING] "I've beaten you again" – not necessarily the others: I've beaten the car, I've beaten the track and I've beaten staying alive. You go "wow, I just did it, I've just brought it all together that one moment in time."'

It is the hunter speaking.

So, Irvine was always going to make it, Watson was a highly accomplished driver, Räikkönen had what Sauber saw as valuable potential, Donnelly got in without having to calculate at all, Palmer thought his way in, Bailey sold his way in, and McCarthy burst his way in. Allan McNish was quite different in that, as for Palmer, Formula 1 seemed to be coming towards him, and quickly.

'A lot of factors happened to arrive pretty much at the same time, and it took a long time to separate it all down and a long time for me to look – not back on it, because I never try to look back – but forward through it.

'The first thing, I was probably too young. I was 19 when I raced a Formula 3000 car for the first time and at that stage I'd done one season of Formula Ford, one season of Vauxhall Lotus, one season of Formula 3. I'd won races in each category and I had to go forward. I'd no choice because when you win in a category you're bound to. You don't stop. So I was 19, I had a testing contract with McLaren, I was going for a season in 3000 and everything looked rosy.'

You were actually going to be able to compare yourself to Senna because he was driving for McLaren then.

'It was just that little bit early. I was, I think, a second or 1.1 or something like that off Senna in the first test. I drove about 25 laps, they put new tyres on and I couldn't go any quicker. I simply wasn't ready for it, ready for the whole G-force thing. It was my neck, actually. I had never done any training – I think I'd been running twice in my life – and suddenly I found myself in this situation and I thought "Christ, I'm going to have to do something about this."

'I'd come from Formula 3 which is 160bhp cars and the races

are 25–30 minutes. I jumped into a Formula 1 car and it was like "you go out and do your 30 minutes – and then go faster." It was stupid little things like the helmet: my helmet was probably about 50% heavier than Senna's, and those are the things you learn afterwards. At the time you don't think of it because you don't have the experience.'

That first time in a McLaren, did you think 'this is what I really want?'

'It just seemed natural although it was still a test and I still had to perform. There was a little bit of nervousness. The whole operation was very silky, they treated me extremely well and didn't make me feel like someone that was being spied upon. Everything was there to help you. However I didn't necessarily think "yeah, that's what I wanted to achieve when I was 15 years old, and this is how I am going to do it." Your career goes from one step to the next step to the next. I don't think the 15-year-old has necessarily thought out masterplans like that. What they are doing is just something they're good at naturally, and that brings them the opportunities to move forward.'

Like Mika Häkkinen, who you partnered in Formula Vauxhall-Lotus in 1988?

'It happens. There was certainly no structure to my personal thoughts of where I was going to go. After the test I did the 1990 season in Formula 3000 [with the DAMS team] and in 1991 stayed with DAMS, which wasn't really my first choice. They are a French team and I don't think it worked in the best way possible. A French team is a French team and you tend to fight a bit sometimes in these circumstances. If it was a Scottish team, a French driver might find it more difficult.

'I stayed in Formula 3000 that second season because, even

although there was interest from people in Formula 1, I personally felt I needed another year. It was generally adjudged by Marlboro, who were my sponsors, and also Ron [Dennis] that it would be the best thing, so I continued to test with McLaren and to race in 3000. However the regulations changed from cross-ply to radial tyres, I was in a Lola chassis and the Lola was rubbish on radial tyres! It didn't work all year, and the fancied runners for the championship – Damon Hill, Marco Apicella, myself and so on – were all in Lolas and all had a dismal year. Christian Fittipaldi won the championship and second was [Sandro] Zanardi, an unknown from Italy.

'DAMS had sort of disbanded a little bit through the winter before. I don't think they had the motivation they needed and, with the chassis being bad, it turned out to be a very bad year, but I was testing a lot with McLaren and that was going well. I was in the wrong place at the wrong time in 3000 but the right place at the right time at McLaren. It was curious because the 3000 was not good for my confidence: that's what gets highlighted in the media, not anonymous afternoons of testing.'

A heavy readjustment by Marlboro left McNish in January of 1992 with no money and 'the first race was in March or April. Without money in 3000 you don't have a drive, and there was a recession coming. Together with Ron Dennis and Mike Earle of the 3001 International team we concocted a deal to run six races at the start of the year and I'd do less testing with McLaren so I could concentrate on that, then we'd see where we go.

'It was the wrong decision. The first really wrong decision I made was not forcing my point at the end of 1990 that I really didn't want to go back to DAMS. This decision in 1992 was the second, although at the time it seemed correct. That was the point when I had a virus and it meant the first three races were a waste of time. I went to the Prof [Sid Watkins] as soon as I didn't feel very good and he did some tests but they never really found out. He said "you've got a virus, it's going to take some time to go but I don't know how long" and he was right. By August I was OK but the damage had been done for the season. I have to say Mike Earle fought for me and he made more of what we had than what we actually had. I really, really appreciated that.'

And it was at a very important time.

'It was a really important time because other people were thinking "maybe McNish is not ..."'

Did you have self doubts?

'I don't know. I was probably a bit confused by what was going wrong, because everything goes right and then suddenly it goes wrong and what are you doing differently? [McNish had been involved in an accident at Donington in 1990 in which a spectator died. The impact on his career is explored in the chapter headed 'Darkness'.] The accident on its own wouldn't necessarily have had dramatic effects without the next bit and the next bit. And it added up at the end of 1992 to a few bad runs. I came out of it feeling 100% fit but without anything to show for the last two seasons, and that was the hard bit. The momentum had gone and once the momentum goes it's very difficult.

'That is when you have got to knuckle down and think "right, OK, where do we want to go?" I still wanted to go to Formula 1 and I tried to achieve it in different ways but the doors just never opened – well, they were open but they required $2m. "How are you going to do it? Realistically McNish, you come from Dumfries, you think you're a very good driver and you've some good results but the fact is you are not in a position to pull that sort of money together for racing Formula 1." And it was right in the middle of the downturn in the UK economy. That was when I joined Porsche in sportscars.'

Did you feel you had failed or was your thinking 'no, I will come back at this' knowing how very difficult that is?

'I was disappointed it all went off the rails but more disappointed that I didn't realise and understand why. One thing I did learn – and this is why I say I was too young – was that I didn't stand up for myself as much as I should have done.'

Who can, so young?

'Probably nobody can. What I needed more than anything else was a manager who could have said "we can't go on like this, you are treating my guy wrongly", but I didn't have that. Now I can stand up for myself, as anybody who works with me knows. Do I look as though I have failed?'

This is a merciless activity.

'I treated it like that in myself. I was quite hard with myself. I was disappointed because I hadn't won that battle.'

If it had been Minardi at the back of the grid – or Andrea Moda like McCarthy – at least you'd have been in.

'I sat down and thought it through. There were a couple of years when I decided not to take drives because of the experience of 1992. My thinking was to do it right or not at all.'

Did you have genuine chances to get into Formula 1?

'In 1991 there was a chance which sort of disappeared and after that yes, there were chances, there were people saying "yes, OK" but it was again back to your Minardis and the $2m. They weren't necessarily chances for Allan McNish. Well, let me put it like this: maybe they would have preferred Allan McNish to Driver X or Y if he'd had the same sort of backing they had, but Allan McNish didn't.'

The last step may be the longest of all, but if the driver takes it he has the chance to wade into the fame and fortune.

NOTES

1. This was in September 1987 and round the Indy circuit at Brands, not the full Grand Prix course. Herbert was 0.3 seconds quicker than the Belgian Thierry Boutsen, who'd been in Formula 1 since 1983. Teo Fabi (Italy) had been in Formula 1 since 1982 and was in his second season with Benetton.

2. Paddock Hill Bend is the adverse camber corner at the end of the start-finish straight at Brands, Druids is the uphill-downhill horseshoe and Graham Hill is the left-hander after that.

3. I'm indebted to Stan Piecha of *The Sun* for these Button quotes.

4. Schumacher and Hill crashed in highly controversial circumstances on lap 36 of the 1994 Australian Grand Prix. It decided the championship in favour of Schumacher.

5. Schumacher and Villeneuve crashed in highly controversial circumstances on lap 48 of the 1997 European Grand Prix. It decided the championship in favour of Villeneuve.

6. International Management Group, founded by an American, Mark McCormack. It promotes leading sports people.

7. This pre-British Grand Prix test involved 32 drivers and Donnelly finished eighth (1m 11.80s against Alain Prost, quickest in the McLaren, on 1m 09.46s). Alesi was not among the 32.

8. Ron Tauranac, an Englishman brought up in Australia, became a leading Formula 2 constructor with his company Ralt.

9. Palmer won the Marlboro British Formula 3 Championship and, between 1 March and 12 April, won all four F3 races in a Ralt-Toyota. He finished the season on 105 points, Thierry Tassin (Belgium) 92, Raul Boesel (Brazil) 81. He tested the McLaren at Silverstone in November and British magazine *Autosport* described his performance as 'sensational'. Palmer did some 40 laps with a remarkable best of 1m

12.49s, which would have put him on the second row for that year's British Grand Prix.

10. Jackie Oliver raced over 50 Grands Prix and Alan Rees achieved success in Formula 2. Oliver and Rees formed the backbone of the Arrows Grand Prix team, founded in 1978.

11. ATS were a small, unsuccessful German team who competed in Grands Prix from 1977 to 1984. Incidentally, Gerhard Berger made his début in an ATS.

12. RAM were a small, unsuccessful British team – formed by John McDonald and Mick Ralph – who competed in Grands Prix from 1976 to 1984.

13. Peter de Savary, wealthy businessman and British patriot.

14. John Webb owned and ran Brands Hatch.

15. Formula 3000, the successor to Formula 2, was in its third season in 1987. On 23 August, Bailey beat Mauricio Gugelmin (Brazil) and Roberto Moreno (Brazil) to win the seventh round of the championship. Tyrrell was able to attend because the race fell between the German and Hungarian Grands Prix.

THE PLACE

Chapter 4

BOTH SIDES NOW

*'You have to accept a certain unpleasant combination
of things in every job, because in every job it
isn't pleasant all the way. Everyone has to
carry this unpleasant part of life'*
– Michael Schumacher

A mong the modern drivers there are two extremes of
character: the careful, methodical family man disciplining
himself so that his surroundings function as a wheel rotates,
precisely and predictably; and the intuitive man, abrasive and
provocative rather in the style of the earlier daredevil racers,
with a fashion model on his arm, and firing from the lip.

That Schumacher – the careful one – is occasionally so consumed by the ferocity of the hunt that he does something rash
brings a sense of human frailty to him (as well as enraging
sizeable portions of the planet); that Irvine – the provocative
one – can drive in the most disciplined, professional, un-
emotional way brings a sense of wonder.

Schumacher and Irvine were team-mates at Ferrari for four
years, with Schumacher contractually number one. In theory it
made life hell for Irvine, as if being directly compared to
Schumacher wasn't hell enough. That Irvine took the four years
of this, and survived and prospered, says a lot about his mental
strength. Schumacher's mental strength was never in doubt –
although Irvine has some revealing things to say about that.

SCENE 1: *Michael Schumacher*

Backdrop

Michael Schumacher made his début with the Jordan team at Spa in 1991 and was immediately outstanding. His team-mate was Andrea de Cesaris, then 32 and extremely experienced. Schumacher outqualified him. 'I thought to myself "this guy is going to be a pain in the arse,"' de Cesaris remembers. He was not wrong.

Schumacher would become the standard all others measured themselves against. I pointed out to Heinz-Harald Frentzen that he'd beaten Schumacher in the past, in German Formula 3, and wondered if he felt he could beat him again.

'Oh yes, sure. I find that easy to say because first of all every racing driver must believe in himself. That's quite normal. Michael is a very good racing driver, I am a very good racing driver and this kind of question is, in one respect, telling quite a lot about whether the racing driver has the mental strength or not. If I would say "no, I will never beat him" everybody would judge I'd already given up.'

Fiorano

A fine August day in the Romagna region of northern Italy, hot enough to make shade seem a good place to be. Derick Allsop, who covered Grand Prix racing for the London *Independent* and had written a book with Schumacher, asked for a chance to do an in-depth interview with him in the summer of 2000. 'I applied to his press secretary, Sabine Kehm, who organises his interviews. I suggested it could be done in Italy because I was going to be on holiday with my family there – wife Sue, daughter Kate and her boyfriend Peter. We were planning to go to Florence, anyway. I got a call from Sabine saying that he was testing at Fiorano and would be available on the Thursday after the German Grand Prix. We went to Fiorano and he was testing that morning.'

Testing had begun at 10am and would continue to 9pm. Luca Badoer, the Ferrari test driver, was out first working on set-ups. Schumacher, concentrating on preparations for the Hungarian Grand Prix, would cover 85 laps during the day. Rubens Barrichello, now partnering Schumacher, was not present.

'At the main entrance people waited and some had brought little seats with them,' recalls Allsop. 'They were obviously prepared to sit there all day for a glimpse of Schumacher. I had to get permission to bring the family in but that was OK and Sabine sat them down in a mini-grandstand – two or three rows of seats – positioned under some trees. There are always a few people there, guests of sponsors and so on, who sit and watch the cars go round. Many more were standing with their faces up to the fencing on the flyover [overlooking the track].

'He is supposed to be anything from unco-operative to downright rude. Far from it. He was in the process of doing a television interview for, I think, Marlboro. As soon as he saw me he broke away from this huddle with the TV people, came over, shook hands, said hello and "see you later." He is just like Senna, very professional, very correct. He knew we had an appointment. Having done that he tested for another hour or so.

'There was talk that we'd do the interview in the hospitality tent or maybe in Enzo's house which he gets the use of[1] but because it was a nice day and we were sitting in the shade under the trees they said "let's do it here." There was a German journalist there [Wolfgang Reuter of *Focus*], but everything was in English – the German journalist asking the German mega-hero questions in English. It's the way the world, and Formula 1, operates. Schumacher was not only relaxed and very co-operative but also, I thought, very frank. The whole interview was handled in an orderly, dignified way.

'There was a gaggle of Italian press men who are always at these tests, and he did 15 minutes with them before he even came and sat down with us. Then there was the television interview. Then he went on until nine at night testing. I think he sees his world more and more clearly as he's got older. They are no different than the rest of us. Certainly as they get older and have a family they take on that bit more of an air of responsibility and maturity.

'When the interview was over I was chatting casually with him. I said "would you like to meet my family?" and he came over. He was very relaxed then because we were talking about kids. He wanted to know where we were holidaying, he wanted to know what the sea was like – he is very conscious of clean sea and things like that. We really were just chatting. Then we talked about kids, and the fact that he's got a girl and a boy, Miki. Schumacher said Miki is very much a boy, into the racing, wants to sit on his dad's lap and hold the steering wheel whereas Gina-Maria is not so keen and already he could see the difference between them, the boy coming along keen to do it. Schumacher's eyes were lighting up as he was talking about this, just as a father's would.'

Dialogue

How are you feeling now? It has been an extraordinary run you have had.[2] In many ways you could say 'well, it could be so much worse' because you are still leading the championship but do you have to be philosophical in a situation like this?

'I am a man of fact, and the fact is we have had a bad last part of the season, where we are right now. I am still leading with 2 points and that is all that counts at the end of the day. If I am still leading by 2 points when the championship closes, that will be enough. It's obviously a shame that the last races have gone as they have gone but races can turn that way. I have always said since the beginning of the season "don't write that I'm champion" until I am mathematically.'

Do you ever think 'maybe there is some kind of curse on me, maybe it is my fate not to win it with Ferrari?'

'No. I feel I am fated to win it with Ferrari – but not in an easy way. Jean Todt is quite right: if we win it in the end it will mean so much more because we have been through such a tough time. I thought my luck would have been back at Hockenheim because I really felt optimistic.'

We saw the car was good.

'But then that's the way it goes, and we still have a long way to go. Honestly, I feel it will be our year.'

It's not just being on the track, it's been off it as well with the polemics, the clashes with other drivers. Does this disturb you?

'It is always the point, what you consider is serious and what you consider isn't. You have got various experiences from all sorts of guys around and you know what you consider serious and what you don't. Naturally it would be nicer if everything is smooth and there was none of those polemics, but honestly it has never happened in anybody's career: smooth and never in these kinds of situations, especially for the guys who are always up front. I prefer that situation … because it means I am up front!'

Do you think these situations are inevitable?

'Yes. If you look at the past, they are.'

You never think 'is it all worth it, do I need all this?'

'No, no. I am far away from being frustrated, far away from "I don't need this." No, no, no, that's part of the business.'

But it can't always be pleasant.

'No, it is not pleasant. Naturally you would like it to be but, as I said before, it never has been. You have to accept a certain unpleasant combination of things in every job – a journalist's job isn't always pleasant either. Everyone has to carry this unpleasant part of life.'

Do you ever try and work it out in your own mind why? There are theories ...

'There are many theories on this but, at the end of the day, it's not worth continuing to talk about it. It's too far away from being true and real. Different people have different views and I am open to letting them express their views but it doesn't need to influence me or come close to me. That's the way I feel about it: there is no point in discussing particular words that Jacques[3] is saying. Obviously I have been told about it but there is no need for a reaction.'

Do you take the view 'well if I just get on with my job I am comfortable with that job' and, also, maybe there are more people who understand me than don't?

'You know, in life you never get everybody to agree with what you feel, what you think and what you do. I have learnt that however you do it there will always be people who won't agree. So ...'

Reuter: You mentioned the frustration. After Hockenheim, how long will it take to get rid of it? A matter of minutes, a matter of hours, a matter of days?

'That is a good question. The first part goes within, say, half an hour but then the rest may take a day or two. It depends how big it is. Obviously at Hockenheim I was a little more frustrated than I was after Zeltweg, because after Zeltweg I thought "well." But twice getting zero points is obviously not ideal.'

But Barrichello winning at Hockenheim softened the blow.

'Yeah, to some degree that, particularly as we are team-mates and we know each other well. He'd already been close in Canada but he had a mechanical problem so that is why he was slowing down, not to force me into problems.[4] He could have done it there and his first victory meant a lot to him. I am happy that he finally got that in and he is obviously very much delighted, in particular by the way it happened. He beat everyone by being perfect and doing a very good race. So 1), he took points away from my competitors but 2) I think more of his pleasure. I know what is going through him and that's the best way to have a good team relationship: if the other guy is having success and is a 100% happy about himself, about the team and his team-mate.'

He also made the point that he thought you were very sincere in the way you came up to him at the end and congratulated him. He appreciated that as part of the team.

'Yeah, exactly. It was his first victory and, as I say, I know what has gone through him. I wanted to leave half way through the race, I wanted to go home and avoid the traffic. "Let's go!" Then the race started to become interesting and I said "I can't go" and it really kept me there, it was fascinating to watch.'

Reuter: You have probably read some headline in German newspapers that there is a hate campaign against you. Would you agree with that headline?

'Unfortunately I haven't read this because I live in Switzerland, I have to go to a special shop to buy German magazines and I didn't bother. I have been told about it. This is one part of the business for magazines, to highlight the issue from various directions. I don't think it is really a hate campaign, because what happened is that there was a race accident. Giancarlo [Fisichella] and me, we went off the circuit: unfortunate for him and myself, but that's about it.[5] I would call Giancarlo one of my friends in Formula 1 and not one of my enemies.'

Reuter: I think you play football together.

'Yes. We have a good relationship.'

Reuter: Is there anybody in Formula 1 besides Giancarlo who you are not so involved with?

'It's like everything in life. You have friends, you have people you don't talk to and you may have your enemies. I'd say I have quite a lot of friends but I have, as well, some people I am not "related" to and I have others who don't like me in particular. I think it's normal that these guys who don't like me will have other drivers who don't like them. I call it nothing unusual.'

On that theme, you will have heard that people say 'Michael is still arrogant' and all that. Does that still bother you? Do you ever think 'well, maybe I should look at myself more'?

'I do. It depends who it comes from and where it comes from. If it comes from your enemies then you know it's not worth thinking about. Obviously I try to look at myself to see what is true and what is not true.'

What do you see?

'I believe there is a non-arrogant person there. I appear sometimes like this to people because of the kind of protection I build up to block things out and keep concentration rather than be open for anything. I am doing a job here. I have to be concentrated for it and that means that I cannot be available to everyone. I am sorry but that's part of my job. Most people understand it and most of the media don't call me arrogant. A few do. Maybe sometimes they are right, maybe sometimes they are wrong but, when I say maybe sometimes they are right, they may not have actually looked deep into the situation to discover why it is like this.'

But in your position it must be very difficult to trust people who try to be friendly with you.

'Put it this way. Our life is quite artificial – not to all journalists, but to a lot of them. They basically don't know you. You don't have the time to know them. I don't know how many colleagues you have in the paddock. More than 200? And I am one person! You never can be right [for all 200 journalists]. Since I came into Formula 1 I have been kind of highlighted. I was the first German driver to be rather successful from the beginning, and something has drawn a lot of attention to me. It was always an unbalanced relationship between me alone and how many journalists were interested in me. Certain "directions" were fixed early in my career and these directions still run after me without being true in reality, but every time something comes which fits these directions it will all be taken out again. It has always been like this.'

Your affection for animals: didn't you pick up another two dogs recently in Italy?

'No, we have four and two children and that's enough.'

I just wondered whether sometimes you think 'well, at least with animals I can trust them, no problem there'?

'Yes, but I have friends and I have my kids, I have my family. I have enough people in my area I trust and where I know what is going on.'

How do you think generally you get on with the Italian public and followers. I know it is not your nature to go out and court people.

'No. I am probably too much German for a lot of the tifosi, I'd say.'

Reuter: What do you mean by too much German?

'Too serious, not enough ups and downs, not enough emotions – not like Alesi. People love that, particularly in Italy. Plus there is the language barrier which I believe I have improved quite a bit because if I go out with my friends – and I have some good friends down here in Maranello – I can talk to them, so my conversation has been much better than it has ever been. Again, though, how many tifosi are there and how many of them actually know me? They see me in my racing car and that is about it.'

It is not in your nature to go out and embrace them?

'No, no, it is not. I am a person who likes quiet, who likes the balance between the business – the job – and the privacy. Again that may not attract the tifosi to me but you have to keep your own balance, you have to find out what is important for you.'

Talking about hate campaigns, you may not have heard that Bernie Ecclestone spoke out very much in your favour this week about people moaning about you.

'No, I didn't know.'

Bernie spoke very long and hard, but I wonder if another part of this is a feeling that there's too much bias towards Ferrari.

'There has always been a person or a team at the centre of attention. I am happy that it is like this because I can deal quite well with the negative things going on around me. The percentage of them is probably less than 10%. The main part is good side but, you know, unfortunately in life if you have a story which is 90% good and 10% bad it is the bad which becomes the centre of attention. Therefore it looks worse than it really is.'

But on balance you can still enjoy it?

'Yeah. The main balance should be taken over all the years – not Hockenheim now as an example, but over the years and it has always been in my favour.'

And Ferrari – that is still worthwhile? If you'd gone to McLaren you'd have won championships.

'Yeah.'

You'd have three or four titles now.

'Yeah.'

Do you think about that?

'No, not very much. I was going to say it is not my way of thinking. I decided at the time that Ferrari was my future and I want to go there. It has been harder than I thought but it is still enjoyable. There are moments when it is not so enjoyable but again the balance is more in favour of wanting to be around Ferrari and being happy in what I am doing. That is especially true this year. How many races have I won? Four? Five?'

I spoke to Ross Brawn last week. He made the point that even now you check everything and you are absolutely meticulous in making sure no way to improve has been overlooked. It must be hard to keep that sort of motivation, trying to be perfect all the time – or is that the real enjoyment, the real challenge?

'I would say I am not perfect, not at all, and there are areas where I may sometimes lean back a little bit. If that comes to my attention I raise it again. However there are certain important things and certain disciplines which are simply natural. You do them without thinking about it. It's part of the game so I don't need to force myself to do that. There are other things like training where sometimes maybe I'll take a day off. It doesn't happen very often, but here and there it does happen and I feel bad afterwards, which is good because it keeps me doing it.'

When you have bad days, such as Hockenheim, do you ever think 'I wish I did something else' – doctor, teacher, footballer, but they might also bring controversy.

'All of our jobs bring controversy – your job, a doctor's job, a footballer's job. All our jobs do have side effects. There is never in this world a job without any bad stuff. Naturally sometimes I feel "yes, well, I am unhappy and things could be better" but it doesn't go far enough to make me say "I want to stop it, that's enough." No, no, because so often there is the opportunity to go out in your car and feel you are doing a good job. That makes you forget the other things.'

That stuff wouldn't ever force you out – you will decide when it is time to go.

'Yeah, one day it may come to the point where I don't have enough opportunities to prove myself and feel this happiness any more. Then the unhappy side of it is too much and you may say "OK, it's time" but right now I am not close to that.'

You have been talking about going on to 40. Is that possible?

'I think that is probably about the time when you are close to reaching your physical limit and the limits of your reactions. That is what I've said before. You can do it to then. Whether I will we'll have to see.'

And afterwards become a team manager?

'No, quite clearly no. I think you have to have certain abilities. I have the ability to drive a racing car fast but I don't see myself having the ability to run a team plus having the passion to do that. I want to have a different life with my family afterwards.'

I wonder if you want to reiterate that you would find it interesting if a young driver came up to really challenge you.

'Yes. That is what I said. It could be one thing where I think I see an indication of the time to stop.'

But you don't see it yet?

'To really see him, he has to be in my team – although Rubens for sure is the fastest team-mate I have ever had.'

And next season Ralf and Montoya will make a good pair?

'Exactly.'

Young …

'Too young! Well, Ralf is only 25 but already these days you're not young any more at 25, which is strange …'

Reuter: Michael, whenever I see you, you seem to look very relaxed. Do you have any anti-stress training or do you just do it?

'No, it is natural. It is always a matter of balance: what you have at home, what is your success, what is your personal situation, which mood you are in. For sure I have bad moods as well, but in general this year – because I know the car is strong and I can believe in it – I am obviously relaxed.'

Looking at the last few races, second places would have …

'But there's no point in thinking that way. Maybe you can after the season is finished.'

Reuter: Looking back on the past nine years of your career, what was the worst point – apart from Silverstone last year [crash on the opening lap] – and the finest moment?

'I had two bad moments. Obviously Silverstone is one, and second is the two race bans I got in 1994, which I didn't think were right. These kinds of moments were quite bad. Nice moments? Obviously the relief at the end of '94 and '95 and then there were so many single races which gave me an amazing amount of pleasure: Hungary '98, Spa '95, Nürburgring '95? I have plenty of these races which made me feel extraordinarily good.'

Spain in the wet.

'That's another example.'

Reuter: Some people say you are very cold and some people say you are very impulsive. Which is right?

'I am sure the people who say I am cold are wrong.'

Not cold as a man, cold in the car.

'I see. Well, that's true, I am.'

Reuter: Did you ever measure your heartbeat, for example?

'Yes, just actually two tests ago we did this. I was ... I don't really want to mention the figure because you'd think I am taking a cup of coffee! It was very low. It was below 100 actually. I couldn't believe it because I did tests some years ago ...'

... must have been a slow car this time.

'No, no, I was driving round Mugello on a long run. I was doing 1m 25s, so good lap times. It was between 95 and 103. We couldn't check it afterwards but on the straight and in some corners I was constantly looking at the monitor. The time before was in the 1995 Benetton, a difficult car, and my heart rate was 130, 140.'

Which is more normal.

'Even that was a bit low because I remember I made some comparison – Ayrton in Brazil was 160, 170 – so I was surprised. The present Ferrari feels good and you don't have to fight it that much to be fast. That obviously helps you to be relaxed. I enjoy it. The last run I just did here, those ten laps, were within a few hundredths. You feel "oh, great." It is fun and if you have fun the job is easy.'

Is there something wrong with a sport where the driver who almost everybody accepts is the best has not won the championship for five years?

'It is not a "single" man's sport any more. It may have been a little bit more in the past. Now it's a team sport and if everything isn't together you don't do it. To a degree we both – myself and the team – weren't prepared. Some years it was the car and one year it was me failing. Both parts have paid their price and I hope we get back what I think we deserve.'

SCENE 2: *Eddie Irvine*

Backdrop

Johnny Herbert on Eddie Irvine: 'He's OK. You've just to accept Eddie as Eddie. He's got a very different outlook on life and doesn't care what anybody thinks about him, and that's fine. He may not be popular, women may find him rude, guys may find him rude, but that's his way. He's in the right sport for that type of attitude and it hasn't done him any harm.'

Is it true about all the girls?

'Not as true as it used to be. Eddie likes that side of it, he tries to play on it. It's out there if you want it, but I was content with what I've got. It is still, however, that special thing. Being a racing driver has that sex appeal.'

Eddie Irvine talking to the *Radio Times* in April 2000: 'I hate bullshitters. I know a lot of girls in Milan have guys hanging around who say "I love you, you're special for me." I don't tell girls they're the biggest thing that ever happened, da-di-da. I never leave them. I let them catch me out. Then they get annoyed and leave me. Afterwards, they appreciate my honesty. We all like the same things, don't we? If sex was such a chore there'd only be a few thousand in the whole world. I'm not thinking about marrying. I'm looking for a place in New York now because I love different places. I get bored easily. My mind needs to be challenged a lot.'

Irvine on Schumacher, and specifically the Japanese Grand Prix in 1999 when Irvine could in theory have become World Champion, with Schumacher – whose season had been destroyed by the Silverstone crash – helping him. How had it been with Michael that weekend? 'No problem at all. The weekend before he'd helped me win the race in Malaysia so no problem. Ferrari have always operated what was best for the team, which I fully understood.'

There is also the question of the mental aspect, you measuring yourself against him – the ultimate test.

'I enjoyed that. I learnt some things that made me drive the car quicker that I wouldn't have learnt if I hadn't been his team-mate.'

Yes, but going in against him mentally?

'Mentally I'm a lot stronger than Michael. I've never seen that as an issue. I just am. I know. I've worked with him. But he's a quicker driver. Because you're a quick racing driver doesn't mean you are mentally strong.'

Schumacher radiates strength.

'He didn't radiate strength to me. He's a quick driver, end of story. I know him. I know how he works. I know his weaknesses better than anybody.'

But he does radiate that Teutonic strength.

'That's the way people can read it. It's like the emperor with no clothes. Everyone saying what lovely clothes except the lad at the end who said "he's got no clothes!" It's exactly that.'

Luton Airport

Even millionaires' corner is raked by the wind, drowned in English greyness. The chauffeur sits and waits. He's concerned about appearances: the Jaguar saloon which has been freshly through a carwash; the *Financial Times* arranged unobtrusively in the back because he's heard racing drivers have a lot of money and like to read about what's happening to it; motoring magazines; small bottles of mineral water in the pouches in the rear of the front seats. Everything is positioned for harmony and symmetry.

Late winter, 2001. Irvine is to attend a Grand Prix Party at the Royal Albert Hall in aid of Professor Watkins' Brain and Spine Foundation.

Millionaires who come to this corner of Luton Airport (so far away from the passenger terminals you use a different road to reach it) have to observe certain procedures. The chauffeur is told these procedures in detail. To meet Irvine's jet he must follow a van escorting him to it, with dire warnings about what will befall him if he deviates. I get in the back of the Jaguar and want to leave my briefcase there but the chauffeur thinks that will mess up the symmetry. Effortlessly he transfers it to the boot. We follow the van, driven by one of those women who must be obeyed, out onto the tarmac to where the small jet has just been parked.

Irvine emerges from it, lean and tanned, his hair a strange shade of straw blond. His girlfriend emerges, dark-haired, encased in denim, sexy in her slightness. If she is not a New York model she ought to be. The chauffeur moves deftly, almost diplomatically, making sure that doors are opened and people are seated: the model, Irvine and myself in the back; James Thomas, the Jaguar PR man, in the front.

The wind rakes the Jaguar, the spitting rain goes on and on and even before we've moved off he says 'Jeez, why does anyone live in this country?' I say that a lot of people have no choice, as if he didn't know that already. The model says nothing.

The Jaguar moves effortlessly away into the aquatics of the M1 and the wider embrace of the greyness.

Dialogue

Drivers are much more interesting than they give themselves credit for.

'Not the ones I know!'

It always starts like that and then it develops into interesting areas.

'Like girls and toys.'

No. We assume that you have girls and toys.

He half turns towards the model. 'Girl and toys.'

It's what you do in a racing car which separates you, because if you were a pop star you'd have girl and toys, if you were a wealthy City chap you'd have girl and toys, but they don't get in the car and you do. That's the difference. They're money machines.

'I'm a motor racing machine. Pop stars are interesting and everyone to their own.'

But you could work in the City and not do anything that might threaten your physical well-being.

'Yes, but I don't think motor racing is something which will threaten my physical well-being. I like my life. I don't want to be [makes squeaking noise which I interpret as dead-dead-dead]'.

But you could be.

'Yeah, but you don't think that. You do it well within your ability.'

The car can break.

'That's the only issue, but it's the same if the aeroplane fails or if this guy [the chauffeur] has a heart attack so there are unforeseen circumstances that you can't do anything about. You just have to pray it's not your time. Your story of life, I believe, is sort of mapped out. And the car failing or plane failing, that's not your story. At the same time you've got to avoid knocking on too many doors. People who go round with a death wish eventually find that it's granted. Someone opens the door for them. So ...'

One of the basic differences with the driver is that his mind seems to be in compartments and he can isolate the compartments.

'I think that's what all people who operate machinery have to do. Pilots are the same. Driving a Formula 1 car takes more of a will, more of a feeling than a pilot needs.'

Let's just suppose you come into the pits and the pit stop goes wrong ...

'... happens ...'

... and a member of the crew like Nigel Stepney[6] has been knocked sideways. Can you isolate that when you get back out on the track or do you take it with you?

'I wouldn't even care. My daughter if I ran over her, yes. My mother, my sister, yeah. But someone that I work with? No, because they're not my family. My family is my family and the racing is the racing. I could go round Suzuka and not think for a second. The only thing I would maybe think is what they're going to do when I get back to the pits, but I have to say I wouldn't worry about it. Which is probably not the thing I should say, really.'

There's also the social side to being Irish.

'I don't really drink that much. I have good fun and I've learnt that you don't need to drink to have good fun.'

The pleasure of driving: it obviously gives you something.

'I get more fun out of it now than I did before. Every year I appreciate more being a Formula 1 driver. When you're young you just take everything for granted. Like today[7] I had to do two long runs and I actually really enjoyed doing the two long runs. When I was young I hated doing long runs. Today I felt I was achieving something and I was working towards that.'

Is that a physical pleasure or an intellectual pleasure?

'Intellectual. Everything I hate is physical. I'm not into the physical. The only physical pleasure I like is sex. I don't like running, I don't like canoeing, I don't like bicycle riding, I don't like any physical exertion at all.'

Sex keeps coming up, and I was going to ask you …

'Yes, that is the only physical exertion I like and that again is mental because it's in the head, isn't it?'

Is there a comparison between sex and the qualifying lap?

'No. The qualifying lap, the pleasure is at the end of it. Sex, the pleasure is in the beginning, the middle and the end. A qualifying lap? The pleasure is when you see the lap time. It's not a finished product until the lap time is delivered. I think about it the minute I'm out of the last corner because then there's nothing I can do about it, the lap's over. That's beautiful if you've done a really good lap. Last year I did some fantastic qualifying laps, I really did. The car was very nervous at the rear end, you had very little understeer which makes for very good qualifying. So it's totally different from sex. Thank God, because sex would be very boring if my job was the same feeling as well. I'm glad it's not …'

The enemy within: your team-mate.

'You have no option, that's the story, and you get on with it. There's nothing you can do about it. You've just got to beat him. The fact that he's trying to beat you always makes the relationship a bit awkward. It doesn't happen to me now because I'm established, I've made it, but when I was young and came into Jordan I had to beat Barrichello, he had to beat me. We fought like hell the year of '95. I was lucky, I came out on top and ended up going to Ferrari. That was the situation: if I hadn't got ahead of him that year I wouldn't have gone to Ferrari, I wouldn't have won Grands Prix. Now I've got to beat Burti and for sure I'll try just as hard but it's not going to break me in any sense. I'm more mature. When you're young you can never separate the two things – that you can actually like the person as well.'

You don't have to fall in love with the bloke.

'No, but Luciano[8] is a sensible guy, he works well with the team and he's fair. That's important. There's other people I've been with who were totally unfair. I don't like that. I'm not talking about Michael.'

Your contract with Ferrari probably contravened most human rights legislation.

'You obey team orders or you obey the Director of the team. It's the same in any team. Some teams say they won't do it. I had an agreement with Johnny last year: if you're quicker than me and you come up behind me I'll move out of your way and vice versa. There's no point in me holding up Johnny and then him missing out.'

It wasn't the same with Schumacher though?

'No, I had to stay behind him but I can understand that because they didn't have a car that was quick enough to win the World Championship on its own.'

How did you cope with that?

'It was my best option.'

It's a bit like Manchester United coming and saying 'how do you fancy playing in our reserves' rather than the Millwall first team.

'I'd rather be in Man. United reserves because you get a chance to move yourself and you've a chance of getting into the first team. I'm looking at it very pragmatically and deciding what's best for me. It was a great education. With Todt and Ross I learnt how a Formula 1 team should run. Rory [Byrne, Ferrari chief designer] delivered the car to Ross and Ross ran the show. That's pretty much the way it works. I'd seen the blueprint of a fantastic Formula 1 team and that's where we've got to get Jaguar to.'

If you had been driving 25 years ago you'd have been one of the boys, not exceptional as you are now. Then, many of them were like you.

'I don't know what they were like then.'

They liked being fully alive in every sense.

'They didn't have the life that I have.'

No, but they weren't robotic.

'I'm the one that's known not to be. There's a few who are like me. I know one driver who flies anywhere in the world in his private plane to get laid. No-one knows that. He'll fly anywhere to ride anything. He's desperado. You hear that the modern driver doesn't like drink. You go into a pub in Tokyo and there was a group of seven or eight Formula 1 drivers in this pub. I wasn't with them, I was sitting in a corner with other people and the group was having a bit of a laugh. The trouble is the job's so … it makes people very independent and it's very difficult to fall out of the lifestyle that you can have. They end up flying back to their flat in Monaco and when you do that the chances of having a nice life are restricted. You isolate yourself from the real world. I've got a good bunch of friends – three or four – who have nothing to do with motor racing and they're all very, very different. This group that we have, each one of us has a very specific role within the group and we have a blast. That's what life's for. We've got the sensible one, we've got the mad one, we've got the organiser …'

Which one are you?

'I'm the magnet. I bring it all together pretty much.'

Martin Donnelly said …

'Martin would have been a lot more friendly with other drivers than I'd have been. I'm not into drivers. I don't find them amusing. There is much more possibility to find better company in other walks of life than down the pit lane. Oh yeah. J-e-s-u-s. For sure.'

That separates you from them.

'I don't see many are great buddies with each other, you know.'

Is that in the nature of being a hunter?

'I really don't know but there's a good chance of that. If you get together with a racing driver, ultimately you talk about cars and tyres and it gets boring. You talk about that all day at work. The last thing I want to talk about is motor racing when I go out at night.'

About the film which we all enjoyed so much, 'Eddie Irvine: The Inside Track'[9]. Was it you?

'Everyone says it was me then. I'm different now. You move on, you change, you learn, blah-blah-blah. I only watched it once, when it came out. I watched part of it again and switched off because I got bored. It looks very dated now.'

It struck me watching it that here is a man who says 'I am going to have a terrific life and I could be World Champion but I'm not going to sacrifice a terrific life for that.' Senna did.

'Senna was that type of guy. He wouldn't have fun living my life because he wouldn't have the personality for it.'

You're about the only driver in the past ten years who could have been the subject of a film like that.

'Yeah.'

There aren't others.

'Probably Huntey [James Hunt] before me.'

Yes, but that's 1976–1978 time.

'What happened was Senna came along and lived his life the way it suited him. It just so happened that he was the best driver at that time. I have my personality and I cannot change my personality. If you try to encroach on that you [expletive] everything else up.'

There was a moment in the film which I remember vividly. You are leaving Monza on a moped overtaking two pretty girls on another moped. You say 'we're having a party at my place, come along, I'll tell you where it is' and they say 'we know where it is – we've already been'.

I express astonishment at the episode because it seemed so normal to him, that pretty girls would know where he lived. By now the Jaguar is moving stop-start in the traffic along Kilburn High Road. The place looks exhausted and sodden and dreary, and people are walking by, heads bowed against the rain.

Has it crossed your mind that something like that has never happened even once to those people out there?

'But I'm not in that life any more. My life is somewhere else and there's nothing I can do about that. There's nothing I want to do about that. I have a personality that takes me that way and that's all there is to it. Some people don't have the personality and it takes them a different way.'

How are you, waiting at the lights at the start of a race?

'You're just thinking where you're going, concentrating on the lights, what you're going to do with the wheels, what you're going to do with the clutch. You're not excited. Your heartbeat is high because there's stress, I know that, but I am just focused. Very calm mentally, although not physically because of your heartbeat. But your body is ready for action. The guy sitting on top of an Apollo rocket is not thinking ... well, maybe he is ...'

... about getting blown to bits, presumably. I once heard an astronaut describe what he was thinking at the precise moment of launch: 'that every part of this rocket was probably built by the companies tendering the lowest offers ...'

'Is he thinking that? I don't know. I thought he would be looking at all his dials making sure everything is correct. I don't think he's thinking about 30,000 kilos of whatever rocket fuel is underneath him.'

I find even watching the start of a Grand Prix frightening.

'That's fear of the unknown. I know what it's like. We went to Universal Studios the other day and the first time on a ride it was like oh-oh-oh-oh! The second time it was no big deal.'

The model says, softly but audibly, 'second time you were still scared!'

'I don't like these rides.'

'I'm OK about them,' she says.

That one on the fairground at Suzuka overlooking the track [a platform in the air that you stand on and it suddenly drops], you can hear them screaming ...

'You could have heard me screaming!'

The Japanese seem to like that.

'I don't. Girls do. I didn't enjoy some of the rides really but I have to say she' – the model – 'really did and you could see that. I was scared.' She laughs.

Genuinely scared?

'Genuinely scared.'

Is that because you were not in control?

'Afraid of the unknown. I'm not in control, I don't know what can go wrong, and I'm getting older – but even when I was young I didn't like these rides.'

We're going round Marble Arch, which is no distance from the Albert Hall, and the interview is moving to a natural conclusion. I wondered if Irvine felt international in the sense of having his own jet, homes on the Continent, taking part in a global sport, a New York model on his arm. He looked at me and spoke very deliberately into my tape recorder so each word would be clear for transcribing.

'I am very proud that I have the personality of an Irish person: open, friendly, hard working, fun loving, all the good things in life – and can speak.'

We came to the Albert Hall and a cluster of autograph hunters lurked by the door. The Jaguar PR enquired how Irvine wanted to play it, stand and have a signing session or cut straight through. He said he didn't mind either way. Perhaps that summed everything up.

Noises off

Johnny Herbert partnered Schumacher at Benetton in 1994 and 1995 and, subsequently and untypically, complained in public that he had not been given equal treatment. I explain to Herbert what I'd said to Irvine: that in joining Ferrari he'd taken on the ultimate mental challenge against Schumacher and Irvine replied he was mentally stronger.

'Yes, in Eddie's way, and that was the best way to be.'

But it got to you because you felt the playing field wasn't level.

'What I couldn't agree with was that they took all my computer data away so I couldn't do a comparison.'

Now here's a mental exercise: two cars – yours and Schumacher's – both set up the way you want them. What happens next?

'I have always said I could accept that.'

Yes, but would you have given him a run for his money?

'I think so.'

Were you intimidated by him?

'No, not at all. Never been intimidated by anybody. By any other driver.'

Why?

'He's only human.'

In his mind he's so strong.

'He believes he's invincible. I remember having that, I know what it feels like. You believe you can do anything. Ayrton had the invincibility in a slightly different way because he was religious and he was protected by God. It's sort of similar.'

And frightening because he might do things on the track believing God would look after him?

'No, no. He was still human. He never did anything in a dangerous way.'

Except with Prost.

'Ah, well. Prost started it, anyway ...'[10]

Mika Salo deputised at Ferrari in 1999 after Schumacher broke his leg. Salo led the German Grand Prix and was within sight of his first Grand Prix victory until team orders decreed otherwise.

Was it hard for you at Ferrari?

'It taught me a lot. I saw how good a team could be and it really opened my eyes because I'd been in very small teams before and suddenly I was at the front. Now I saw what you needed. You put Michael Schumacher in a Minardi, he can't win the race.'

Did you find it easier to run at the front?

'The same. It's the same guys I've been racing with all my life so there was no difference, just more attention.'

How did you feel at the moment you had to let Eddie past?

'I was sad but then it was my job to help Eddie win the championship.'

Did you have a moment's hesitation?

'I let him go as soon as I heard it on the radio. When Eddie didn't win the championship at the end I was sad again because ... I could have won that race.'

Rubens Barrichello took on the ultimate mental challenge against Schumacher when he joined Ferrari in 2000. 'I'm tinkering with my head and really working on myself,' Barrichello would say in the spring of 2001.[11] 'At Jordan in 1996, I felt that I wasn't wanted any more but I knew that those tough times would do me good. It was a learning period and it helped me at Stewart. I wanted to learn all that was possible. I signed with Ferrari because they are the best team and because I wanted to rub shoulders with Michael. After seven years in Formula 1, I know how to deal with my head. Now it's one of my strong points.'

David Coulthard overtook Schumacher in the wet in Brazil, 2001, and would explain that the mind of the hunter works like this: every car you come up to is prey, doesn't matter who is in it, and you must think like this.

The last insight comes from Frentzen.

One of my local postmen, Ian, follows your career avidly and he tells me that in 1999 you were voted German Sportsman of the Year, above Michael.

'This was in the past ...'

It means they liked you more.

'I don't want to comment.'

Bless my soul, after all these years of searching I've found a Grand Prix driver who places self-effacement before accepting his dues, and that's the final twist to a chapter involving the mysteries of Michael Schumacher and Eddie Irvine.

NOTES

1. Enzo Ferrari's house is broad, detached and three storeys high. The shutters are painted Ferrari red. It stands in a courtyard near the track.
2. Schumacher's run was potentially crippling to a World Championship bid: retirement at Monaco, victory in Canada, retirements in France, Austria and Germany.
3. In July, Jacques Villeneuve had said that Schumacher was unethical at the start of races. Coulthard had complained that Schumacher swerved across to defend his position at the French Grand Prix. 'It does bother me,' Villeneuve said. 'It is always the same person doing it. But why should he stop? He always gets away with it.'
4. In Canada, in heavy rain, both Ferraris wanted to pit at the same time. Barrichello waited until Schumacher had a set of wet tyres fitted.

5. Schumacher and Fisichella crashed at the start of the German Grand Prix.

6. Nigel Stepney, a senior Ferrari mechanic, was knocked over and broke his ankle in the Spanish Grand Prix when Schumacher made a pit stop and was waved away fractionally early. Stepney held the refuelling nozzle.

7. Irvine was testing at Valencia.

8. Luciano Burti, a 25-year-old Brazilian, had been Jaguar's test driver and deputised at the 2000 Austrian Grand Prix when Irvine was ill. He left Jaguar to join the Prost team in the spring of 2001.

9. © Formula One Administration Ltd.

10. The crash at the chicane at Suzuka in 1989 when Senna went up the inside, Prost turned in and the laws of physics asserted themselves.

11. Quoted in *F1 Racing*, April 2001.

Chapter 5

GILDED CAGE

*'I'd never have done that, but then I'm not a three-times World
Champion who made a lot of enemies as well as friends.
And you know what? Maybe that's some of my downfall.
Maybe if I was a lot harder, a lot more cut-throat, I'd still be
sitting in a Grand Prix car today. I had the ability, I had the talent
but probably I was too nice.'*
– Mark Blundell

The paddock is public and private. Here, behind the pits
and encircled by enough fencing to keep outsiders out, the
insiders scurry about their business. There are a lot of insiders
bumping shoulders, arranging and re-arranging the dozen things
which constantly crop up, always going somewhere, always
coming back. Here, lavish hospitality is dispensed under
awnings and, as it seems, regardless of cost. Mechanics of
modest means and corporate creatures meet on common
ground. Celebrities sit looking lost or getting in the way.
Drivers' agents sit siphoning money. PR people in team livery
pretend to listen to journalists bemoaning the fact that the
world is not constructed as journalists would wish. Here – a
bastion of male chauvinism – women decorate the grid, hand
out press releases or do the cooking. Women are girlfriends
who seem to be models. Women are wives and mothers but,
often as not, they stay at home having had more than enough of
the paddock across these long years, when their husband's

team deciding to change tyre manufacturer was almost a religious moment of salvation to him – and a complete mystery to her.

Because so many dozens of insiders are in perpetual motion you can easily make the mistake which Ernest Hemingway warned against, and confuse movement with action. The action takes place in the motorhomes which stand like citadels amongst all the scurrying. These are the epi-centres of power. They are private places. You cannot see in and you won't be invited in.

The driver will be pursued, almost buffeted, from his pit to his sanctuary within the motorhome and each footstep of the way he'll have little chance, in Mario Andretti's delightful phrase, 'to walk the walk and talk the talk'. A knot of media people will be hemming him in, television cameras will loom, autograph hunters will wonder if they dare seize the fleeting moment, well-wishers will want to shake his hand or slap his back. The driver is semi-hunted until he is gone up the stairwell and into the air-conditioning of the upper deck. When he was the kid going home after a race – the van towing kart or car on the trailer – his second home was motorway cafés and formica tables. Now it is the motorhome.

The paddock has a feeling of self-importance and under-standably so. The newcomer, suddenly confronted by its size and scale, must make himself comfortable within it, and that may not be easy. He must learn the tricks of celebrity, of accepting that outside the car, the pits and the citadel he belongs to everybody but himself.

Behind the inscrutable faces are many private tensions and, sometimes, terribly vulnerable people. Julian Bailey, with his miserable season at Tyrrell in 1988 and his miserable three out of four Grand Prix meetings for Lotus in 1991, found his induction anything but easy.

When you look at your record, you must think you're better than that. Deep down you must know that truth.

'Obviously I do.'

You're better than Did Not Qualify, Did Not Qualify ...

'You've got to look at it this way in my days of Tyrrell: it was the most competitive time ever in Formula 1. You had a struggle to get into the races [on Bailey's début, Brazil, 31 drivers contested 26 places for the Grand Prix]. It's self-confidence, self-belief, and obviously sometimes I didn't get the balance right on that.'

But as a person you don't lack self-confidence, do you?

'Well, I think everyone does, don't they? You know you're not the best in the world at everything.

'I'd like to go back and do it again, I must admit I would. I am a better driver now than I was then and that's the thing that upsets me. I was a little bit too early into the Formula 1 game. I think also my background didn't help. I felt I didn't belong sometimes, because I was a working class kid from a council house. I was aware of it. Johnny Herbert's a different guy because he comes from the same background but I don't think he cares. I did care. That's my problem: I thought about it too much and I did feel that sometimes I didn't belong in that razzmatazz multi-million dollar scene because I'd actually come from a council house in Woolwich. That was the lack of self-confidence there, if you like. Left school when I was 12, and even though I can speak fluent Spanish because I lived there, and so I've got two languages, I never had any education and I felt a bit sort of ... lacking the self confidence.'

I put this to Herbert.

Julian Bailey said he felt very uncomfortable when he got to Formula 1.

'I never had that complex. I think I've been very fortunate. My career went very well in karting and Bill Sisley used to help me – I was sponsored by him. Then I had Quest who sponsored me. Then I got involved with Eddie Jordan which in some respects wasn't a bad thing. Then in 3000 we had no money whatsoever but Alex Hawkridge[1] helped out with engines, Reynard helped with the chassis, Eddie stuck Camel on the side of the car, we went to Jerez and I won that race. Then when I got to Formula 1 I was lucky because I had Peter Collins. I did my first test through him and even after the accident Peter was still very keen for it to happen anyway. Peter wanted me in the team and so I have never had those complexes at all.'

But you've never been bothered by what people thought.

'No, not really. I get peed off when people say things, yes, because sometimes they are very unnecessary things that are said, but that is the game of Formula 1. I never had a complex with it. My first time at Benetton[2] it wasn't that I felt pushed out, it was as if I wasn't there. I had a big problem [feet] but that was different from Julian's. At the time it was very hurtful but looking back it was the right thing.'

What Bailey said remains striking, and he expanded on it.

Normally motor racing people are tremendous achievers who think positively and, as it seems, can disregard their past if they need to.

'Some people do.'

Say they're from Finland. Who cares about that? 'I'm not in Finland any more, I'm here.' You couldn't leave that part behind you?

'Not really. It's like if I go to Monaco and I have a look round. I think "oh yes, it's all right" but I actually don't feel like I belong there, I don't like it. Not that I belong in Woolwich either. So … I don't know. Anyway, that's the sort of thing that would play on my mind a bit sometimes.'

And did you feel when it was preying on your mind that it shouldn't have been – that in many ways you'd got there in spite of Woolwich and the council house.

'Yes.'

Therefore you really did have the right to be there – more than many of the others.

'Yeah, but … I don't know. You compare yourself to the best, don't you? You compare yourself with someone like Senna who had the ultimate self-belief all the time.'

When you looked at Senna did you think 'yes, but you had a rich dad who bought you a kart when you were four, yes he financed you to come to England?'

'I look at some drivers like that but not him, because he was the best. Money can help you along the way but it can't make you the best. Beyond a certain point you are on your own.'

Did you feel that other people looked down on you?

'I did a bit. Yes.'

I once interviewed Lord Hesketh[3] and he said he'd noticed in Formula 1 how frightfully grand people were, even if they came from the Goldhawk Road.

'A lot of it was to do with that: people who'd made it flaunting it, and I couldn't.'

You may compare this with when Gerhard Berger arrived in the paddock for the first time as a Grand Prix driver in Austria in 1984 and saw it as an Aladdin's Cave of everything he desired. Niki Lauda once told Berger: 'Formula 1 is full of people who think they're so important. I can't stand the people in this paddock any longer.' This puzzled Berger. 'I was just starting and I thought he was crazy! Look at the girls, and the people giving you money everywhere, you get the best hotels, eat the best food. What more could you want?' Only much later did Berger understand.

It's a fair question to raise here, although it will be more fully explored in the next chapter: whether, in the midst of everything, genuine friendship between drivers is possible. Martin Donnelly was happy to answer. 'Yes, it is possible. I'd say I had good friendships with Johnny Herbert, Damon Hill, Julian Bailey and Perry McCarthy. In 1989 Jean Alesi and I were team-mates [in Formula 3000] and became close friends but he went off to Tyrrell and I went off to Lotus. Although he was towards the front of the grid we used to have our usual banter and carry-on but the circumstances of being a Grand Prix driver don't allow you to have a drink afterwards or play a round of golf. You have the debrief and the sponsors. After that you are away from the circuit, straight back to the hotel to get cleaned up, then I'd be at a Camel dinner and he'd be at a Marlboro dinner, or you have something else to do, and you don't get the opportunity. It is possible to team up at the circuit but these days it's very much a rarity.

'You're in close proximity, you're there in the paddock, but outside the motorhome these are our sponsors, you've got to do this presentation, that presentation, meet those people and these days it's even worse. Senna had the power to say "I am not driving an F1 car from 30 November to 5 February" – Schumacher too. Let the monkeys go out and do the testing and two weeks before the first race a Senna will come back in and say "you've done your job, boys, the car's all right." Bang.'

The driver faces many examinations, as we have seen, but none so full of nuance, undercurrent and subtle shifts as his relationship with his team-mate. Here is the core of the hunt: the two drivers are constantly compared because (in theory and mostly in practice) they are the only drivers on the whole grid who have the same cars. That is the only valid comparison to make. On the track, in the pits, in the paddock and in the citadels this taut human situation is arguably the most interesting of them all. The driver will have to accommodate the fact that the man sitting opposite him hour after hour can only be the enemy within. Sometimes it degenerates to the point where, as with Senna and Prost, it threatens the well-being of a whole team.

John Watson partnered Lauda at Brabham in 1978 and at McLaren in 1982 and 1983.

How can you survive a relationship like that?

'First of all, the relationship that Niki and I had was a very good one because, I believe, it was based on a genuine liking of each other. I like him, he likes me and before McLaren we were team-mates at Brabham, of course. Bernie [Ecclestone, who owned Brabham] came to me and said "what do you think about having Niki as a team-mate next year?" I said I'd have anybody in the world as long as we were given equal treatment. Bernie said that would be no problem. I said I didn't want to be number two, I wanted recognition – acknowledgement – of us being given equal status as drivers and equal status within the team. Bernie said "it's no problem."

'In the course of 1978 I realised the swing in the team had gone towards Niki and I had a moan about it at one stage. I said "Bernie, you know you promised me we would be equal number ones and I don't feel I am getting number one treatment." He said "John, let me just tell you something. It is a fact of life that there are some people who through their personality, their motivation or whatever is their core being, instil confidence, belief, respect into others and you can't put that on a bit of paper. It is about that single person and another single person."

'The thing that Niki brought to the show at that particular time was his presence as two-times World Champion [1975, 1977], a successful sponsorship with Parmalat and – I think it was the first time I'd come up against it – he was a team-mate who didn't believe in fairness in the way that I did.

'I realised that what happens in motor racing is that a team-mate isn't there to be fair and equal, he's there to win, and if he is a character like Niki he will use every strength in his make-up – ability as a driver, intelligence, reputation – to enhance his position and ensure he gets the latest modification, engine update, chassis change. Fairness has damn all to do with it. It is about survival of the strongest and showing you are that person: the strongest.'

How do you cope with that in your mind?

'I wasn't prepared for that and wasn't able to deal with it. I wasn't a two-times World Champion, I hadn't got a face which was famous all over the world. The only way was to fall back on the qualities that I had, which were my driving qualities, and try and resurrect myself through driving. It's difficult, because when you've got a team-mate like Niki who's an outstanding driver as well, you're not suddenly going to be a second a lap quicker consistently.

'I remember a shakedown[4] at Donington Park prior to going to a Grand Prix. I had my car and drove it, then I drove Niki's car and it felt better. I said to Gordon Murray[5] "his car feels much nicer than mine, what's different about it?" He said "it's got a stiffer rear roll bar on it." I said "well, why don't I have it?" "Because," he said "you haven't asked for it." What happens is – and I've seen this with Senna, with Prost – the natural born leaders have understood that teams look for leadership and commitment from the driver in much the same way that a driver looks for support from the team to assure him, or re-assure him, or reconfirm to him that he is a good racing driver.

'I lacked the outward confidence, or the arrogance, but Niki had achieved it through his success, and the reason he had achieved the success was because he had demonstrated it to the teams he'd driven for. I had it but didn't know how to express it.'

Is that a conscious decision by such as Lauda? I'm sure it was conscious on the part of Senna, and Schumacher – but the others?

'It goes back all the way to childhood, it's a process of evolution. Fundamentally I was an extremely shy person, still am, but there are techniques and mechanisms to overcome that. I probably never fully appreciated or believed in myself to the level that other people might have done and, therefore, I was much, much too introverted as opposed to acknowledging my own ability. More important, though, I was too self-effacing to make teams appreciate and understand. This is the value which people like Lauda have throughout all walks of life. They come into a room and they demand your attention: everybody is galvanised by them. You can't teach that. Other people come in and they blend, you don't see them, they stand on the edge.'

When you're in a team it's everything to you – home,

protection – but the moment you're leaving or you're fired it's as if they've never seen you before. It's a very cold leaving. How do you cope?

'Funnily enough, at the end of 1978 I began to get the message that Bernie was not going to keep Niki and me and I was the expendable one. My contract was for two years and it was up. Also Nelson Piquet was beginning to come along and Bernie was showing signs of wanting a young up-and-coming charger for no money – I was paid virtually no money anyway. I got the message that my staying with Brabham was not likely to happen, then Ronnie Peterson had his accident at Monza[6] and he'd already signed to drive for McLaren so I was straight in there on the back of that. It was negotiated in the early part of September and concluded before the final two races, and I knew that I had a place to go. I remember in Canada Bernie saying "you can't wait to leave can you?" and I said "absolutely bloody right, I just can't wait." That was a shame, on reflection, because it was a negative reaction from me, a reaction to the circumstance.'

So, how do you cope?

'In theoretical terms it was actually a better deal for me because I was going to McLaren as the de facto number one driver as opposed to finding myself subjugated. I have to say I am guilty of that, it wasn't the fault of the team. The team gravitated to the power source – Lauda – projecting the message "support me and I'll win the Championship for you."

'Now look at the case of Stefan Bellof.[7] He had this ability to jump into the car and on his first flying lap go quicker than his team-mate had done. Be it Derek Bell,[8] or me in Japan, it is a psychologically damaging tactic. In the same way today, Michael Schumacher has done that to his team-mates. He destroys them, but it is not as if he does the destroying himself: he creates the circumstance where he allows them to doubt themselves.

'Take some of Schumacher's team-mates, Eddie Irvine or Rubens Barrichello or Johnny Herbert. It just does their brains in, and it is very difficult because everybody has an ego about them. They think, as I thought and Derek thought, that they are the best driver in the world, and then you get a special guy like Schumacher or Bellof coming along and it knocks you bandy. It's very, very difficult to find ways to cope. I remember when Herbert became team-mate to Schumacher at Benetton and he thought he was going into a level playing field. I wrote that Johnny was there as Michael's number two and Johnny was slightly miffed about that. I said: "Johnny, that is Schumacher's team. You are there only to win if Michael doesn't win. You are not there to beat Michael and you won't."'

That is a very daunting thing to have to live with in a competitive environment.

'It is. Stefan Johansson, for example, is a less intense, much easier going person and that's what I mean about Senna having it.[9] Prost had it, although not quite as obviously as Senna, and Schumacher has it. They are natural born leaders in whichever sphere they are operating and believe in themselves emphatically. It may be that that actual belief is not as strong as you see it, but they are able to persuade a team principal that it is. Therefore the team will go through hoops of fire for them. In the same way, Senna would not have been able to deal with someone like Stefan, who in his mind wasn't even in the equation, suddenly being quicker.'

John Watson chose his words carefully but what he meant was that Senna would have been dumb-struck if Johansson had out-qualified him and would have adopted immediate and massive retaliation. In 1993 Michael Andretti retreated to the United States after a sad, foreshortened season with McLaren, and Häkkinen, the McLaren test driver, replaced him for the Portuguese Grand Prix at Estoril. This is what happened:

Practice 1	Häkkinen	1m 13.857s		Senna	1m 13.868s
Qualifying 1	Senna	1m 12.954s		Häkkinen	1m 12.956s
Practice 2	Senna	1m 13.434s		Häkkinen	1m 13.817s
Qualifying 2	Häkkinen	1m 12.443s		Senna	1m 12.491s
Warm up	Senna	1m 16.493s		Häkkinen	1m 16.769s

To match Senna so closely throughout, and out-qualify him – Häkkinen third fastest overall, Senna fourth – was rightly regarded as a sensation. In the race Senna ran for 19 laps before his engine failed while Häkkinen ran 32 laps before he had an accident. The truth of Senna's immediate and massive response lies behind all that, however. When Häkkinen was back in the pits Jo Ramirez, long-time McLaren team-member, asked what had been wrong with the car before the accident and Häkkinen replied, nothing wrong but he'd just learned from Senna that one lap in qualifying is not the same as sustaining that, lap after lap in the race.

In Japan, Senna out-qualified Häkkinen and took pole in Adelaide with 1m 13.371s while Häkkinen was on the third row with 1m 14.106s. Senna won Suzuka, Häkkinen finishing 26 seconds behind him. Senna won Adelaide while Häkkinen retired with a brake problem after 28 laps. The point about the mind of the great driver is not that he can draw from it masterpieces of movement but that he can reach a mental plateau which enables him to do this regularly and for as long as he needs; and always keep a certain percentage in reserve.

John Watson sums it up. 'Partly the key to the success of certain drivers is that there is no self-doubt, no question of self-analysis and even less question of the team ever thinking about it, because these drivers only project one thing and that is why they win and that is why they're good and that is why they have the position and that is why they have the respect within the team that they do.'

Mark Blundell had direct experience of this.

Every driver worth his salt believes he is the best, and here you were being compared with Senna because you were McLaren's test driver in 1992. You're going to find out.

'Yeah, but it doesn't happen in reality because you soon discover what the pecking order is. I didn't really learn it until I got inside a Grand Prix team and saw how it functioned. I got wind of it when I was doing a little bit of testing at Williams in 1990 but, to be fair, I had some very good runs there and I was competitive in times compared to Patrese and Boutsen. In fact I would have done my first Grand Prix with Williams if there had been that unofficial Grand Prix at Donington but it didn't happen.

'When I went to McLaren testing after my year in Grands Prix with Brabham I ran at Imola on a couple of occasions and was blindingly fast. Senna had all my sheet times and data, looking where I was quick. He'd analyse it. At Silverstone testing he ran in the morning, set a time, I went out with the same engineer and did the same time. The first thing he said was "I'm impressed, you've done the job," but it didn't get played up and you couldn't go and shout your mouth off about it because that would be highly unpopular.

'That was the way things were. I was fulfilling a role but I wasn't able to use it as a publicity vehicle. I was able to use it in terms of learning, abilities and so forth ... but to make capital out of it, to go to people and say "hey, look at this," that wasn't going to be allowed. Come the end of the day, if there was a press release I wouldn't be all over it. What happened testing at Monza that year was the classic and it hit home to me.'

Senna was really telling you something very hard, almost uncivilised.

'Yeah. At that point he was outright rude. I was the new kid on the block. What happened was this: when I went to McLaren I received approval. I ran for a couple of days then these guys [Senna, Berger] saunter along. When they've checked out what I've done they judged "what the kid says is on the button, that's good for us, we trust what he is about to do for us." Through that year I did a lot of testing and a lot of development work, new floors, underwings. Then the new stuff would be tested, Senna would put his stamp of approval on and McLaren would produce it in two days like they do – their normal way – and it would be in the next Grand Prix.'

They'd say 'if Mark is happy with it, we are'?

'Yes, and at that stage of my career as well [Blundell had only driven 14 races in an uncompetitive Brabham]. Internally I knew that, but externally it was never allowed to get out. Not like today. Look at the role Olivier Panis has just done testing for McLaren where they've made something out of it, which has given him a credibility. I was the first generation of test drivers and it was like being a child, seen but not heard.

'The Monza thing was feeling the wrath of Senna. I'd done a good job, I'd tested well, I'd been very, very quick, and the physiotherapist Josef Leberer was going to give me a lift back to the airport. No big deal, a 25-minute journey, but I had to get there because I had a flight to catch. Senna was staying on for another day's testing. As we sat there, he said very clearly and coldly to Josef "no, you stay here." I'm sitting there not making even a thin response.'

How did you take that moment?

'I'd never have done that, but then I'm not three times World Champion and I haven't made a lot of enemies as well as friends. And you know what? Maybe that's some of my downfall. Maybe if I was a lot harder, and a lot more cut-throat, I'd still be sitting in a Grand Prix car today. I had the ability, I had the talent, but probably I was too nice. I was Mr Nice Guy way too much.'

You'd have had to become something that you weren't.

'Right. I just didn't want to live through that all the time to get what I wanted. I wanted to try to get there as myself.'

So the argument would be that you didn't want it enough.

'It's not that. I think some of it is the way you get there and the effect that can have. It's how you manage yourself, how you cope. You can be a little bit in awe of the whole deal, you're reluctant to rock any boats, you're a little bit wary that [snaps fingers] you'll be just out. As I've gone on in my career I've learnt that if you don't speak up you don't get heard, and Formula 1 is such an animal that you have to be like that.'

Looking back now, would you have made a conscious effort to change yourself?

'On reflection, and to achieve what I wanted to achieve then, yes – but you can only do that with knowledge and experience. Another thing. I never had the support team some drivers do. I had family and I had people, but that was not the same as having a management. I didn't have the voice of experience which was strong enough to say "enough of that. I've seen all this before, I know how this functions, stay your ground a bit, don't buckle" – because afterwards you'll get a lot more respect out of it. [These sentiments are hauntingly similar to those of McNish, and will be echoed by Jonathan Palmer.]

'Stand your ground and people say "hey, he really does want it, he is adamant about it." Take Johnny Herbert. For what it was worth he had Peter Collins[10] behind him. Collins was running Lotus, he was a good, strong guy. You analyse it, you look at the guys, you look at their generation, a lot of the guys had a support team with them – somebody like an ex-driver looking after them, or somebody who'd been in the sport and saw it all coming.'

Karl Wendlinger went through a searching mental examination against his team-mates and he, too, faced the dilemma of whether to change himself.

When you reflect on your Grand Prix career, what do you think?

'I am quite happy with some parts but then when I think back I was not ... in German you say *konsequent* but it's not the same meaning as the English word. In English *consequence* means what comes out of something. In German it means step by step. I had very good parts. I remember the first races in 1993 with Sauber – Donington, Imola, Barcelona, Monaco as well. After Monaco was Canada, Magny-Cours. These races I was very fast compared to JJ Lehto, my team-mate. I thought "it's easy, no problem." In Imola I think it was 1.6 seconds, in Monaco it was 1.2 seconds in qualifying, in Barcelona it was more than one second so it's easy – but I was not strong enough in my head to continue this. I was maybe lying at home thinking "I don't have to prepare my race any more mentally, I just arrive and I'm fast." Then suddenly at Silverstone I was slower than him, Hockenheim I took speed back again [1:41.6 against Lehto's 1:42.0] but then from Budapest through Spa to Monza I had troubles because I was not concentrating enough. I was young and maybe I should have been a lot stronger and only think about the next race – nothing else – but maybe I would not have been relaxed. I don't know. The problem was that I didn't feel as mentally good as I had done a few races before. The difficulty is to find a way out of the problem.'

At the end of 1993 you were very highly regarded, you were the next generation.

'I think it was quite good, even the ups and downs that I had had in the second part of 1993, especially in qualifying. But I brought the car into the points: Budapest it was one point, once I finished fourth [Monza] and once fifth [Portugal]. I showed that I could drive a race from the tactical point of view and be consistent. Then, end of 1993, the season was finished and I started a very hard physical training programme. I thought it was necessary to do it. I believed in it. It was not a pain for me to do this – I liked doing it. Every day running and in the evening I played ice hockey. My physical condition was my best that I ever had. Maybe because of that I lost a little bit of easy going in the car, just jumping in the car and going fast. Then Heinz-Harald arrived at Sauber and he was fast right from the beginning. I knew him from German Formula 3, and it didn't make me too nervous. I said "OK, when the first qualifying comes at Interlagos I'll be there." Even the Friday qualifying I was faster than him. Saturday morning I had an engine blow up, the change of engines took too long and second qualifying started, I was not on the circuit and it started to rain. So Heinz-Harald was in front of me by two hundredths of a second.

'Then I was not relaxed any more. I said "I have to be faster than him the next time – I have to be faster than Frentzen, I don't care about the race." This was a mistake and this destroyed my head. If this was the reason for my accident I don't know. Maybe yes …'

Because you and your team-mate are competing for the same thing. Doesn't matter about, say, Schumacher because he's got a Ferrari.

'It was not difficult with Heinz-Harald. He's fast, of course, but as I now realise I made a mistake – I've read books about mental preparation, books about the brain, about positive thinking and so on. The problem was that I was not relaxed any more because I was only thinking "the next race I have to be faster than my team-mate" and this I think stopped me beating him.'

You see the mental complexities because at first Wendlinger is convinced that thinking about nothing else is the solution and a bit later that it is the problem.

'When I went home after the first race in Brazil, I said "[expletive] it doesn't matter – he was faster in qualifying but I was in the points. Next race I'll beat him no problem." I should have gone into the mountains to a little house to drink milk with the old farmers. This would have helped. I found out that this worked a lot better not just as a racing driver or sportsman generally but applied to a normal working guy. You have to find the right middle way between what you want to achieve and staying relaxed. You don't push yourself too hard. You think about it once, you forget about it and it happens anyway. In my racing career I got that wrong, mentally I was too aggressive against my team-mate. Not that I didn't like him or I hated him or whatever, it was just that I wanted to beat him. It was not only Heinz-Harald: it had been JJ before. In 1992, my first full season in Formula 1 with March, I had Jean-Paul Belmondo and he is a very nice guy but it was difficult for him to be fast in a Formula 1 car so that was never any problem for me.

'There was only one race, in Budapest. I arrived there, I had friends with me. In the evening we didn't go to a disco but also not to bed and if you'd have said "what about the de-brief" I'd have said "ah-ha! The de-brief!" Friday qualifying he was faster and I made a mistake. Then in second qualifying I spun, I was on the gravel and he was in front of me again. That showed me that when you want to have something 100% and you're not relaxed any more and you cannot accept somebody is better than you, it's even worse than if you do accept it.'

Perry McCarthy is convinced that drivers are prey without the mental strength, and there can be little or no doubt that the great ones had it from the beginning. They brought it with them. 'Look how many times that Ayrton or Michael have been seen by nearly everybody else in the world as being wrong about something. They will not accept it. What happens is that life walks into what you want it to be and it re-supports your confidence in how you go about something like motor racing. Doesn't matter what's happening around you, you will turn life to yourself – so drivers like Senna and Schumacher say "no, no, no" because they know to them-selves that they are right.

'I am like this in business and it's the same as being a racing driver: straight out, nose-to-nose, keep charging after what I want and getting it. I have set myself some very harsh challenges in this, as I did in motor racing. What that says to me is when I get a deal nobody else has thought of –

and I've put it together – I'm fastest. It's the same mentality.'

The hunting ground is so crowded that rookies need to stamp their authority immediately.

'Your first half dozen races in Formula 1 will do a lot to create the impression you are going to have,' Jonathan Palmer says. 'Alesi did it, Alesi came in and looked good immediately. Look at Schumacher with Jordan, look at Berger when he came in with ATS in Austria. A few races in a decent car is worth a number of seasons in a bad one. The European Grand Prix at Brands in 1983 was my first opportunity. I was thrilled to bits to do my first Grand Prix and with Williams.[11] OK, it wasn't the best time for Williams because they were still running a Cosworth DFV against the turbos. That was an interesting era because you pitted in the race but for fuel, not tyres. It was also a time when Keke Rosberg with his gung-ho confidence and aggressive driving style was able to make a much better fist of the job and get some heat into the tyres. He qualified sixteenth but Jacques Laffite [the other regular Williams driver] didn't qualify at all – he was a neater driver. I was pretty neat and I just about managed to out-qualify him. I was twenty-fifth on the grid.

'I never had a manager and in some ways it would have been better if I had but I was always my own person. Everyone around, particularly the team, were saying "don't worry about the result, make sure you finish" and all that stuff. What I'd say to anybody now is "what people are looking for is the guy who gives it the big send the moment they get off the grid." You're better off overtaking four people and then shunting it at Druids or wherever.'"

The team will think 'we can calm that bit out of him but he can do it.'

'Absolutely, and the biggest mistake I made was listening to what people were saying.'

I'd guess that your instinct would be towards prudence and caution.

'Yes, and it was the kind of approach that brought me championship wins in Formula 3 and Formula 2. If you are getting results, it's hard – even if somebody says "look, go at it" – to change the result-based approach. I think it would have made a difference to try and change, but it's difficult.'

They are inviting you to become somebody else.

'It's up to you to see whether or not you a) want to and b) are capable of evolving your character in a way that's more appropriate to what you're trying to do. With the benefit of hindsight, that was a mistake-time for me. I should have been a lot more relaxed and a lot more gung-ho. I should have paid lip service to all those telling me to keep it on the island[12] – "yeah, yeah, yeah" – and gone out and given it the big send and seen what happened. An experienced manager might have taken me to one side and said "look, your team are bound to tell you all that stuff but ignore that and make an impression on this race."'

Julian Bailey suffered the anguish of the young man drawn into a début season which was going very wrong. (Paradoxically he was partnering Palmer at Tyrrell.)

If you hadn't had strength of character, that could have damaged you.

'I'm all right now. Obviously you have to be an optimist in motor racing because if you aren't you'd think you were going to die. You think things are going to get better: you've just got to get through this bit and the car will be better at the next race or you'll get on with it a bit better. You keep going.'

You had no doubts that you were doing the right thing?

'I had no doubts until probably about three races into the season, four races, and I realised that I hadn't enough experience. I'd done six Formula 3000 races, no testing, and obviously there was very little budget in the team. It wasn't three weeks in Barcelona going round and round testing and getting to know you. I sat in the car at Imola and did about 20 laps. I had no problem driving the car although I felt there was no downforce on it. I said this to Ken and he said "well, everyone says that when they get into Formula 1" – but when we looked at the speed trap figures I was quicker than the Ferrari into Tosa and I thought "well ..."'

Next came Brazil, where Bailey's car had mechanical problems and he failed to qualify. He did a 1m 36.137s to be twenty seventh (Oscar Larrauri in the Euro Brun did 1m 35.711s to be twenty sixth).

I remember going over to the pub before you flew out and you were completely relaxed.

'Yes. I didn't know what was ahead of me.'

At no stage before did you have any self-doubts?

'Not that I remember. Self-doubt came as the season wore on.'

So you go to Brazil ...

'... and the steering rack wouldn't go on, so I lost the first 45 minutes of the first session. Now bear in mind that this is my second time ever in the car and I hadn't a clue about the circuit. You weren't allowed to go out in a road car and go round. They said if you want to learn the circuit you can walk round. Well, you can do it but it's a long straight to walk up three or four times. The first session in those days was an hour and a half. When I got out onto the circuit everybody was up to speed. I didn't know if the corner coming at me would be a right-hander or a left-hander – and the mirrors fell off the car as I went out of the pit lane ...'

But you're in for a season and there is no way out of this.

'I didn't want to get out of it, I wanted it to get better. The next race was good because we went to Imola where I'd done a few laps and I out-qualified Jonathan. I retired with gearbox trouble, and I was running well ahead of Jonathan at the time so I thought that's not too bad. I was quite optimistic after that.'

It can't have been helped by them all queuing up to complain in Brazil.

'Yes, but I couldn't learn the circuit, couldn't go round on a motor bike, couldn't go round in a saloon car and then I had no mirrors on. It doesn't help when Nelson Piquet comes down and starts ranting and raving at you and Prost is behind him – and I knew they had a valid point. It was dangerous.'

The paddock may represent an Aladdin's Cave to a Gerhard Berger, but for some F1 newcomers it can be a stage full of leading players for ever trying to assert themselves – over you.

NOTES

1. Hawkridge ran the Toleman team in the early 1980s and hired Senna.
2. Herbert raced five times for Benetton in 1989 before being in effect fired.
3. Lord Alexander Hesketh ran his own Formula 1 team in the 1970s (starring James Hunt) and became a senior politician in the House of Lords.
4. Shakedown – usually a new car's first test, shaking down any problems.
5. Gordon Murray, a South African, designed the championship-winning Brabhams of 1981 and 1983.
6. Ronnie Peterson (Sweden) died in hospital after a crash in the 1978 Italian Grand Prix at Monza.
7. Stefan Bellof, who drove 20 Grands Prix for Tyrrell in 1984–85, was

regarded as one of the outstanding talents of his generation. He was killed in the 1000kms sportscar race at Spa.

8. Derek Bell had an unusual Grand Prix career (nine races between 1968 and 1974) but became a celebrated sportscar driver, winning Le Mans five times. Ickx holds the record with six.

9. Johansson competed in the last three races of 1984 for Toleman: Italy, which Senna missed, the European at the Nürburgring (in qualifying Senna 1:22.349, Johansson 1:41.178), Portugal (Senna 1:21.936, Johansson 1:22.942).

10. Peter Collins, who emigrated from Australia to Britain in 1977, was employed by Colin Chapman, the founder of Lotus. He worked for Williams and Benetton before rescuing Lotus in 1990. The team struggled on until the end of 1994.

11. Williams ran three cars in the 1983 European Grand Prix, for Rosberg, Laffite and Palmer who qualified on the last row of the grid. He finished the race thirteenth, two laps behind the winner (Nelson Piquet/ Brabham).

12. 'Keep it on the Island' is motor racing-speak for keeping a car on the track.

Chapter 6

THE SWITCH

'In the warm-up I was running more fuel or something and I remember he chopped me. He did something to try and say "hey, I'm Ayrton Senna" and I was thinking "what a wanker, you know, grow up. It's the warm-up and you want to overtake me, fine, overtake me, but in the races ..."'
– Eddie Irvine

Anyone reaching Formula 1 who does not have a solid mental picture of who he is and what he wants probably won't survive. Without that the settling-in period can be ... unsettling.

In 1993 Irvine made his Grand Prix début with the Jordan team at the Japanese Grand Prix. He had driven for Jordan in Formula 3000 and, from 1991, competed in the Japanese Formula 3000 Championship, so he knew his way round Suzuka.

'Guys coming up have less respect for the guys above them than you do when you're in it for even a while because you think these guys are old tossers hanging on for the money, and that's what I thought. You were very arrogant.'

Senna clearly wasn't hanging on for the money.

'No. I thought he was the business as a driver, but none of the rest, I felt, were any good.'

Irvine qualified on the fourth row of the grid. Senna led from Prost and Irvine made a superb start, up to fifth with

Schumacher behind him. Schumacher got past on lap 3 and Irvine had a strange race – as high as fourth – before Senna came up and lapped him. At this point Irvine ran just behind Damon Hill (Williams).

'I am in a Jordan which has never scored a point that year and I am racing with a Williams for fourth. Senna comes up behind me, I let him through and Damon holds him up for a lap and a half. So then I see the opportunity to overtake Senna and then overtake Hill, which I did – then Hill overtook me again, then I overtook Hill and the battle went on but Damon was the one who was totally in the wrong. He should have let Senna through straight away, as I did.'

Let's picture the situation with, on a wet track, them running in order Hill, Senna, Irvine. Senna dropped back a little way from Hill and Irvine hustled Senna, tried one overtaking move then another, putting the Jordan alongside him and squeezing it ahead. Irvine advanced on Hill and went inside him at the chicane. Irvine slithered (a little) coming out of the chicane and Hill immediately retook him. They went down the long start-finish straight with Senna trying to hustle Irvine who, in the long spoon of turn one, darted inside Hill. As they moved into the next left Hill retook him on the outside although their wheels almost touched. They ran in order Hill, Irvine, Senna until Irvine slithered (a little) in a left-hander and Senna sneaked through. Senna was enraged that Irvine had had the temerity to unlap himself rather than meekly get out of Senna's way. Irvine finished sixth.

Did you have any doubts about overtaking Senna?

'No, because he wasn't going to overtake Hill. Hill was chopping him and Senna was leading the race by a long way and there was no need for him to take a risk. I needed to get past Hill as soon as I could.'

Is this also a way of you saying 'I've arrived'?

'No, I didn't think of that at all. Honestly, it wasn't even Senna in that car. That was the car between me and Hill.'

And afterwards he came looking for you but he didn't know what you looked like and kept saying 'which one's Irvine?'

'I know. In the warm-up I was running more fuel or something and I remember he chopped me. He did something to try and say "hey, I'm Ayrton Senna" and I was thinking what a wanker, you know, grow up. It's the warm-up and you want to overtake me, fine, overtake me, but in the races ...

'I thought it was very sad that a guy with his reputation and his record had to show a little guy who's just come into Formula 1 that he is the king. You shouldn't need to show it. Childish.'

(Irvine, as it seems, has never modified his position on all this. In an interview in 1995 he said: 'When you come into Formula 1 a lot of people try and intimidate you. That's what happened with me and Senna in Japan. He tried to intimidate and I told him to get stuffed. You have to start as you intend to go on.')

And what about the incident itself when he came down and 'attacked' you?

'He lost control and I was totally calm, sitting there just arguing. I was standing up for what I had done, for what my thoughts on the situation were. He lost the plot, screaming and shouting.'

What did you feel about that?

'I thought he should calm down.'

Have you ever been in that situation?

'Ah, loads of times but not at the racing, that's my job. I'm very in control.'

What about outside your job? What would make you blow your mind outside?

'Erm ... injustice. That ban that I got for three races (after a crash in Brazil in 1994). It was embarrassing for the FIA to be honest.'[1]

It was the punish-the-kids syndrome?

'I'm not into that. You judge every case on its merits and that was bollocks. There's supposed to be a tribunal which decides each case on its merits and how those guys got to that judgement is just mind-blowing. There shouldn't be politics. A court is not about politics. And that's the thing that really winds me up in the world – whenever you have political decisions over really what should be the right outcome of a court case. I think that's Irish. The Northern Irish, we're very strong on that sort of thing.'

The Jordan was powered by Hart engines and Brian Hart was at Suzuka. 'Eddie was justified in what he did on the track despite all the comments afterwards. Gary [Anderson, Jordan designer] and I had left the track so we didn't know about what happened until we got to Tokyo. Ayrton had lost his cool and Irvine, being Irvine, acted as you'd expect. I'd only met him a few weeks before because he'd been doing 3000 in Japan. I was immensely interested in how he approached testing a Formula 1 car. He wasn't overawed by it or the fact that Rubens Barrichello was going to be his team-mate. "It's a racing car. That's my job."

'When we got to Tokyo we went to the Hard Rock club to get some food and a drink because it had been a grim year and we'd just got Jordan's first points – fifth [Barrichello] and sixth

[Irvine]. And Eddie had been on the pace. The guy in the bar in the club was telling us "oh, you've come from Suzuka, have you heard about Ayrton Senna and Eddie Irvine?" We had to work it out from what we remembered of the race.

'Eddie could just have sat behind Senna and Hill but he didn't because he was racing Damon. What he was saying was "I'm here. If you're the best guy in the world you should have got past Hill because you were lapping him, but I was racing Hill." Eddie let Ayrton pass him and then there was all these shenanigans between Senna and Hill so "I'll overtake both of them." Eddie was correct.'

Senna demonstrated a more humane side of his character when Martin Donnelly prepared for his first season in Formula 1 with Lotus in 1990. Donnelly's friend Ed Devlin – who had run the café outside Snetterton where young drivers ate during breaks from testing[2] – recounts the incident.

'When Martin went pre-season tyre testing at Imola he took me with him and I walked up the pit lane. As usual round the McLaren pit there were loads of photographers and press and Senna was sat in the car. He looked over and couldn't work out what Ed from the café was doing here. He got out and walked over to me.

'He'd had the problem with Prost the year before [at the Suzuka chicane when they crashed in bitter circumstances] and had been undecided about whether to retire or not. I'd written to him and asked him not to retire. Now at Imola he said "your letter was very important to me. Thank you very much." He'd not only read it, he'd remembered I'd written it – and it was a very heartfelt letter because I felt close to him, as I did with a lot of drivers. He asked if I brought his *baurú*, a toasted cheese, ham and tomato sandwich which we made for him every day. My wife used to cut his hair: when he came back after the winter break it was long! He said "is your wife here with the scissors?" He put his arm round me, he walked into the Lotus pit and said "hi, Martin, welcome to the club. I hope you have a successful time." I spent an hour with him on a couple of days during the testing and it was absolutely magic.'

Donnelly has precious memories of this side of Senna too. 'I was in a BBC Grandstand race at Brands Hatch in 1984 and won but lost my front wing – it came off the nosebox. Ayrton came up to me afterwards and looked at the car. "That was brilliant," he said. "I never thought you could have done that." I'd held everybody else up because although I was quick on the straight I'd been slow in the corners. However from 1984 until I got into the Grands Prix I hadn't really been speaking to him, then he came along and said "good to see you, Martin, and welcome to the club." That was a good five, six years later.'

Senna's mind truly was arranged into a series of compartments, and often the contents seemed so contradictory that they defied rational analysis. He could be brutal with Irvine and tender with Donnelly. He could be utterly diplomatic or publicly insensitive. He could preach the sanctity of life and endanger the lives of others. He could argue vehemently against poverty while amassing vast wealth. But he is not here now to explain the contradictions (or if they were contradictions to him), so we'll let that rest.

Looking at the reverse of the Irvine incident, the seasoned F1 driver faces a particular challenge when he confronts the newcomer. Kimi Räikkönen seemed to pose just such a problem before the 2001 season because of his youth and lack of experience. I asked Heinz-Harald Frentzen about this.

If you are on a fast lap in qualifying and you see Räikkönen ahead, what are you going to do?

'You have to be aware that an inexperienced driver could, in reacting, do something wrong. As you approach him you ask yourself questions. Is he looking in the mirror? Is he creating space? Can he see you as you go to overtake him? You can see and estimate the answers way before you reach him, and you give yourself a margin. For example if he is on the racing line going slowly then you know he has not seen you and you make a decision on that.'

And what's the decision?

'To abort!'

Now let's look at it from Räikkönen's vantage point, with Frentzen coming so urgently towards him. What does he do?

'I think exactly similar!' said Räikkönen. 'Sometimes you catch them on the straight or they see you in their mirrors and when you are turning into the corners they just let you by. Otherwise you can't because you'll have a shunt. You need to slow down then.'

But you will be keeping your eyes open ...

'Yeah, yes, for sure but there is no point in holding people up if they are doing a heavy lap.' Räikkönen smiled at this moment and murmured that if you baulk them they tend not to forget. The kid is thinking, as Mario Andretti once remarked in another context altogether.

Jonathan Palmer's path into F1 was smoothed by his benevolent sponsor, Peter Millward. 'I used to go along and say "I need another £25,000" and he'd write out a cheque. It seemed so incongruous to have these huge sums of money and then in your everyday life you'd be writing out a cheque for ten quid. I did 1984 with the RAM team and at the end of the year I paid John McDonald. He said "you're the first driver who's ever paid me what he should!" I wouldn't have done it any other way.

'My team-mate was Philippe Alliot. We got on well but he was as tricky as they come. Those were the days of the turbo cars and he was forever winding up the boost. We never had a spare car. I had an aluminium composite chassis and he had a carbon one and his car was obviously better than mine but he was paying half a million and I was paying the £250,000. Most qualifying sessions we'd end up sharing one car anyway [because the other one broke]. The car was a dog at first and it was a very difficult time.

'That season Senna came in with Toleman, who had a pretty good car and he had some good results. Thinking about it, they'd done a good job too with Brian Henton and Derek Warwick. Brundle came in with Tyrrell and he had 1984 with Stefan Bellof – Tyrrell had a normally-aspirated car and at least it handled well, he could chuck it about on a street circuit. I'd come in brimful of confidence from being Formula 2 champion and it really knocked the stuffing out of me having what proved to be two or three difficult years. The confidence can't help but ebb away. I came into Formula 1 thinking that I could win in anything but, particularly after the first year lumbering around getting in people's way, you do begin to doubt your own ability to drive a car quickly.'

And an opinion may be solidifying within Formula 1 that you're not good enough.

'That's very difficult. Anyway, at the end of that season I remember testing for Toleman. They were looking for next year and I was substantially quickest of a number of drivers they tested. It was an Estoril test.[3] Politics or money became involved and I didn't get the drive but Zakspeed[4] was starting up. They got in touch with Andrew Marriott [who worked for CSS, a promotions company with close links to motorsport] and said "who should we get to drive the thing?" He said "put Jonathan Palmer in." I met Erich Zakowski[5] and I joined. That was another baptism of fire. If you look at the results you can see what a confidence-shattering time that was.'

Palmer drove seven Grands Prix in 1985, retiring with mechanical problems six times and not starting at all at Imola because the car had a misfire which, despite frantic work, could not be cured. Palmer had qualified on the ninth row of the grid and his thinking was that, if the misfire persisted at the green light, he would endanger the nine drivers accelerating as hard as they could behind him. He was eleventh at the next race, Monaco, the only race he finished.

'That season I did sportscars as well but I was out because I broke my leg quite badly in a Porsche at Spa. The irony! Then the following day Bellof was killed – that was a really dreadful weekend. My big worry at that time was would I stay in Formula 1 and would I stay with Zakspeed? I was desperate to stay in Formula 1 and stay with the team.' Palmer missed the last five Grands Prix and 'Christian Danner drove instead of me. Anyway, I stayed with Zakspeed in 1986 and partnered Huub Rothengatter, who wasn't particularly competitive. I had a slightly better time that year – qualified sixteenth in Spain and that was a pretty good effort. I also qualified nineteenth at Monaco. Actually I nearly got sixth place in the Mexican Grand Prix and that was a pretty good effort too.'

You look at the finishes. You are finishing fairly consistently.

'Well, I don't know, there are retirements everywhere. There was a huge amount of frustration but, and it's the same old thing, I knew I needed the car in order to do the job. At the end of that year Zakspeed felt they wanted to get somebody else, they wanted to do better. They felt I had done a good job for them but they wanted to move on to somebody else. I think it was probably ditto at Tyrrell with Martin [Brundle], so he and I swapped places. I got the better end of the stick because although he had a fifth somewhere [Imola] and the Zakspeed was definitely getting better, I had a fifth at Monaco, a fifth in Germany and a fourth at Adelaide' – plus three finishes just outside the points.

'I was really pleased to join Tyrrell, very excited, because it was a major team although I can't remember how it came about! The first year we had the dual series[6] and I won the Jim Clark Trophy [for non-turbo cars]. The best result was at Adelaide after I'd won the Trophy, when Senna was disqualified [oversize brake ducts]. I'd collided with Warwick on the first lap, had to come into the pits, dead last, came back out and got up to fifth on the road by the end of the race.

'I did experience frustration because whenever I got a chance, like the Toleman test, I was there. When we had the new Tyrrell in 1989 I was there. When Alboreto started with the team he had the new car at Imola. I qualified the old one on the last row of the grid and he didn't qualify at all. He promptly said the car was undrivable. I thought the car was so much better than before.'

The driver will have to master what John Watson calls The Switch, which 'is a funny thing because to me it was automatic and I can give a little anecdote to illustrate that. In 1976 I was driving for the Penske team [owned by Roger

Penske, an American]. We got to the Dutch Grand Prix on the back of winning in Austria and prior to the beginning of qualifying I was sitting on the pit lane wall with, I think, Heinz Hofer, the team manager. We were bullshitting, talking about anything under the sun – but not motor racing. Roger got really intense. "I don't understand you guys, I don't know how you can sit there and be so cool and relaxed and then get into the car and drive. It's like you've a Jekyll and Hyde personality."

'I think it is an unconscious mechanism that we have which enables us to keep that pressure in control. Different people have different mechanisms. In qualifying I'd be fairly relaxed but come the race I'd like to be fairly alone in the half hour before you moved into the process of getting into the car. I wouldn't want to be bothered by people. Jackie Stewart thrived on being busy-busy-busy, being in the public eye – that was his mechanism and he released it that way. Others have got theirs.

'I watched Michael Schumacher in Malaysia in 2000 and he didn't do anything for 15, 20 minutes before the race except stand around chatting, smiling, whatever. He wasn't actually doing that. What you were seeing was the image of him doing that. Inside there's still a pressure but it's being disguised by this way of handling it.

'The underlying thing is a chemical effect because what we're doing is controlling the flow of adrenalin. Adrenalin is an essential commodity in any sportsperson's make-up at any high level but particularly in motorsport because of the obvious physical aspects – danger. As drivers we understand how to switch it on and how to switch it off.'

Let's say a race goes an hour and three quarters, and you're driving pretty much on the limit. Does your mind think about non-racing things?

'Not the menial things like "did I put the cat out?" There will be lots of things that go through your mind, like maybe "what the hell am I doing driving this heap of scrap today?" That's a racing thing ...'

Is it possible to go an hour and three-quarters and not let the world intrude at all?

'The intrusion will be principally about things that have been occurring around you over the weekend. I don't think you are going to go through a race distance thinking about personal things. Those thoughts might be there in your subconscious because adrenalin heightens awareness in the same way that it polarises your eyes like a camera lens and gives you a huge depth of peripheral vision. That is a physical change. Probably your mind is equally expansive in that context. You're taking in huge amounts of information but not in a forward planning sense. You are being bombarded with it because you are so receptive. I have seen people use this analogy in a TV programme.'

[It was called *Full Throttle: the technology of speed*[7] and was shown on British television in 2000. Alexander Wurz described the nuances of controlling a car at speed and the commentator said that Professor Mike Land of the University of Sussex 'believes these images and feelings that a driver has help him to refine a sophisticated map of the circuit he has created in his mind.' A driver, Tomas Scheckter – son of Jody and, that season, driving Formula 3 with the Stewart team – was to cover some laps so that what he was doing could be analysed by Professor Land.

'Scheckter,' the commentator said, 'glances at the same part of the road as ordinary drivers but it turns out his mental map of the circuit allows him to use the information differently. Tomas doesn't have time to use feed-back information from the side of the track to position the car – he's travelling too fast to react to it – but, because he knows the circuit so well, his brain is able to use the feed-forward information in conjunction with his mental map to predict the tiny reactions he needs to make to position the car on the track. Surprisingly, throughout the six laps that the Professor analysed, Tomas only glanced at his instruments once.'

'There is information which is positive, and you take that on board,' says Watson, 'and there is irrelevant information. Interestingly, the commentary in the TV programme said that Scheckter only once consciously looked down at his instrument panel, and you might have thought "ah, there's a guy who doesn't look at his instruments." Bullshit! The driver knows what the water temperature, oil temperature, oil pressure and all that stuff should be reading so he doesn't look down. What is happening at the conscious level is that the driver is being fed information but, because there's so much of it, he has to disseminate what is important and ignore the rest. He stores the important. Now suppose without warning something is happening, for example the water temperature going off the clock. Mechanisms are triggered to make the driver look down.'

Why?

'That I don't know. It's a function of how our brains work, or at least how we take information and process it. You are dealing with huge amounts – I can't even put it into computer terms – but it's the bit in front of you that's the most important. If something in that information changes, you react. You've this super computer, if you like, programmed to accept information and suddenly one of the messages is different – coming from a different direction or at a different speed or whatever – and that triggers something. In Scheckter's case no different message came – he'd know approximately what the engine should be doing, approximately where he should change gear – and it was not necessary to glance at the instruments.'

Perry McCarthy expands the theme. 'A lot of a racing driver's job is to take on information quite coldly. As we go faster and faster and faster we are acting, to a degree, like a micro-processor. You go into a corner and you store what happened to the car out of feeling. It's rather like people who are able to speed-read. They are taking it in intravenously as it were, and that is what we are doing with a car. To articulate our feelings takes an awful lot longer than a lap, and you just know what's happening. You can't say to yourself "I am approaching this corner, I had a little bit of understeer there last time so maybe if I go a bit deeper on the brakes, turn in a bit harder, I'll do it better." You're not doing that. It's rather like a flow chart and you say "right, I'm going there, I'm going there, I'm going there" because of what you felt the last time.'

Is that subconscious or conscious?

'A bit of both. The feeling is subconscious but you've stored it consciously. It's in you. I can tell you when I come in from a lap, as many, many other drivers can, exactly what the car's been doing at every single corner, under braking, at the turn-in, by the apex, the exit, power on, whatever. I can re-live it.'

But you haven't been trying to remember that, have you?

'No. You are concentrating in the car and you have an open mind, an open disk. So I've had the feeling on one lap and, next time I come around, part of me is flagging that I can go faster here or do this or do that. You might pick a visual object and "that's where I'm going to brake." No discussing it: you're going too fast.

'Then maybe when you get there the bloody thing locks up. It says no-no-no. Next thought: I've still got control of the car, I'll still try and get the lap time even though I've made a real big booboo. You've gone onto another level: "got to control this, got to try and not smash the car to pieces." It just works like that.'

Mark Blundell puts it this way: 'One of the advantages a racing driver has over an ordinary driver is to look ahead so much and absorb so much. The racing driver can already read the situation far quicker. It's like the snooker player. He's at the shot but he's already worked out the next shot.'

Do you do that automatically when you drive a car on the road?

'Yeah. The thing is, I'm always looking for an escape route. I've already thought "ditch there, lamp-post there, if something happens where do you go?" It's just a natural process. "Where's the way out?" It's like a micro-processor, processing information all the time.'

Were you born with this?

'I guess that's the old question of asking whether someone is a natural or manufactured driver. I don't know what I am. Someone else would have to give that opinion. I don't come from a racing background. To me, Mansell was more manufactured. He had to work overtime to get what he got but there's no doubt about it, he got it and he was good. Senna was the other end of the spectrum, naturally gifted. There's no right and wrong about this, about what's fastest or what's best. It's just the way it is.'

When you drive the car competitively, how far ahead can you see?

'You know the track so you are already calculating like the snooker player, planning ahead. You are following a guy, tagging him, and you're trying to set the guy up as well. You take on board the weaknesses and strengths of where you're going to try and make your move.'

Johnny Herbert drives intuitively and this is how, on the way to Formula 1, he solved the problem of feeling he wasn't driving at his best. 'I remember what I did, remember doing it once at Silverstone. I went out and I was driving like an old woman. I pitted because I knew that if it wasn't right it wasn't going to get any better. I got out, went to the back of the garage and spent ten minutes there wiping it from my mind. Then I got back in, went out again and the good feeling was back. Pole. I used to be able to do that.'

In the matter of overtaking, John Watson was a master, wielding what Ken Tyrrell memorably described as a 'burn from the stern' as he seared up through the field.

Mentally you have summed up the character and likely conduct of the driver you're about to overtake. Suppose it was de Cesaris or Arnoux,[8] you'd give them a wide berth?

'Arnoux was a very skilful, very competitive racer,' Watson says. 'I remember in Brazil in the early 1980s coming up through the field and Arnoux was a walk in the park to pass. I manipulated him: made one move and he countered, went into the gap he'd left and bomp, bomp, bomp it was done, calculated and executed sweet as a nut. Tried the same on Prost, much more difficult person, intellectually much brighter. I eventually got past him but it was harder work.

'Let me give you another example. In Detroit in 1982 I had a very good race, won and I started behind Niki.[9] We had a re-start and Niki got in behind Pironi and Eddie Cheever and Niki couldn't get past, sat behind them lap after lap. I came up behind with momentum into Turn One. Niki saw me coming and knew my strengths. Niki was a missile when he was on his own in clear air and very, very difficult to beat but when it got to street fighting, getting down and getting dirty, I was a more complete driver. So he saw me coming and you know when somebody is on a mission behind you. They are going to come past you, they don't sit there and say "please may I?" In a sense, I was actually doing to him what he did to me at Brabham – taking a place away.

'Niki let me go through and he was saying to himself "you're a clever guy, OK, you passed me but now get past Cheever and Pironi." In one lap I did the three of them. Niki had sat behind those guys for six or seven laps like a metronome. When he saw me pass he reprogrammed his own mental state, thought maybe you can get past and he passed them. Then he tripped over Rosberg which was a bit pathetic because Keke was cute. I had no trouble passing Keke because all the passing had been done in the laps when I was catching him at three seconds a lap. I had already passed him in his mind before I got near him. Then he saw Niki and he knew Niki wouldn't be quite as decisive as I was so he squeezed Niki and Niki didn't know whether to go or stop and clipped the wall.'

That's the psychology of it when you say you'd overtaken Rosberg before you reached him.

'He said to me afterwards "John, I knew I wasn't going to

win because you were catching me so quickly. I did my best lap and you took two and a half seconds out of me."'

How much of that is mind games? How much is it a driver who has a reputation for preferring to crash you than back off?

'It's a very good tactic and it's very intimidating. Senna had it, I think Michael [Schumacher] has it, but I don't know of anybody else to that degree. In terms of overtaking I don't think Senna was, in fact, a natural or the best but he was a bloody good intimidator. In my view, someone like Mansell was a better racer, whereas as soon as people saw the McLaren and then put the yellow helmet and the car together – Senna coming! – they got out of the way. It can be a career strategy but you have to create it.'

You create it from a rational decision: I will take this to the stage where people see red and white car + yellow helmet and think Armageddon – Ah'm a geddon outta here![10]

'I imagine that, once he had established his power over others, those thoughts would have been automatic. This is about understanding yourself, being able to recognise the fact that you possess that ability. It is like a power of mind over somebody else's mind. You are mentally manipulating your competitor.

'In the summer of 1987 I went over to Willy Dungl's[11] training camp for a few days and Ayrton was there as well, bicycling and so on. He asked me "what do you think about McLaren, what sort of team is it?" I said it was a fantastic team, obviously, and "I know there have been discussions, or there are rumours, that you might be going there. If you go, remember that McLaren is 100% Alain Prost's team.[12] They think the sun shines out of him, he's very good friends with Mansour Ojjeh,[13] he's done a really good French job on the team and Mansour and everybody. If you go there just bide your time, don't take on Alain, don't challenge him because you know he's very strong." Ayrton said "no I don't agree with that. I'm going to go there and I'm going to be physically stronger than Alain, I'm going to be mentally stronger than Alain, I'm going to knock his socks off, I'm going to lift the whole game." And that is what he did.

'Monaco 1988. Prost had pole position, then Senna got it back. Ten minutes to go. Prost went out, got pole position back, came into the pits. I stood and watched this. He stood up in the seat of the car and all the French press gathered round him like moths round a candle. "Oh, Alain, fantastic time, pole position, Alain." Two minutes to go Senna went out and did a time which was almost a second quicker. [It didn't happen exactly like this: see Breaking Point.] In the eyes of the team and the public and most notably himself, suddenly the robes had been stripped from the Emperor – metaphorically Alain was left naked. Because he is such an insecure person Alain was deeply, deeply psychologically wounded by what Senna did. In the race Senna made a mistake and Alain won but the key was qualifying. He seized Prost and threw him away.

'Ron Dennis and all the team went up to Senna and they grabbed him and they loved him because the team had seen the centre of power shift, and that's why a man like Senna can control a situation.'

This same year, the intricate demands of Monaco worked hard against Julian Bailey, driving the Tyrrell in his maiden F1 season.

'Couldn't get to grips with it. Tyrrell had two different cars, long wheelbase and short wheelbase. Jonathan Palmer took the one that worked better and I was left with the other one and didn't qualify it, just didn't get on with it. I'd been to Monaco in the Formula 3 support race to the Grand Prix two or three years before so I knew which way it went but I just couldn't drive the car.'

The one thing the Grand Prix drivers can't survive is self-doubt.

'I did get self-doubt and driving the car became not something I looked forward to, which is a serious flaw. And I'm in for the whole year hoping that things are going to get better.

'Some time during the season Harvey Postlethwaite joined from Ferrari so there was a bit of a new atmosphere. His first race was Hungary. I remember getting up that morning, looking out the window of the hotel overlooking the Danube and seeing it absolutely bucketing down. I thought "hmmm, this is good, now it's going to be a bit more of a level playing field."[14] In practice I went out immediately and was really quite quick. I saw everybody else spinning off through the puddles and I thought "strange, because I can get through them." When you get big puddles on a circuit you don't accelerate or brake, you just go through them and do what you've got to do afterwards. Berger went off and everyone was spinning. I came past and I saw P3 on the board, third quickest. I came in. I was under no illusions because I knew Senna and Mansell hadn't been out yet. Harvey made a few changes and said something like "you're a bit of a superstar, aren't you?" I thought "well, actually I am quite good in the wet." I went out again and all of a sudden I was quickest, P1, and everyone was out then, everybody.'

That's an instructive moment because from nowhere you are proving that you can compete with these people.

'Yeah, but the problem is that towards the end of that session, still being quickest, I nearly had a moment at the next corner because I was thinking [expletive] – "ten, fifteen minutes left, right, I don't want to crash because it will look really bad," which is still a touch of self-doubt. I'll leave that in the bag now because I've done that, and I'm still P1. It had stopped raining and the circuit was getting a bit drier and I came in and said to Ken "look, I don't want to do anything stupid, the car's good in the wet, we know that, we'll leave it at that." He said "fine, OK." Then I watched the monitor and I ended up third. I think Mansell went quickest, then Nannini, then me. I was quite pleased with that.

'Then I didn't qualify for the race. The last qualifying session started damp and it dried out and at the end it was dry. In that dry I didn't drive the car hard enough and that was it.'

And then you've got Belgium did not qualify, Italy twelfth, Portugal DNQ, Spain DNQ, Japan 14, Australia DNQ.

'We were of course naturally aspirated cars against the turbos and they could run much more downforce, they were just quicker everywhere by a country mile. You are in a second league.'

So you come to the end of the season, no pub …

'I think we had 30 grand left in the bank between us and I got a phone call from Lola – Eric Broadley – out of the blue. "Would you like to do some testing for Nissan?" I said, "rather than test it I'd like to race it because I'm not doing anything next year." I got a two-year contract and over that period I paid my brother his money, paid what else I owed and had some money left over.

'And I had a good time there, because I was number one driver, I really enjoyed it and again there was a good atmosphere in the team. It was back to how I think teams should be run, where you nurture a driver. A driver has to be told he's good. If you turn up at a circuit and you get the feeling that they don't want you there, that you're a pain in the behind, you're not going to perform. You don't look forward to it and they don't look forward to seeing you. It has to be a family-type atmosphere.'

When you got the Nissan drive did you think 'that's it' with Formula 1? Or did you think 'no, I'll go away and come back at it?'

'I didn't totally discount it because I'd always look for the opportunity. I am an opportunist and if there is something on the go I'll go for it.'

At some point the driver will arrive at Spa and have to confront *Eau Rouge* where, as Senna once said, 'you can only believe so much.' Because much of the circuit is public roads you can drive up *Eau Rouge* yourself. A television camera diminishes distance and levels the contours so what will astonish you about *Eau Rouge* if you have only seen it on TV is the steepness of the descent from *La Source* hairpin, the tightness of the left–right kink at the bottom and the sharp angle of ascent. You are travelling uphill and you can't see anything beyond the brow way up there at the top.

Nick Heidfeld spent his first season of Grand Prix racing in 2000 with Prost and then joined Sauber.

Which was the moment that has given you the most pleasure?

'I cannot point out one single thing because there has not been a lot of success so far.'

Has there been one lap?

'It happens sometimes and you know that that was a really very good lap. Take the end of testing with the Sauber at Barcelona. I was very happy with the car, it behaved better than it had been doing, and the set-up was right. I did a good lap and I felt there was not a lot left in it. You can never do a perfect lap, but that was a big pleasure to me.'

Is that an intellectual pleasure or is it physical and intellectual?

'Both together. It happens more in your head, definitely. You have to move your body and use all your muscles to do that but you don't say to yourself "body do this" or "body do that" – it is more the concentration.'

When you go into Eau Rouge at racing speed, what do you feel? Fear?

'It is not really fear but … respect. Last year it was not a big pleasure driving through there. My car was not set up so nicely. However each lap is something special arriving there.'

When you come round La Source and you are going down, do you feel it in your stomach?

'Yes, but it's virtually the only corner where it is that special.'

Then you're going up the hill and you can't see over it.

'You can't see but once you have done so many laps you roughly know where to go.'

Do you like it?

'Um … well. It was … how do you say it? In German we say *Herausforderung* [a challenge which is a provocation]. It was something you have to do, have to get over.'

Perry McCarthy would agree with that, and we'll follow him in sequence to *Eau Rouge*. At Silverstone he failed in pre-qualifying. 'What people don't realise is that the team kept me in the pits waiting and in the end they sent me on to the track with about 20 minutes of the session remaining, with wet tyres, old wet tyres, and the track's dry now. They didn't have any money. Bob Constanduros [on-track commentator] was giving them so much gip in the pit lane on the microphone to the entire circuit.

'By now the situation was getting ridiculous. I'm out there on the wrong tyres. I thought: to hell with everything. To hell with you, to hell with me, to hell with the team, to hell with the car. That's it: flat! I went round that circuit and I came across the start-finish line on wets which were being destroyed, right, and I've gone absolutely gorilla on that one lap. I've come into Bridge sideways flat out holding it like *that*, come round the final curve, Woodcote, and I'm on the grass, I've changed up on the grass getting grip there just trying to get back on the track. I've got to the pit straight on the grass still trying to get the car back on, still flat. I've come past, I have equalled the fastest time set in the last 35 minutes on that one lap and then the clutch blew and thank God it did because I was about to get myself in big trouble. I was going to crash the car.

'With me, when it comes to qualifying and when it comes to what I've got to do, it's as if you have these blinkers that open then gradually come back-back-back and they close and I see one thing. I know what I want and that's what I've got to do to get it. That's it!'

The next race was at Hockenheim. Six cars were to be involved in pre-qualifying on the Friday morning and Julian Bailey, Mark Blundell and JJ Lehto were out on the circuit at a corner, watching as the session began. McCarthy, who certainly did not know Hockenheim in a Formula 1 car, approached.

McCarthy: 'where are they braking for this corner?'

Bailey ruminated, because he was thinking about where good cars braked. 'Just after the 100-metre board.'

McCarthy: 'right.' He continued his recce.

Bailey to Blundell: 'I don't believe he is going to do this.'

They stood waiting and after a while they heard the distinctive high-pitched wail of a Formula 1 engine on its way towards them. It burst into view – what Bailey describes as 'that black Andrea Moda thing going *whaaaaang*.'

Bailey shouted 'no, don't do it.' Bailey was deeply, deeply sure McCarthy couldn't make it.

Lehto put a finger to his forehead, the international sign for madness.

McCarthy was absolutely determined to brake after the 100-metre board, and still believes he did.

'How he made that corner that day I don't know,' Bailey says. 'We were actually scared and we told him that, which we should never have done I suppose. We should have said "well, it was nothing" but I honestly thought he was going to kill himself there.'

Now to Spa where for the first time that season McCarthy did not fail to pre-qualify. 'The only reason I managed to elevate above DNQ was that the Brabham team didn't turn up and pre-qualifying was abolished for that race only. I knew Spa and I thought I might be able to do something.

'In my qualifying lap I went absolutely head-first into *Eau Rouge* – flat out, maybe 170, 180mph in that thing – and as I turned the steering wheel it jammed. I thought this is *it*, a cold feeling. To be honest, it was the first time I had had the feeling: this *is* it, this is the one, there's no way out. I pushed and prodded everything that the car bleedin' had on it, slammed the brakes on and I was pushing the steering wheel as hard as I possibly could at the same time. So part of my mind was saying this is it but the other part was still fighting.

'Suddenly I just got a bit of turn on the car and I'd gone off onto the grass and the more it slowed down the more I was able to steer, and, I tell you, I pulled my shoulder something rotten doing that – and I'm a fairly strong boy. I got to the top of *Eau Rouge* and I had really hurt my shoulder badly but I'd survived. Luck and judgement, and I've put those two in the right order.

'I tested the car on a couple of slow-speed corners after *Eau Rouge* and I realised what it was, the downforce causing the steering rack to flex and it jammed. I got back to the pits and said "I think the steering rack's flexing." Tony Dodgins [a journalist] was begging me not to get back in the car but luckily enough the thing went wrong and I couldn't do anything anyway. Tony Dodgins was white. He was looking and he was going "Perry, you're going to die here." He was convinced and to be quite honest I wasn't far behind him.'

(Dodgins, unassuming, quiet and soft-spoken, is a purist among the purists. He fell in love with the racing somewhere back there and never fell out. He has no qualms about the legitimacy of persuading a Formula 1 driver to abort a run. It was a humanitarian gesture. Dodgins remembers sharing his hotel room with McCarthy circa 1992 because McCarthy had no money and remembers, too, this delicious anecdote. McCarthy flew to America for a drive, left his beaten-up banger in the short-term car park at Heathrow and, upon his return, discovered that the time he had been away cost more in parking fees than the car was worth. He handed the keys to the attendant, explained that the attendant was now the proud owner of the car, and went home by train.)

What seems utterly remarkable, separating the mental processes of the driver from just about everybody else, is that at Spa, having survived *Eau Rouge* and wrenched his back doing it, McCarthy was quite prepared to get back in that car there.

Why?

'Decision: yes or no, bang. Then if you make that decision: flat out or slow. Next decision: flat out. But the thing broke on me so I was lucky in that I couldn't get back in.'

In a curious way you were an object of bemusement but not derision. People were laughing at the Andrea Moda soap opera but not at you. You were well on the way to becoming a cult.

'I've been called a few things in my time but a cult, no. That's really nice to think about. It was funny at the end of the year because I had about two or three different Grand Prix offers. Some other team managers had seen what I'd done and seen that determination that I will not let go.'

How did you feel going through that season? Bemusement and laughter are quite something for a driver to live with.

'I didn't like myself.'

What does that mean?

'What it means is that I am looking at Perry McCarthy and Perry McCarthy's no good, Perry McCarthy's at the back of the grid, Perry McCarthy's not qualifying, Perry McCarthy's not even on the grid, Perry McCarthy's not mega, Perry McCarthy's not a superstar. And I don't like that.

'I tell you one thing though. You get into Grand Prix and you are a star even at the very back of the grid, even nonqualifying, because you are in that environment.'

You seem to have spent a career seizing chances in desperate situations.

'We had a situation in 1999 where we'd had big problems with the Audi at Paul Ricard. Finally they thought some of the problems had been fixed and I got in it, did three, four, five laps. The thing was absolutely all over the place. I came in. John Wickham [running it] knows me very well and I couldn't talk to him. I was so upset I felt on the verge of tears. What I'm trying to say is, when you love this, when it's go-kill-crush-destroy and it's not happening, it's like being married and not consummating the marriage. You're wound up. That is my release, that stopwatch says I'm right, that stopwatch says yes, this is why you're in it, this is why you think like that and focus on these levels. And then I've come out of it and I've got no reward for it. It's that lactic acid that hasn't gone away ...'

I'd have thought at your age you'd have said 'OK, let's come back tomorrow and try again.'

'This is where other drivers are different. I have thought about the psychology of motor racing and I am very similar to Nigel Mansell. We are both fighters, both bruisers.'

Nick Heidfeld has faced quite different pressures.

Michael Schumacher, Ralf Schumacher and Frentzen are all German, from nearly the same area and you are as well. Are you compared to them in Germany?

'Not so much really. Everybody is taken as an individual.'

Do you compare yourself, say, to Michael?

'I watch not only Michael but also all the other drivers and it's very difficult to make comparisons because we are all in different teams. I want to achieve the same things as other very successful drivers. I don't compare myself to him in how he behaves or how he is as a person.'

An ordinary German might say 'Heidfeld, he's not as good as Michael Schumacher.'

'Yes, I think so, I think they will do that.'

Does that worry you?

'No, not much. First of all, I have learned that what people say or what is written in newspapers and magazines is not so important. Quite often it's not true. That's not easy to accept: you have to learn it. If somebody writes something bad about me I am very angry, which is why I try and be careful about saying things, but if each time you say to yourself "I must do something about it" you get crazy. So you have to rely on yourself and in a way I think it makes you stronger in your self-belief. You can say "just ignore it" – but it's not that easy.'

When you look in your mind, can you see things slowly? I know you can in a car but can you do it when you watch TV?

'No, no. I know what you mean with reference to driving. If I see a race on TV and I am not concentrating on it so much it looks very quick, but being in a car it seems a lot slower.'

Is that true when you drive on the autobahn?

'Yes. But compared with Formula 1 it is nothing.'

Can you slow that down so the lorry isn't coming at you so quickly?

'Maybe a bit more than other people. Obviously you have to be concentrating driving on the road but it is something different to driving a Formula 1 car.'

I am interested in concentration because you have to do it for nearly two hours.

'It comes quite easily to me and I have never had big problems with it. As you progress through the different stages – karting, Formula 3, Formula 3000 – the races get longer and you get more used to it. I think I can apply it to go very deeply into something, 100% concentrated.'

Is that true in your life?

'A couple of years ago it was like this for many things but now they've separated from Formula 1 because it's the only thing I really do to the extreme.'

The driver has a shifting mosaic of other people constantly around him. He will be in competition with some, not just in the races but for the drives, and the unavoidable sense of competition creates unusual relationships between people who, otherwise, would have everything in common. Is genuine friendship possible? Allan McNish has a revealing anecdote about that.

They used to say about Jimmy Clark that he was mild-mannered before he got in the car but you took him on into turn one and you'd see him grow horns.

'There are two types of hard: people who are hard and fair. You know you can take them to the limit, right to the last limits and, yeah, they won't step over and do something bad. One example. I have raced a lot against David Brabham, I have had some extremely hard fights with David and also in Formula 3. I will push him right to that limit and he will push me right to that limit and when I need that inch I know I will get it.'

He knows that from you as well.

'It has to be on both sides. I was reading an article on Gregor Foitek. It was Johnny Herbert talking about Foitek and their crash at Brands Hatch.[15] That was hard but in a different way. For some people there is a fine line between the two, that you can push them to an edge nine times but the tenth time something happens and they lose it. Certainly there are few people I would trust as much as David because I know through experience that he would not put me in a situation where I could crash.'

Do you know him as a person, have you talked?

'Not really talked about it, you tend not to do these things.'

You spend your whole life in proximity with these people and they are strangers.

'David I know quite well now because there are so many trips to the same venues.'

Would you see it as a sign of weakness approaching a subject like that?

'No, it's not something that has ever entered my head. I would never say to him, and I would never say to *anybody* whether I thought it or not, "I tell you what, I reckon you are a bit quicker than me over whatever." You don't want to give them any help. I've only been friends with six or seven drivers in my career and one ended up in the wall.[16] That was a separate issue, it wasn't just driving: driving gave me the opportunity to meet him and then we had a friendship which developed from there but generally the friends are not drivers that I have raced against.

'Racing in America has created situations where I have flown on the same flight as David for example, probably about five or six times this year, and you check in generally at similar times, you meet in the lounge. Now take Damon Hill. I raced against Damon for three or four years and the only time I can really remember sitting down and speaking to him was when we had a flight delay in Rome airport. We were going to Sicily. We were on the same inbound flight, we were on the same connection and it was delayed. In the end, you were standing there and you said hello.'

What was that conversation like?

'I wouldn't say it was the most natural conversation that I had in my life. I think the younger you are the harder it is, certainly for me. The older I get, the better I am socially. I can balance things up and separate things a little bit better. Remember, when I started testing with McLaren and doing Formula 3000 I was 20, 21 years old. I looked at a picture the other day and you can't believe how young and little I looked, almost like a jockey.'

McCarthy, Bailey, Blundell, Herbert and Hill were contemporaries and certainly the first four became known as the Essex rat-pack.

'I'll tell you one of the reasons why we are all such close friends,' McCarthy will say. 'If ever I talk about the fast lap, the close shave or whatever – which I don't very often – ordinary people have no idea what I am talking about. No idea. It's only another driver who knows how you're feeling, your personality, what you're about, what you've put up with.'

But say there was a plum drive going and it was between you and Julian.

'I'd do everything I could to take him out of it. End of story. And he would do the same to me, absolutely.'

And that wouldn't affect the friendship?

'No way. I would never tell tales on Julian, ever. You just don't do that.'

But what if it was you and, say, de Cesaris for a number 2 Arrows drive and Arrows said 'well, if you raise 300 grand you've got it.' Would you fight dirty for that drive?

'It depends how dirty because if you are seen to do that, how much can anybody trust you in the future?'

But how can you trust all the others to start off with?

'It doesn't come down to that. Normally if you're going to get a drive, it's somebody hearing what you're saying, that they believe in you and then it might come down to the factors of price. If I thought I'd get a drive over Julian by chipping in what it took, I'd chip in what it took. Sorry, that's business. But I would not say anything against Julian. I wouldn't say anything against that driver if he was a personal friend.'

In 1991 Bailey partnered Häkkinen at Lotus.

Is it possible to have a friendship with somebody like that?

'No, I don't think so. Not unless you're Finnish, I suppose, and you've got the same sort of outlook on life. At that time of course he was very young and immature but he was the sort of bloke who's never got any money on him. He'd sit down for a meal and expect you to have the money. It was a bit like having a child with you. I think from what other people say he's not changed much. I'm not saying there's anything wrong with that but it just struck me as odd.'

Is friendship possible in Formula 1?

'I think it is. Mark Blundell was in Formula 1 at the same time as me and we were friends. It wouldn't have mattered whether we were or weren't in the same team. It depends on your culture. It's difficult to have friends, I think, outside that, although Berger and Senna were friends.'

Blundell thinks friendship is possible. 'Martin Brundle and I have been team-mates in two teams and we speak every two or three weeks. Normally your team-mate is the enemy, the comparison, but with me and Martin it was a situation where when I started I looked up to the guy full stop. When I first got in a racing car in 1984 in Formula Ford 1600 he'd just reached Formula 1. Senna had started at Toleman and he had started at Tyrrell.

'Those guys, they were idols. When I got to my first year at Brabham [in 1991], Martin was there. I looked and I learnt a great deal from him although I treated it in such a way that, yes, he was my competitor. Every time I got in the race car he was the first guy I wanted to beat and I did on several occasions. That gave me credibility. In theory it puts a strain on a relationship but we could relate to each other so well because we came from very similar backgrounds: the same area, East Anglia, and our fathers were both in the car business. I'm being very blunt about it, though. He was probably better educated than I was. I am a little bit more of a street-wise guy, part of the rat pack – a lot of self-education in me – which meant there were differences as well as similarities. Even though he was a little bit older, he learnt from me and I learnt from him.'

(During Imola qualifying in 2001, Brundle – commentating on the British television channel ITV – said it was not unknown for a driver to go out with an adjustment to the car, come back and say to his team-mate "much better" but whisper to the mechanics to change it back because it's worse. Brundle chuckled. I say this, Brundle continued, even though I know a former team-mate Mark Blundell can hear because he's in the studio preparing to comment on the qualifying.)

Friendship happened with Senna and Berger, but only because Berger was no threat.

'There was friendship, definitely, and it was friendship with some depth, but if there had ever come a point when Berger was outdriving him – and I have been on the receiving end of it – that might well have changed everything,' Blundell will say. 'Maybe the situation between Martin and I was unique because we speak to each other and tell each other a lot of things. It's a good steady friendship.'

A question to Heidfeld, so fresh to F1.

What relationships do you have with other drivers?

'I don't see it as strange relationships. I have been used to this since I drove in karting. Definitely there you know most of the people better, especially if you are young because you play together: you drive against them but you still get to know them. It's just a pretty normal thing for me. It's not as if you have to hate them or something like this. You can be friends without a problem, even I think in Formula 1. People say it isn't possible but I don't agree although I only have a couple of friends who are important to me and they are outside Formula 1. I have known them from school. There is not much chance that you meet 21 other people [the current number of Formula 1 drivers] and one of these happens to become your best friend. If you are really good friends it doesn't matter, or shouldn't matter, that you are also competitors. That may make it harder but, for me, it should still be possible.'

NOTES

1. Irvine was involved in a four-car crash during the 1994 Brazilian Grand Prix (involving Brundle/McLaren, Jos Verstappen/Benetton, Eric Bernard/Ligier). Initially Irvine was given a one-race ban and fined $10,000 after the stewards said he 'committed a very dangerous manoeuvre' which caused the crash. Irvine appealed but on 7 April 1994 the FIA Review Board rejected this. 'It is the Board's opinion that Mr. Irvine failed to evaluate the situation in the way that he ought

to have done and recklessly pulled out to pass the car driven by Mr. Bernard.' The Board suspended Irvine's Superlicence until 16 May, and he missed the Pacific, San Marino and Monaco races.

2. Van Diemen, manufacturers of single-seaters in the smaller formulae, are based opposite the Snetterton circuit.

3. Toleman tested four drivers immediately after the Portuguese Grand Prix, last race of 1984: Senna was leaving and they needed a replacement. Palmer was quickest (1m 22.80) from Roberto Moreno (1m 24.10) and Manfred Winkelhock (1m 24.14). Ivan Capelli took over an engine now pushed far beyond its normal rebuild and it blew so his time (1m 30.10) was not relevant.

4. A small German team which took part in 52 Grands Prix between 1985 and 1988.

5. Erich Zakowski, a talented engine tuner, founded Zakspeed.

6. One for turbo charged cars, the other for normally-aspirated (the Jim Clark Trophy). Palmer won it with 87 points from Philippe Streiff (74) and Philippe Alliot (43).

7. The film was made by Uden Associates, commissioned by the British TV company Channel 4 and shown on their *Equinox* programme.

8. Andrea de Cesaris (Italy) and Rene Arnoux (France) were not known for their diplomacy on the track.

9. Watson qualified on the ninth row for the 1982 United States East Grand Prix at Detroit. He was thirteenth at the re-start and won, beating Cheever (USA/Ligier) by 15.726s.

10. A joke poached from the BBC radio series *Goon Show* from the 1950s.

11. Willy Dungl, Austrian fitness guru who treated Lauda after his horrific crash in 1976 and has achieved an almost mystical reputation among racing drivers since.

12. Prost had been at McLaren since 1984. To 1987, in sequence he finished the World Championship 2, 1, 1, 4.

13. Mansour Ojjeh was behind the TAG (Techniques d'Avant Garde) involvement in Formula 1. TAG was a 'Saudi-connected corporation established in 1977 by Akram Ojjeh to consolidate his family's commercial activities between Europe and the nations of the Middle East' (Doug Nye, *McLaren*, Hazleton Publishing).

14. Traditionally rain negates the advantage that leading teams have

because it slows everyone. How a driver handles the wet is a mark of his skill.

15. Gregor Foitek (Switzerland) drove in seven Grands Prix in 1990. That he was involved in the Herbert crash at Brands Hatch is not disputed but the exact part he played remains conjectural. As Herbert's wife Becky told me: 'Even Johnny doesn't know!'

16. He was referring to Ayrton Senna, who he had known for years (both were sponsored by Marlboro).

THE MOMENT

Chapter 7

HERE TODAY ...

*'I cried inside for years afterwards. Am I over it yet? That's the
difficult part, living with the knowledge that it was unfulfilled'*
– Ivan Capelli

You see drivers seeming so sure of themselves. You see them
bestriding the paddock, creating a swell of interest as they
move around bearing with them a certain mystique, but in
reality the impermanence is striking and ought to occupy the
thoughts of every driver. Between the birth of the World
Championship in 1950 and the 2000 season, for example, 24
drivers competed whose names began with A. Ten of them
competed in fewer than ten Grands Prix and failed to score a
single point. A career may be over very quickly. Mauricio
Gugelmin's wife Stella once said to me with undisguised feeling
'Formula 1 can screw you up real quick and you're gone.'
Mauricio did 74 races between 1988 and 1992 for a total of ten
points. Then he was gone ...

Points are a surprisingly scarce commodity. Philippe Alliot
drove for a full decade, in five different teams and 109 races, for
seven points. The man-hours expended by designers, construc-
tors and mechanics, the money raised and invested, Alliot's own
mental and physical efforts, not to mention incessant travel – in
short, the overall duration and scale of the effort for seven
points – defies rational analysis.

Moreover, to do nothing but Grand Prix racing and its

associated activities is a constant temptation. Consider this Ferrari schedule for the beginning of February 2001.

Thursday: Vairano – Fabrizio Giovanardi (deputising for test driver Luca Badoer, injured) 38 runs of 'aerodynamic tests' on the main straight. Barcelona – Barrichello 78 laps testing tyres. Fiorano – Schumacher 68 laps débuting the new F2001 car.

Friday: Vairano – Giovanardi 32 runs on the main straight trying 'aerodynamic solutions.' Barcelona – Barrichello 68 laps on 'tyre and electronic testing.' Fiorano – Schumacher 102 laps on 'development work.'

Saturday: Barcelona – Barrichello 58 laps on 'tyres, electronic testing and several practice starts.' Fiorano – Schumacher 55 laps on 'development … and three pit-stop practices.'

Multiply something like this over eight months of the year, thread in 16 or 17 races (each a four or five day trip), add the sponsors' demands, thrust in the constant media hunger, remember that Schumacher cannot go anywhere without being mobbed and the hunter becomes a captive. How he deals with this pressure will decide whether he survives.

Every successful Grand Prix career is initially a triumph of hope over inexperience, but every unsuccessful career is harder to quantify.

Ivan Capelli came to understand quickly and conclusively what he had done in joining Ferrari for the 1992 season. 'I realised it the first day I was presented as the new driver. Going down from Milan to Maranello I stopped at a petrol station and nobody recognised me, nobody asked me for anything. Coming back in the night when the radio and television had been saying "ah, Capelli is now a Ferrari driver" I stopped at the same point of the highway but the other side and they wanted autographs and pictures from me: just 12 hours of difference.'

That gave you an idea of what was waiting for you?

'Absolutely.'

Capelli had served a proper apprenticeship, beginning with Tyrrell in 1985 and moving through AGS, March and Leyton House and had driven 78 races.

'I received a call from Claudio Lombardi who was in charge of the team and obviously it was a great honour to partner Alesi. It was like finding the end of a dream.'

Did you hesitate?

'No, absolutely not because I was already a Scuderia Italia driver[1] but my contract had been switched to the Ferrari team so I became a Ferrari driver.'

Every other drive in the world is a normal drive but an Italian in a Ferrari is more important than the government.

'Yes, there is a big pressure for sure and especially for me because I came back as the first Italian driver after Alboreto and it was obviously a very, very big challenge but it was an extremely difficult year and my dream became a nightmare.'

In South Africa the engine failed; in Mexico he had a start-line crash; in Brazil he was fifth but a lap down; in Spain he spun off; at Imola he spun off; at Monaco he spun off. Around about then, five months before he was fired, Capelli sensed that Ferrari were essentially finished with him. 'My mechanics formed a team within a team' and it worked in something approaching isolation. Capelli remains fiercely loyal to those who, in his mounting distress, remained loyal to him. 'I am still proud of what I did with Ferrari. I realised that with the situation that we had I did my maximum and I still think that the Ferrari mechanics are the most wonderful people in the world.'

In Canada he crashed; in France the engine failed; in Britain he finished ninth a lap down. 'It was difficult and I had some overstress, let's put it like that. It began to really affect me: all the pressure of the team was on me. I was living in Monte Carlo at the time and so I didn't face it every day but when I went back to Milan to see my parents I did.'

When it went wrong, was it more difficult for you as an Italian with Ferrari?

'Well, I hadn't been able to pay in a restaurant! They wouldn't let me. Before Ferrari I had to pay, during Ferrari I didn't and afterwards I had to pay again!'

In Germany the engine failed; in Hungary he was sixth but a lap down; in Belgium the engine failed; in Italy he spun off; in Portugal the engine failed. He had three points (and Alesi 13).

'I was in my house in Monaco and received a phone call from Luca di Montezemolo's secretary. "Please come down immediately, the President has to talk to you." So I took the car and went immediately to Maranello. I arrived in the afternoon at 2.30 but instead of going to the President's office, the guy in charge of the press took me to the racing team. There, Harvey Postlethwaite told me "this is the statement we are going to put out in half an hour." It said that they were not retaining me. I did not cry at the time. Maybe I had been crying inside for months and maybe I cried inside for years afterwards. Am I over it yet? Maybe you never get over it. I am living with it now and I think I will have to live with it forever. The problem is when I look back I see my dream and it was not completed. If a Formula 1 team went crazy and rang me today and offered me a drive I'd take it. That's how I feel inside.'

Capelli drove one more Grand Prix, for Jordan in South Africa in 1993. 'It was too soon, I was worried about sponsors and I hadn't got my self-confidence back. I was not thinking about doing the fastest lap I could. Somehow I was pushed into it and I should not have allowed myself to be.'

Capelli joined *RAI*, the Italian television channel which covers the Grands Prix, in 1997. 'When I came back into Formula 1 and started to do my new job as a commentator I met again some of the guys who'd been at Ferrari then – some were now working for other teams – and they looked away when I looked at them.'

Because they were ashamed?

'Yes, they were ashamed. Luca di Montezemolo was always embarrassed when I went to Maranello for the annual launch of the new car. And then he came just two years ago and said that in 1992 the car had been so bad nobody could have done anything with it.'

It was a little bit too late.

'Especially for my career.'

Everybody loves football in Italy. How many Italians have played football for Italy compared to how many Italians have driven for Ferrari?

'Yes, but you know the problem? I'm too good as a person – not too good, too soft. People that are going to the top are so tough and they are not looking at anything else, they are just tough.'

Mark Blundell says he was not hard enough and he didn't want to change himself and become someone else.

'I am with Mark Blundell one hundred per cent.'

In 1991 Julian Bailey went to Lotus and was instantly confronted with the impermanence. 'That was a strange deal. Here's an example of how you can psychologically be ... well, not damaged but how you should be wary. I went to sign my contract with Peter Collins at Hethel.[2] Johnny Herbert was supposed to be joining Häkkinen, who'd already signed a contract, but Herbert was in Japan and I think he had some contractual problems so I was a good bet. I signed my contract, sat there in the famous Colin Chapman office, and Peter Collins was a guy I got on with. You could talk to him and he'd help you. I thought "this is a much better atmosphere for me than Tyrrell." He said to someone "can you go and get Julian's overalls from upstairs?" This chap did that, came down, gave them to me and said "you'd better try them on to make sure there's no major problem with them." They didn't fit. I looked and they had Johnny Herbert's name on them: they were Johnny Herbert's overalls. They knew that Johnny was joining the team later in the year and I knew now too. I thought "that's nice, thanks very much." I was on the way out before I'd got in but I reasoned "I've got a chance, I've got nothing else to do, let's do it."

'We get to Phoenix [the USA Grand Prix in March, first race of the season] and after about three or four laps I was fifth quickest, and as I was going down the back straight I looked in my mirrors and I saw this huge fire coming out: huge. The whole oil system had gone up. That meant I missed all the rest of free practice and the next session, and I'd had no time on the circuit at all. I'd never seen Phoenix but I quite liked it. I didn't qualify.

'Then Brazil. I did a couple of laps, came in, they jacked my car up and a wheel fell off. They said "oh, right, we thought we might have a problem with those axles." I said "what about Mika's car?" They said "oh, no, we've changed the ones on Mika's." So now I can't drive the car. We were waiting for the axle and part of the brakes to be flown out from England. Come the end of the final qualifying session Häkkinen has qualified and they said "jump in his car." I hadn't been round the circuit. I'd missed all the free practice and everything. I didn't qualify. I thought there were reasons for all this happening, it wasn't just down to me.

'Then we went to Imola and we qualified twenty-fifth and twenty-sixth. Häkkinen out-qualified me [1m 27.324s against 1m 27.976s]. We get to the race and that weekend was a bit

Previous page: *The eyes have it. Michael Schumacher seeing everything clearly* (Allsport).

Left: *The eyes no-one will ever forget. Ayrton Senna, storing everything* (ICN).

Below: *It was partly a question of boxes. Schumacher at Maranello on a test day, moving his mind from the racing to the social box. Derick Allsop prepares to interview him, and he'll give absolute concentration to that, but first a happy pose with Allsop's daughter Kate and her boyfriend Peter Kopczyk* (Derick Allsop).

Mid-summer 2003, and Johnny Herbert prepares to tackle Le Mans in the No 8 Bentley he shared with Mark Blundell and David Brabham. For the three drivers, used to the egotism of single-seater racing, this called for a completely different mental approach (both LAT).

It takes profound self-belief and commitment to even break into the sport. Nigel Mihell (above) was sure he could beat the world and still smiled when he couldn't (both courtesy Nigel Mihell). Perry McCarthy (below) survived a season with the Andrea Moda team alive and sane (Formula One Pictures).

Life's tough at the top, as Niki Lauda (above) found trying to run the Jaguar team and Antonio Pizzonia (below) discovered in 2003 trying to drive for them (both LAT).

Whether they talk about it or not, all Formula One drivers know the risks. Martin Donnelly (top), Lotus, Jerez, 1990 (Allsport); Ivan Capelli's Jordan (above), South Africa, 1993 (Formula One Pictures); Karl Wendlinger (below and right), Sauber, Monaco, 1994 (Allsport).

Philippe Streiff in Rio in 1989 before disaster struck (Formula One
Pictures); *the aftermath of the crash in testing* (Formula One Pictures);
but the will to drive fast still dominates (J. F. Galeron, courtesy Streiff).

Different drivers have their own way of coping with the stress. Mika Hakkinen (above left) did it in private (Allsport)*; John Surtees (above right), the only man to win World Championships on two wheels and four, believed in the importance of being able to switch off* (LAT)*; Eddie Irvine (below) favoured the laid-back approach* (Formula One Pictures)*.*

Monza, 1990. While his disintegrating Lotus was travelling upside down at 140mph, Derek Warwick *thought with perfect clarity* (Formula One Pictures).

Jonathan Palmer (above left) believes in working things out (Formula One Pictures); Mark Blundell (above right) – with a reminder of mortality, the Indy Car he crashed – feels he's the luckiest fellow alive (Formula One Pictures); and, to relieve the tension, occasionally the sport itself does a bit of clowning (below), even if this is carefully staged for the cameras (ICN).

There are moments when joy, fun and even sentiment are permitted. After achieving his first pole position Jean Alesi (above) glows with pleasure, and Lauda enjoys the moment too, Italy, 1994 (ICN); Rubens Barrichello (below left) never concealed his delight and smiled his sunshine smile, especially when he won the 2003 British Grand Prix (LAT); Frank Williams with Carlos Reutemann (below right) who drove for him in the early 1980s, pictured at Argentina in 1997 (ICN).

Few drivers were more competitive than Ayrton Senna (above), especially in the bitter mental and physical war with his McLaren team-mate Alain Prost, who he leads in Canada in 1988 (Marlboro). And (below) few were more charming than Michele Alboreto (Formula One Pictures).

Ralph Firman – a rookie in 2003 – brought past and present with him to Jordan. Here (above) at the Goodwood Festival of Speed he helps unveil a sculpture by Tim Tolkein to mark the 45th anniversary of Cosworth (Paul Nicholls). Ralf Schumacher brought lively sibling rivalry. Joining F1 as a Jordan driver, he was quick to learn and never got lost in Michael's shadow, despite moment like this (below), after hitting the guardrail in Canada, 1997 (ICN).

To the drivers it may be 'just winning another race', as Jonathan Palmer believes, but the three on the podium usually manage to seem wildly happy, as Damon Hill (opposite top left), Jacques Villeneuve (opposite top right), Alain Prost (opposite bottom left), Gerhard Berger (opposite bottom right) and Michael Schumacher (above) demonstrate.

Overleaf: David Coulthard, the serious face of Formula One – envisaging a lap to a tenth of a second? (Allsport)

traumatic for Lotus because we'd a mechanic die during the week in an accident. It was a bit of a difficult time for Peter and the whole team.

'For the race it's absolutely bucketing down. Off we go and as a consequence of being last on the grid you can't see a thing, it's impossible. You've got 20-odd cars all going down to Tosa in an incredible wall of water. People were going off and I went past Häkkinen. I was flying along. I kept passing people, passing people. I ended up in fifth position and then Peter Collins is waving at me over the pit wall to come in. I wouldn't. I thought "I know why he's waving me in – because Häkkinen's behind me. He's quite a long way behind and he wants him to beat me." Peter couldn't tell me on the radio because it wasn't working. I thought "I'm not going in, I'm not giving Häkkinen fifth place." And I was catching people, looking for maybe a rostrum finish. Collins is frantic over the pit wall, frantic. He was nearly jumping on the track to get me to come in.

'Eventually I did come in [on lap 29] and asked what was going on. When they'd done the tyre change from wets to slicks [on lap 16] they hadn't taken the tape off my front brake ducts, so Collins is thinking that the brakes are going to catch fire. They did take them off Häkkinen's but they didn't do mine by mistake. That's why he wanted me in – it was nothing to do with Häkkinen at all but, of course, I didn't know that. By now, however, I'd made the pit stop, Häkkinen was miles down the road and I dropped to seventh but then I caught him up and I think I ended up crossing the line about two-tenths behind him. I was quite pleased and there was no doubt that in that race I was a lot quicker than Häkkinen.

'Then we get to Monaco, which is obviously some sort of bogey circuit for me: crashed at the Loews hairpin, just steamed into the barrier [Bailey didn't qualify for the race]. The next race was going to be Canada. I really wanted to do it because I love that circuit, I knew I could do a good job there and in my mind I knew I could beat Häkkinen there. I never got the chance because Herbert came, and that was it. So you sit on the sofa and look at the phone and think "what shall I do now?" I picked up a couple of drives in Japan.'

Johnny you knew because of the Essex rat pack.

'I never had a problem with another driver from that point of view. It's not his fault and a lot of it is commercial pressure. Lotus had Japanese sponsors and Johnny was well known in Japan. I never had a problem with Johnny or anybody else taking my drive. If they do, there's a good reason – and from the day I got there I knew Johnny was coming. It was a matter of when he comes, not if.'

John Watson sensed the impermanence coming at him. 'In 1977 at Monaco I took pole position, although Jody Scheckter won the race. In 1978, still with Brabham, I couldn't get the damn thing to work in qualifying but when it did I was very quick. I'd gone out towards the end, done a time and went second quickest to Carlos Reutemann. I came in for my final set of tyres to go for pole. I said "OK, put the new set of tyres on," then I had to ask where they were. Bernie [Ecclestone] had given them to Niki. I went ballistic.

'The reason Bernie gave them to Niki, however, was that Niki had come in and said "I got held up on this lap, I know I can get pole, give me a set of tyres" and Bernie said "where are the tyres? He's got none? Whose are those? Watson's? Put them on his car." Bernie was being led by Niki – Niki was orchestrating it through projecting himself as Superman.

'Another example, in the French Grand Prix. I had pole at Paul Ricard and I think Niki was third quickest. It was the first race after the Swedish Grand Prix with the fan car – Bernie had withdrawn the fan car.[3] We were running a normal car. On Sunday morning, Bernie said "John, if you're leading on the last lap of the race and on the last corner before the flag, I'm asking you if you'll let Niki win." I thought "what? Huh?" Bernie said "I am asking you because Niki has a mathematical chance of the championship."[4] Mark you, this is in July – not exactly the last race of the season. I was about to go out for the morning warm-up and I said "I'll give you an answer after." When I did I said "no." That was me being honest and saying what I felt. I knew also that with Bernie, when you're out, you're out. I sensed that at that point I could have said "OK, I'll do it" thinking that the probability of the situation happening and Lauda being behind me on the last lap was very remote. Therefore saying OK would probably not create a problem. But I didn't. As it turned out, it was an irrelevance because the Lotuses (Andretti, Peterson) vanished into the distance. The irony is that I was almost creating the launch pad not to be retained for 1979.'

How many team-mates did you have?

'The first was at Brabham in 1977,[5] starting off with Carlos Pace and then momentarily Larry Perkins, then Hans Stuck, three in one year. Then Niki came in 1978. After that it was Patrick Tambay in 1979, Alain Prost in 1980, Andrea de Cesaris in 1981 and Niki again in 1982 and 1983.'

Any of those you didn't get on with?

'Not particularly. The most difficult time was probably with Prost but that was the team's fault. They focused on Alain and I think that the way Teddy[6] ran the team at that time was frankly disgraceful, but the team was in trouble and they were fighting for survival. Prost was outstanding in his first year, so they just focused on him and I got the sharp end of the stick. It was not helped by the fact that I got hardly any support from the British press. They jumped on the Prost bandwagon too.'

How did you take that?

'Badly. I am sensitive to that, I am not a thick-skinned, hard-nosed person. Subsequently I have learned techniques and methods of dealing with it, but at that time I needed the wisdom of age – I needed to be like any little guy out there now, skin of a rhinoceros and arrogant as hell.

'Fundamentally I am a very shy person who discovered a talent which in a sense I couldn't come to terms with: that I could be in races with people like Graham Hill, Jackie Stewart and Denny Hulme. The drivers in my first Formula 2 race included Jochen Rindt and Jack Brabham. These were people who were gods, and here's a kid from Northern Ireland who is suddenly on the same grid. It was a time when there was respect for your seniors.'

Mark Blundell reflects on how he ought to have protected himself. 'If I could've gone back to school, started out again and re-run it I'd have approached it in a different way completely. I'd have made sure I had a budget to get a PR machine working. Every time you looked left, right, front or behind, you'd have seen Mark Blundell. It would have been impregnated in people's minds. What I have seen, and what I know now, is that Formula 1 is like the fashion industry. One minute you're in, next minute you're out, and it's very difficult to know which way it's going to go because it's as fickle as that.'

But it's not fickle at the top, not for the leading four or five drivers.

'That's as may be, but the top four or five teams can be fickle. If you look at Williams, and where they have taken some of their drivers over the years, you have to ask about the logic – and I'm not picking out Williams.'

Most people see a Formula 1 driver as ruthless, utterly self-confident, the hunter.

'When I sit in the cockpit of a race car then that is me: I'll get out there and do the job, I'll race with anybody.'

Did you really feel you could be as good as Senna?

'I feel that I could have been as good as anybody given the right opportunity, and maybe I can say that because I feel I have some depth. I sat inside a Grand Prix winning car, whether it be a Williams I was testing or a McLaren, and I was matching their race drivers in speed. Whichever way you look at it, the only way you can accurately reflect on someone's performance is what they do on a stopwatch. Those little digits sitting in that little face have made plenty of decisions. There is no escaping that.

'When I'm in a race car, that's when I'm at my best. I am a race car driver. Outside of the car is where my learning curve begins. I took the year with Martin Brundle, I took the year with Senna and Berger and all of a sudden I learnt how they operated out of a car. That's the big difference.

'With Senna, he continued out of the car as he had been in it and that was my downfall in not being hard enough and firm enough to stay in the game. I didn't learn until too late.'

Heinz-Harald Frentzen spent three seasons with Sauber before joining Williams and might well have won his first race for that team – Australia, 1997 – but for wheel and brake problems. He did win his fourth race, Imola, and finished the season second in the championship. A year later his confidence seemed to have gone so completely that there were doubts about his ability to actually drive the car. Williams have a reputation for being pragmatic rather than paternal with their drivers.

1997 and 1998 were almost lost years.

'No, they weren't lost years,' Frentzen will say. 'The man I am today is a man who has driven for several teams collecting experience everywhere. I think I am on my best level in my career due to gaining experience. I'm pretty much in good shape.'

Frentzen joined Jordan and, with a strong late run, almost became a real championship contender. Eddie Jordan has a reputation for paternalism and pragmatism, applied it, and Frentzen was re-born.

'Nearly ten years ago, I was the wrong man for Eddie,' Frentzen explains, 'but before the start of our first joint season in 1999 I realised we had both changed. Eddie has learned to survive in Formula 1, the toughest category of motorsport in the world, and I have learned this too. I am not as inhibited as I used to be. I learnt many things in the two years before I joined Jordan: Eddie and I are united by the fact that we have both had set-backs in our careers but that, ultimately, our career paths have constantly moved upward, and usually when people least expected it.'

In 1999, at the circuit hotel at Suzuka, with the Japanese Grand Prix over and the championship finally won by Häkkinen, Frentzen was in the corner of the enormous lounge doing a live interview on German television, arc lights illuminating his face. Eddie Jordan entered the lobby, saw Frentzen from afar and began, wonderfully, to heckle him. 'His head's so big I'm surprised it fits in the room!' Equally wonderfully, Frentzen managed to keep his concentration and a straight face until towards the end of the interview when he clamped his jaw into a semi-smile and locked it like that rather than explode in hilarity. It made me think that a driver's mind can absorb and isolate a data stream to an astonishing degree – but not when confronted by Mr. Jordan.

Going into 2001, Jordan had Honda engines. Isn't that making it harder for you?

'Ah, I think this is the right pressure,' Frentzen said. 'You need pressure. You can see it negatively or positively and I think there is no reason why we shouldn't take it positively and get the best out of everybody to build a good car.'

You seem to have blossomed with Jordan.

'Yes, yes, but those weren't lost years at Williams. At Williams I had a big lesson as well in what it means going from a small team to a top team. It was a really big step in my career even if it was short on results – but I was getting experience with leading professional people, setting up cars, talking about the development and things like that. You can only get experience when you are sitting there.'

At Williams did you ever doubt yourself?

'No. I had some hard times but this is the process of development. You must have them. You cannot live in the sunshine the whole day saying "I'm good, I'm good" and not getting any experience. Thank God it was a hard time. You have to fight if you want to achieve good results. Last year it was very difficult to keep my motivation high and there is no way out [with an uncompetitive or unreliable car]. I am responsible for the team, in a sense, because if I lose motivation the members of the team lose it quite quickly as well. Everybody gets influenced[7] by the results on the track.'

There was subsequently a savage irony to all these brave words because Jordan fired Frentzen in mid-season 2001. It had gone wrong and, as EJ said, 'there were several things I was unhappy about.'

In 2001 Frentzen was partnered for the second year by Jarno Trulli, who'd joined after two and a half seasons with the Prost team. Trulli explores another dimension the driver must master in protecting himself: the psychology of language. Although

Trulli had an Italian engineer he resolved, and announced publicly, that they would converse only in English.

Because otherwise you risk having misunderstandings?

'No, it is to make sure that there are no doubts that me and my engineer are fully open in working together with all the team. When I was at Prost it was very difficult because they were French and I had to learn French to understand what was going on. I don't want to give anyone at Jordan any opportunity to tell me I'm doing something illegal or wrong with my engineer. I just want to make sure that everything works well with everybody. I talk in English so if someone is listening they will know what I am talking about. It's very important because let's say you are doing very, very badly. Someone can say you are not fully 100% inside the team – they've heard you talking in Italian. I don't want that.

'Eddie Jordan is very good for the team because he doesn't really get involved with the technology of the car. He is a very important person because he is extremely positive always, doesn't matter what is happening. That does give you the motivation not to give up, to always go for it. If you are in a really bad situation, like we were last year – unfortunately our car wasn't really reliable – he's saying "ah, but next year will be better." It leaves people still hoping for something good.'

How do you regard the team?

'At least at Jordan I have several times a competitive car which gave me the chance to fight. I achieved a front row [at Monaco, 2000] and that gives you a little satisfaction which helps you to carry on through the season, but when you don't have any help, when you don't have any results, when you don't have anything and you keep dropping out of the race it's really bad. I don't want the best car, I just want a car which in several races – not all races – gives me a chance to fight for points.'

Ricardo Zonta stepped out of Grand Prix racing at the end of 2000, after two seasons with BAR, to test drive for Jordan, as he had in 1997. This was either a finely calculated risk or impelled by necessity, but either way it seemed to be flirting with impermanence.

'Of course I would like to be a racing driver again. The opportunity I had was with a small team or maybe a three-year contract with a medium team. I thought it was too much and I got the opportunity to be a test driver again. My thinking was that then I'd have options for the future.'

But it is a risk.

'I don't say it's a risk. Of course there are going to be problems but maybe next year I'll be with a good team who give equal support to both drivers.'

Have you found it difficult to accept that you were not at the front of the grid?

'All my career I won everything I tried, but Formula 1 is too much about the cars. If you are in a small team there is no opportunity to fight for the podium. You lose motivation, you don't want to be just another one on the grid. That is the way I look at it. So many drivers, they want just to be on the grid. I would like to be between the sixth and tenth place.'

Can you make testing mentally interesting for yourself?

'Yes, of course, like in the tests I did for McLaren, and now Jordan, where I was fighting to beat the others at the test. That was the only way to make it exciting. My objective should be to beat my lap times all the time. The racing drivers, they spend all the Grand Prix weekend fighting and fighting and when they go to do the tests they are easy-going, they don't go on the limit.' Then Frentzen was fired and Zonta said 'I have to be in Formula 1 next year. We are in talks now but this is a great chance for me.'

Mika Salo might have been flirting with a subtle variety of the impermanence. He decided to leave Sauber at the end of 2000 and join Toyota, which meant testing a completely new car until it made its début in 2002. That in turn meant missing each Grand Prix of 2001 and the first of them, Australia, hurt a bit. 'I really don't like doing nothing at a circuit.'

What was your thinking in stepping outside racing?

'I've been seven years in Formula 1 and only during my short time at Ferrari was I given the chance to win races. Driving for the same positions – between tenth and sixth, let's say – doesn't make me happy any more. [It was just what Zonta wanted, but Zonta was 25, Salo 35]. I needed to make a change.[8] Toyota gave me the opportunity to start something new. It was a difficult decision. I still had one more year on my contract with Sauber and they were offering a year after that. I was dropping off two guaranteed years of racing for testing so of course it was difficult. Then I saw what Toyota had ...'

I'm interested in how you approach testing mentally, same circuit, on and on.

'Testing is always fun when you have new things to try and it's different with the smaller teams who never have anything. You just keep going round and round doing nothing. With a new team and a new car there will be something new every day and it's much more interesting. It's a big challenge.'

Is it difficult, because the team and car are new and you have no points of reference?

'Yes, you can easily go on the wrong track so that's why we need a two-car team [Salo and McNish] so we can swap around sometimes to see are we doing the right thing in both places.'

Is it frustrating?

'Ah, no, not at all because I know I am working for next year's car. It would be hard if I was working for somebody else's car and I knew they'd be driving it but now it gives me one very long test session.'

For ordinary people it's hard to understand what it's like to be so competitive yet have so often been in a car that you know cannot win. Suddenly you've got a chance here ...

'That was the point. It is giving me a better opportunity than if I stayed racing in Formula 1.'

Do you get more nervous at a function like this [the Toyota launch at Paul Ricard] than driving the car?

'Yes, because this is not really my job. My job is to drive the car and not to talk so I'm really happy that today the talk is over and I can start the driving.'

Do you think with Toyota you are going to be the new Mika [superseding Häkkinen]?

'I'm better than him already! He's been in one of the best teams for years and obviously if he's in a McLaren and I'm in an Arrows I can't race with him. That's another reason why I'm here. At the moment, if you look at Ferrari and McLaren you have no chance to win against them and I don't see any point in racing if I don't have even a little chance of winning any more.'

What about Räikkönen doing well. Did that niggle, a young Finn coming in when you're out?

'Oh, no, no, no, I'm happy for him because I helped him to get there.'

But he's racing and doing well and you're not.

'There was another Finn doing well all the time I was racing so it doesn't bother me, and when you're racing you're racing against everybody, not just one guy.'

When you're testing new things, can your mind separate doing a fast lap from what specific things on the car are doing?

'That's my job, to go fast all the time. I'm going maximum every lap.'

Have you enough mental capacity left to say 'we're trying something new, I'll concentrate on that' and still do the fast lap?

'Yes, no problem. I can feel the difference, I can feel one millimetre change somewhere in the car.'

Is your thought process constant all the way round the lap?

'Yes, it has to be. I have to explain what it does in every corner. It is the same in a race. After doing a 70-lap Grand Prix in Monaco I have to remember what happened every lap. I've been doing it for 27 years. It's something you learn. It's my job and I have no other job – if I had a different job maybe I couldn't do it.'

McNish, who understands impermanence and exile as well as anyone, discusses lengthy runs. 'Sometimes in a car you've got to force yourself a lot, play little mind games with yourself. Le Mans is not a sprint, it's 24 hours, but you do have to drive it flat out. Each person's different. I keep concentrating on trying to make sure those lap times are as fast as I can. I try to be precise all the time, very precise, on my braking, turn-in points every single lap I do: same in practice and qualifying. When I come into the pits I come in fast and when I go out I go out fast. I make sure I hit the markers because even if you only gain one second at each stop, at Le Mans it's going to be 15 seconds. I force myself all the time to try and push those boundaries a wee bit further everywhere. OK, you've got your physical limits in the car. It delivers a certain amount of power. With any set-up there is a point where if you go any faster you will run out of road. However, there are so many other ways you can gain time. I believe you draw confidence and psychological strength from that, and it keeps you focused.'

Zonta faced something similar.

How much running did you do in a McLaren?

'A lot. One time I had a test in Austria. I started to test on Tuesday at Magny-Cours and they kept me to Thursday night. They sent an aeroplane to Magny-Cours to take me to Austria because the test was important for them.'

Did you get a chance to compare yourself with Häkkinen and Coulthard?

'Yes and my times were not better, but close. It looks so easy from the outside to say "if I had that car I could beat them." Well, I had two years and I couldn't beat Jacques. I went to the team and I knew, I knew I could beat Jacques but something was not quite right.' Zonta is being diplomatic about equal-treatment.

Are you worried about watching the races and thinking 'that could have been me?'

'No, I didn't make the wrong decision because it was for the future, not for one year. I am sure I will be racing again.'

D'you think anybody could beat you if you have two cars the same?

'Oh … I don't know. I lost a little bit of confidence in two years. All the problems I had. Of course I need to try again and say I am strong enough so that nobody can beat me, but now I am really saying I don't know.'

McNish, in his exile, reached the point where just getting in at the rear of the grid was no longer an attraction.

You were not really going to give up your successful sportscar career for Minardi any more.

'No I wasn't, because I have more understanding now of what it takes. I realise that if you get into a team like that it's very difficult to get out.'

The thought processes of the mid-to-rear-grid driver are as fascinating as those of the outright winners and losers. The middle men are in the hunt but are rarely hunters themselves. They grind it out season on season, they pass into their thirties and their faces are no longer young, and they must know the truth. That may be a harsh judgement on any driver like Jonathan Palmer [84 races between 1983 and 1989: 14 points] but it is one he is prepared to face. Interestingly, he also went the testing route but in slightly different circumstances to Zonta and McNish.

Was there a moment when you thought 'I've done my seasons with Tyrrell, not bad results, and this is really not going anywhere'?

'I realised when Alesi came to join Tyrrell. Until 1989 I had no doubt I could win races and the championship in the right car. I had been quicker than Alliot at RAM, quicker than Rothengatter at Zakspeed, quicker than Streiff at Tyrrell. I was confident. Alboreto came in and he was quicker than me sometimes, and I was quicker than him more times, so basically I was quicker than him too. The last race he did was in Canada when I outqualified him pretty comprehensively. At Montreal I set the fastest lap of a Grand Prix[9] but I ended up going off in the wet, aquaplaning.

'Anyway, Alboreto came in as the big number one, the Ferrari race winner, and this Jonathan Palmer guy was giving him a hard time. He left. I thought "well, I've now got a clear run to be number one" but what I hadn't reckoned on was this young Alesi guy. First race he did at the French Grand Prix I qualified ninth, and was very good, and he qualified sixteenth. He was effusive in his praise for me and I couldn't understand why. It was because he couldn't think that anybody could ever drive a racing car quicker than him! At Silverstone I qualified eighteenth, he was twenty-second. At Hockenheim, his third race, he qualified ahead of me [Alesi tenth, Palmer nineteenth] and he out-qualified me every race thereafter. At that point I knew.

'It's really tough when you get someone in the same car who is younger and quicker.

'I remember being at the Belgian Grand Prix at Spa – typically wet, pouring with rain – and Alesi wasn't there, he was doing a 3000 race.[10] In the Grand Prix I couldn't see a thing and it was just ridiculous. I went off the line and I think I lost four places on the first lap. Ken was clearly not impressed. He called me into the office afterwards – this was early September – and said "don't you think it's time you stopped? You're not going to be joining us anymore, are you?" I said "well ..."

'I couldn't stop just yet and in fact I was very quick next time out [two races after, Portugal, where he finished sixth]. Anyway at the end of the year I was talking to Arrows about driving for them in 1990 but the Alesi thing was obvious, everyone could see Alesi was blowing me away. I was in my third year at Tyrrell and by the end of it I was effectively on the scrapheap so I decided to jump before I was pushed.

'Then at the final race of the year, Adelaide, I couldn't believe it. Here, where I had had my best-ever result,[11] I failed to qualify. The car wasn't brilliant but it should have qualified. I was twenty-seventh and Alesi was fifteenth. I knew it was my last Grand Prix and I hadn't even qualified for it.

'I was as gutted as I have ever been in my life. It was just such a sad end to a slippery slope year and I couldn't hang around. I went straight off, got myself on a flight at the airport and came home.'

You couldn't face the others or you couldn't face yourself?

'I couldn't face staying around there to watch the race. No way. You walk like a leper – you're the bloke who should have qualified and you haven't. Funnily enough, things go through your mind: "I should have done this or I should have done the other, I should have used this set-up or that set-up."

'I was back in England in time to watch the highlights on television, but when I saw the conditions – the race was run in absolutely atrocious conditions, and Senna hit the back of Brundle – I thought "well, I'm delighted I didn't qualify." My emotion changed from being absolutely gutted to thinking maybe it wasn't such a bad thing. I'd have hated to race in that. I enjoyed driving when it was wet but not when I couldn't see. There were a few of us who were the same – the more intelligent drivers. Prost would pull off, Lauda would pull off, I'd pull off, because then it becomes a game of Russian roulette. Any time it's about judgement and knowing what you're doing, fine, no problem, I'd do that but when it was the roulette, no.'

Alesi is magnanimous about driving with Palmer.

When you were out-qualified by him at Paul Ricard you congratulated him and he was surprised.

'Ah, yes. For me it was a great moment because it was my first race in Formula 1 and to be with Jonathan Palmer was also great because he had good experience. For me he was ... not a teacher but a good level to try to reach. It was what I was trained to do.'

Also he said that very soon you were quicker and he realised then that for him it was finished.

'I was a young driver in a different situation. I was doing Formula 3000 and for him it was the end of his career. It will happen to me also when a young driver comes up next to me and that will be time for me to stop.'

He understood this and did not make excuses.

'Jonathan is a clever guy, he's not like these people who have no idea what racing really is.'

Palmer thought he'd be better off joining McLaren as a test driver. 'I had a good three to four year spell testing what was the Grand Prix car and in the back of my mind was that if anything happened to Senna or Berger ...'

... *like if he broke an ankle* ...

'Berger was unwell prior to Monaco but he got himself well.'

So it was over and, as the poet said, the world ends like this: not with a bang but a whimper. The late Harvey Postlethwaite, once of Ferrari and Tyrrell, put the same sentiment another way. In Formula 1, everyone exits through the back door.

I don't want to create the impression that Grand Prix racing is about people clinging on – surviving the hunt, if you will. To a few there are precious moments when they conquer or come close. We'll approach this with a minor detour. John Watson, who knew such moments, is discussing the passage of time.

'Today the whole value of respect has changed out of all recognition. Jenson Button is an example of the youngsters. I am sure he has respect for Michael Schumacher but he started his career much younger than we did, he's had the benefit of a lot of success at international level and he's out there racing. To some degree I operated on my own. In the 1970s Nick Brittan[12] was around but not as Willi Weber and other managers are these days. You have a guy like Didier Coton with Mika Häkkinen, and every time Mika gets out of bed Didier is there holding his dressing gown. That type of management and support was unusual in my day. Drivers were much more self sufficient.'

Niki Lauda retired in 1979 but returned in 1982 with McLaren, partnering Watson. That season Watson mounted a strong challenge for the championship and went to the last race at Caesars Palace, Las Vegas, with the points like this: Rosberg 42, Pironi 39 (but out of it because of his Hockenheim crash), Watson 33, Prost 31, Lauda 30. In that era a driver could only count his best 11 finishes from the 16 races, a system sometimes demanding nightmarish mental arithmetic.

You were going to do it by yourself, you weren't counting on anybody else.

'No, I wasn't. However, on the Saturday Ron Dennis said: "Niki, can we rely upon you to support him if he's behind you and he can possibly get to a position to win the championship?" It was the first time, possibly the only time, that Niki was asked and I know it must have been extremely difficult. OK, he had a remoter chance but he still felt that he wanted the opportunity. He did agree and I suspect that he just turned off in that race.

'I had to do an awful lot of work and sadly it wasn't sufficient to win it [Watson was second]. It was a bit like Häkkinen in 2000. The championship was lost earlier in the year for a variety of reasons but a lot of people could say the same. Niki could say it in 1982, Pironi might have said it – and you have to put Gilles Villeneuve into the equation. I could say "if only I hadn't retired at Hockenheim, if only it hadn't rained at Spa …"'

In 1991 Nigel Mansell was going hard for the championship and before the Hungarian Grand Prix I called in to see Lauda, who spoke eloquently about the self-control and mental disciplines Mansell would need. Here, by extension, is how Lauda won three.

'The problem with Mansell is very simple. He is a balls-out flat-out racing driver. In the past he was not able to use his head to slow down at the right time, save the car and drive an intelligent race. Prost is the ideal racing driver. This year Mansell has surprised me in a way that suddenly he realises that he has to be safe, use the speed at the right time and not do these crazy things. In the last three races he's won in perfect style using his head, being quick enough at the time he needs to be.

'You know I've been through this many times. He needs more and more brains the more the season progresses. He should not worry about anything because he has the best car. Therefore he can use all of the power in his head to work out how to use this huge jewel of a car to make this thing happen.'

Mansell did not win the title in 1991, but he did in 1992 – by exploiting restraint.

The championship is tantalising because you might only get one chance at it. 'I must talk about this in terms of an obsession,' says Watson. 'You go through your career and you make the sacrifices at every level from your adolescence through your youth into adulthood. You sacrifice friendships, sacrifice professional relationships – perhaps everything – in pursuit of your goal, the championship. Then, for whatever reason, you may be denied the chance to fulfil that, which can be positively dangerous to you.

'It's quite different if you have the chance, as I did, and Eddie Irvine did in 1999. To a lesser extent that applied to Mika Häkkinen in 2000 [going for three consecutive championships]. McLaren said "we lost Mika the championship" and that was them rallying around as a team, encircling to protect itself rather than allowing the snipers to pick out and then pick off individual targets and maybe weaken the fundamental structure.

'It can be damaging if you don't fulfil it, less damaging if you've had a go and didn't make it.'

Irvine went to the 1999 Japanese Grand Prix with an outside

chance. Soon after, he'd be gone to Jaguar and toil a whole season for four points.

At Suzuka that weekend there was a strange atmosphere. Michael didn't quite know how to play it and that was the first time I'd seen him uncertain about what he should be doing, how he should be thinking.[13]

'I wasn't even thinking about what Michael was doing,' Irvine will say. 'I was just trying to get on the pace because I was massively off it and I'd never been like that at Suzuka before and never have been since. It was the Friday morning, I did one or two laps and said to my engineer "it's just like driving on ice." I was off the pace the whole weekend. I don't know what it was. I don't know if it was me but I'm pretty sure it wasn't. I went there so confident because that was my circuit. I wasn't going to a circuit I didn't know or wasn't good at – every time I went there I was king.'

If points are elusive (the 2001 edition of the *Marlboro Grand Prix Guide* lists 333 scoreless drivers), victories are by definition more slippery still. The 1998 update to Hayhoe and Holland's *Grand Prix Databook* gives these totals of most races before a win: Häkkinen 96, Thierry Boutsen 95, Alesi 91, Mansell 72, Herbert 71, Patrese 71. I asked Irvine about his first win, Australia 1999 – his 82nd race – and specifically the final lap.

'I was just backing off.'

You move along the pit lane straight into that final lap …

'You're just hoping nothing happens to the car. I knew I was going to win it. The race had been over since shortly after the re-start[14] and if the car didn't break I was going to win.'

So you can be quite calm on that lap?

'Oh yeah. I was just keeping my distance from Frentzen and

taking care I didn't make a mistake. I honestly cannot remember what I felt when I crossed the line. That was an easy race to win. Austria was a difficult race to win.[15] That was amazing to cross the finish line there because really we shouldn't have won that race.'

D'you let yourself go in the cockpit then?

'You're going whooo, whooo, whooo!'

And that last lap in Austria.

'We won the sort of race that people would say "only Michael can win races like that." It was great because it was my first race as team leader and to win it was fantastic, it was magic, it was perfect.'

Did you feel a sense of fulfilment?

'A sense of proving myself. I didn't really look at it in that much detail, to be honest. I just thought "right, next race." I don't have a lot of sentiment in my life. Maybe when I get older I will have but now I don't have any.'

Few of them do, or will admit to it anyway.

NOTES

1. Scuderia Italia were a small Italian team.
2. Hethel in deepest Norfolk was a country house which became the Lotus headquarters.
3. The fan car was sensational. In 1978 Gordon Murray saw a gap in the regulations under which an extractor fan could be used to reduce air-pressure beneath the car so long as its 'primary function' was not aerodynamic. The Brabham looked astonishingly like a species of jet aeroplane. It was banned.
4. The points position was Mario Andretti 36, Ronnie Peterson 30, Lauda 25, Patrick Depailler 23, Reutemann 22, Jacques Laffite 10, Watson 9.
5. Carlos Pace (Brazil/71 races/killed in a light plane crash); Larry Perkins (USA/11 races); Hans Stuck (Germany/72 races).

6. Teddy Mayer, an American, ran McLaren.

7. At the Jordan launch, on a giant screen, interviews were shown with employees who did not go to the races, and they said in the most heartfelt way how they rejoiced and suffered depending on what happened in qualifying and races. You could tell this made a profound impression on Frentzen.

8. Elsewhere, Salo has been quoted as saying 'I think it will be good for my brain to have a little break.'

9. Palmer did a 1m 31.925s on lap 11, Senna next on 1m 32.143s.

10. Alesi was contracted to Jordan in Formula 3000 and drove in the Grands Prix which did not clash. He was at the Birmingham Superprix and Herbert deputised for him at Spa.

11. Palmer finished fourth in Australia in 1987 behind Berger, Alboreto and Boutsen.

12. Nick Brittan, who acted as Watson's manager, was closely involved in the Lombard RAC Rally and subsequently organised historic rallies.

13. Schumacher's dilemma at Suzuka was that he had been hired at extraordinary expense to win the world drivers' championship for Ferrari, something they had not done since 1979, but – having broken his leg at Silverstone – could not achieve it. Would he help his deputy, Irvine, achieve it instead?

14. The re-start was in fact after three laps of the safety car and Irvine led from there to the end.

15. Coulthard and Häkkinen crashed just after the start of the Austrian Grand Prix and charged to finish second and third – Irvine beating Coulthard by 0.313 of a second.

Chapter 8

BREAKING POINT

'I said "I promised you: you did that in Hockenheim, I do this in
Zeltweg, so stay away from me. Until you say sorry for Hockenheim,
every time I see you I push you in the grass."
He went "um, um, um. Sooner or later somebody will be killed."
I said "yes, but maybe it will not be me"'
– Michele Alboreto

There's a paradox between qualifying and racing because, in absolute terms, qualifying ought to be relatively unimportant. [This chapter appeared before the 2003 qualifying rule-change, but retains its validity in an historical sense. The effect of the rule change is discussed later in the book.] The qualifying sessions carry nothing into any round of the World Championship except grid positions and, while these are relevant to the start, they guarantee nothing.

The driver does not see it like this. To him qualifying is a taut and turbulent mental examination where fast laps are the currency and he has limited opportunities to do them. All manner of circumstances can conspire against him: the track condition if he goes too early or late, the weather, these days a restricted number of laps and tyres, the myriad mechanical problems which a hugely stressed car suffers, and what the drivers unlovingly call 'traffic'.

Qualifying is more than this.

It demands tactics and exquisite timing to maximise everything you've got going for you. It demands that you are constantly ready to respond to anything your opponents produce. You see the driver sit in the car in the pits, his eyes roaming the timing screens, the telemetry, the television pictures. He can move from passivity to counter-attack in seconds.

Qualifying is more than this.

A good lap in a bad car will attract attention even if the time is slow. A very good lap may hoist a driver in a not-so-good car a couple of rows up the grid so he's racing in an elevated position he might have found unreachable otherwise. A pole lap may enable the driver to lead the whole race. This means that the struggle for the grid is always being enacted at several different levels, but at the core are vital aspects of man against man, man against himself.

Qualifying is more than this.

It has a supposed and unwritten etiquette which invites the slower driver, and particularly the newcomer, to get out of the way of the fast men, thereby showing deference to their seniority. The etiquette insists, however, that any driver on a slow lap gives way to any car on a fast lap. Qualifying times are so close that balking, however momentary and involuntary, can wreck the fast lap beyond recovery. The Malaysian Grand Prix, last of the 2000 season, will do nicely as an example.

Michael Schumacher	1m 37.397s
Mika Häkkinen	1m 37.860s
David Coulthard	1m 37.889s
Rubens Barrichello	1m 37.896s

The top 17 drivers were all held within the span of 1m 37.397 to 1m 39.591 (Salo in the Sauber). So 2.194 seconds, gained and lost over 3.4 miles/5.5km, was the difference between pole and the far reaches of anonymity. And within the etiquette, who knows which drivers will move over and which won't? Who can predict, at immense closing speed, what the driver of the slow car ahead will do or even if he'll do anything? What do you decide, when do you decide it and how?

To show the pace at which drivers operate, here is Mark Blundell discussing Spa and specifically *Eau Rouge*.

How do you know your exact entry speed, how do you know exactly where to position the car?

'It's all sensors, all sensitivity factors. The old saying about the seat of your pants is still true to this day. No matter how much telemetry and electronics you've got on the car, the most sophisticated sensor in the world is your backside, and it's still all about that. It's the feel for the wheel, it's the feel of the car, it's the balance of sensitivities, it's references – like the state of the track – it's absorbing this piece of information or that piece of timing, that sign, that differentiation in colour, that piece of turf there which is your marker for turning in because the car feels it's correct to turn in at that point. All this is being processed. Maybe a jet fighter pilot does the same thing except that nine times out of ten he's in a sky which he's got pretty much to himself.'

When you go down into Eau Rouge, *do you get a feeling in the pit of your stomach?*

'You get a sensation of the G forces, yes, but it's not an awareness that you take any notice of. What you are more concerned about is that you're into the corner. Have you found a good way into it? How is the car feeling? How you are going to exit?'

Are you already in the next corner as you come out of Eau Rouge?

'I am already setting myself up for it because I know what's coming. I have already registered that. You have a straight and you are just powering it along there. All you're looking at on that straight is what revs you are pulling and whether you've got a competitively fast lap going. Am I, say, 100rpm up because my exit was good from *Eau Rouge*? Am I carrying that 100 – which is now 150 – down the straight? You think: this is it, this is the lap, this is really a good pointer. It's all about limitations. Can you afford to carry the 150 and then brake the extra *two metres* later? Will the car do it without screwing itself? Two metres might be half of a tenth of a second gained – which could also be the loss of a tenth of a second on a poor exit. Think of it this way. You go a tenth up here, a tenth up there, half a tenth up here and over a lap you might be talking five tenths of a second. Not a lot, you might think, but it is a lot in Formula 1. When the semi-automatic gearchange came out, the thinking was that it takes 60 milliseconds for a human to change gear, we can cut it down to 25 milliseconds. Multiply the number of gearchanges per lap, multiply that by a race distance and suddenly … hey! That's how they look at it, that's why they say let's get to work on that. Part of the fascination with Formula 1 is such things. You get the technology and you get the human side.'

This is the pace at which drivers will be approaching traffic and, very possibly, the Grand Prix novice. The trend now is to hire younger drivers and by definition they have less experience of everything. We have already had the interplay between Frentzen and Räikkönen.

I asked essentially the same question I'd asked Frentzen to Jonathan Palmer, a driver from the generation before Frentzen (Palmer retired in 1989, Frentzen began in 1994, so it's a nice span). Palmer experienced the super-sticky qualifying tyres which lasted almost exactly a single lap at full bore and then began to disintegrate. That loaded even more pressure on the driver to find an unimpeded lap: he only had a limited number of tyres. As Palmer says, 'you had to do it on your first lap' because you couldn't assume your second would be unimpeded.

From the cockpit how difficult is it?

'It's the worst thing because in many ways the qualifying is the most important part of a Grand Prix weekend. As a driver, you tend to think that the race will sort itself out. Qualifying is so crucial because that's when most of the work is done. You've only three or four laps depending on how many sets of tyres you've got, so when you do get someone in the way it is numbing. You're coming up behind them, closing-closing-closing, and you have to try and have some positive thoughts. It's very easy to have negative thoughts – "he's going to block me, he's going to bugger it up" – and you talk yourself out of it. And it may well be that in the last second he doesn't block you. Generally speaking, you have to charge as if you are not going to get blocked and then at the last minute you have to back off if he does.

'Sometimes as you get closer you have to make a do-or-die commitment: "I'm just going to have to assume he's seen me, I'm going to go for it, dive up the inside somewhere." You know the car and probably a third of the time you know which of the two drivers is in it because you've seen the side of the helmet as he's gone through a previous corner or a previous section of the track. Most of the time you'll have an expectation of whether they will pull out of the way or whether they won't, and you're normally right. Inevitably if there is somebody who's new to Formula 1, the chances are they won't pull over and they won't see you because they are too busy looking after themselves. You must also consider that they're on their good lap in a car slower than yours.' In that case they are fully entitled to hog the racing line and if you swarm them, tough.

Qualifying is more than this.

The driver exists through the medium of speed. In the Grand Prix he must pace the car, albeit very fast. In qualifying there are no such constraints. Alboreto once said that when he got back to the pits after a fast lap and the car was 'pinging' – every nut and bolt exhaling, inhaling, exhaling because he'd stretched them to what they could take – 'the Tyrrell mechanics liked that.' Of course they did. That's why they made the car.

The driver is expected to explore the inner places of his desire by taking everything to this limit in one mighty, manic bomb burst. He is urged to translate his masculinity and his high opinion of himself into a sublime peak only he can reach, but the trouble is that they're all doing it, on a narrow ribbon of track, together.

Now, more than any other time in the Grand Prix weekend, the driver is likely to give his temper free rein. But before we reach that here's a genuine laugh or two woven into the tension of a pre-qualifying session. Perry McCarthy is talking about the 1992 season when he partnered the Brazilian Roberto Moreno in the Andrea Moda team. Alan Henry, writing in the *Autocourse* annual, described Andrea Moda as 'the fiasco of the season by any standards.' We join McCarthy at the point where he is explaining his own character.

'I was from the East End and I would get called arrogant at school – not arrogant as far as being snooty goes, not arrogant about refusing to talk to people, but very self-confident. I would stop lessons in applied physics and say "no, I don't agree with that. Please explain it." I suppose I can be very difficult. Conversely when it's all going wrong, I can make the team laugh and get them on my side and gee them up. But if I see things going the way I don't want them to, I'm not very good at disguising my feelings on it.'

Now to Hungary, where Mansell was preparing to become World Champion and McCarthy was preparing for the pre-qualifying. It was 8–9am on the Friday and involved five drivers, Gabriele Tarquini and Eric van de Poele (Fondmetal), Ukyo Katayama (Venturi), Moreno and McCarthy. The four fastest would go forward to qualifying proper.

'The team waited until about 40 seconds before the end of the session to send me out so before I can even come round the chequered flag's been waved. As I've come past the pits I'm shaking my fist at the team – I'm going to take everybody apart. I pulled back in to the pits, got out of the car, I've gone back into the garage and all the team were there, [team principal Andrea] Sassetti, Moreno. I was pushing everyone around. I wanted a fight. Moreno walked past. I body-checked him out of the way. I was screaming at everybody and I just wanted one person to raise a finger ...'

Why did they do this to you?

'Because they were idiots! They just didn't understand. They kept trying to keep my car in reserve for as long as possible in case anything happened to Roberto's, and he would then get in my car. Now here's the McCarthy timing on this: after that little episode, five minutes after it, John Wickham [team manager of Footwork, formerly Arrows] came up and said 'Jackie Oliver wants to talk to you about testing for Arrows.' I said "OK, tell Jackie I'll do it, I'm in, no problem at all." So he said "yes, but he needs a letter from Sassetti releasing you to do it." I asked Sassetti and he just looked at me after what I'd done. Moreno walked past and said "you've just stuffed yourself" – and I didn't need a lot of help in that department, did I?'

You can't act rationally in those circumstances.

'No you can't. I'd lost it. I will say this: most top racing drivers have a fairly good temper on 'em. Oh, yes. It's like [snaps fingers] now! You get crossed up on that, people are not doing what you want, or in a way you want, or they are doing it how you believe is wrong, or they're not helping you, then believe me they find out about it. I've got hold of drivers before now.'

Here, for posterity to contemplate, is the Hungaroring on the dry, warm and sunny morning of 14 August 1992:

Tarquini	1m 22.412s
Van de Poele	1m 23.398s
Katayama	1m 24.421s
Moreno	1m 25.567s
McCarthy	0m 27.565s

During this strange statistical freak of a 'lap,' or rather a fraction of a lap, McCarthy was timed at 126.81mph (204.08kph) which, to the ordinary motorist, seems very fast indeed. A much more telling statistic is that all the other four drivers were timed at 145mph or more, proving, as Albert Einstein might have revealed, that these things are relative.[1]

Now consider the young driver who faces the dilemma of whether to assert himself or not. When Jean Alesi made his début at the 1989 French Grand Prix driving a Tyrrell, Mansell felt he obstructed him in some way and strode down to complain to Ken Tyrrell. Tyrrell explained the situation to Alesi and said that, regardless of the rights and wrongs, if Alesi tendered a tentative apology to Mansell, harmony would be restored: no big deal either way. Alesi weighed this up in his own good time and said 'I don't think I want to do that.' Tyrrell savoured the moment because he knew that the meek are easy prey in the hunt.

This is how Martin Donnelly handled it at Hockenheim in the Lotus in 1990, only his tenth Grand Prix meeting, when he encountered Gerhard Berger (Ferrari), then in his seventh season.

'In those days you had qualifying tyres. I was coming out of the chicane approaching the Stadium and Gerhard was on an out lap so he was going slowly. I came up behind him and got to the braking area. Just when I was turning into the corner Gerhard left me the width of the F1 car to get through. I hit the brakes harder, lost my momentum and basically lost my lap. I took the view that if he had been on his qualifying lap and I'd done that to him I'd have buggered his lap up.

'Afterwards the press loved that, as you can appreciate. "He said this." "Well he said that." I thought "it's not nice having to live the rest of your life under a cloud" so I went back to the FOCA bus to look at the videotape. You could see he hadn't left me much, perhaps deliberately or he'd misjudged it. He said "I left you room." I said "you left me two-fifths of [expletive] all." It was going to be knives at dawn.

'By this stage it was going up and down the pitlane as I've described it, to and fro. It was great because I got headline news in the German papers. We didn't make it up and I had no respect for him for the rest of the year and he had no respect for me. And those are the things that can get out of control. From Formula 1 to 3000 and down to Formula Ford it happens every week and every test day, and that's all the way through the sport. It's just egos. One guy wants to get the upper hand on the other guy – he gets the better of it, then I'll get you next time.'

But Berger was a very senior driver, driving for a big team. And you're driving for what had become a small team. Didn't that make your position difficult?

'At the same time I am in Formula 1. I am among the best 26 drivers in the world. I believe that, given the opportunity, if I am in Berger's car I can do a competent job so I am not going to be intimidated by some bigwig who thinks he's been there for the last few years and is going to push me about.'

Mark Blundell had exactly the opposite experience.

'The incident for me in terms of qualifying was my first year in Grand Prix racing with Brabham, and it was with Michele Alboreto at Adelaide. He came up on his qualifying lap, because in those days we had qualifying tyres so it was one lap. We were running Pirellis and to get one clear lap was a big deal. I was on a warming-up lap, he felt that I got in his way and basically he tried to run me off the road.

'I was fully aware in the mirrors of where he was but he felt that there wasn't enough room. I was quite adamant that I was clear of him. At that point he came up the side of me and that meant I didn't get a chance to start my lap properly. He was so unnerved he gave me a load of hand signals in the Italian way and then started to push me into the wall. It was a street circuit of course. I can deal with an Italian waving his hand but trying to push me into the concrete because he was so aggrieved by the whole situation was a little bit much.

'It's my first year, I'm young, but I'd been around Grand Prix cars since 1989 testing for Williams and I'd been on the track plenty of times. I did my lap but I wasn't very happy so I went to the garage to see him. I actually tried to stick one on him because I was fuming and he did the worst thing in the world that you can do to me: gave me the finger in the chest, the prod. I go over the red light with that. I can't stand it. I tried to hit him and it was a big flare up and the mechanics all tumbled in to prevent it. Tempers calmed down and that was the end of it. I walked away. I have spoken to him since but we didn't discuss it.'

You live in very close proximity to other drivers who may be strangers to you.

'That involves some understanding of the make-up of people because otherwise there's no saying what the guy's going to do. You take a trust and a respect into the racecar and the race, but it will only function in a certain way. Otherwise, without the trust and respect, it's very scary. It doesn't have to be. For instance, the Grand Prix at Hockenheim 1993. I was in a Ligier and I was running with Senna and Berger: a real fight. I knew

Berger, I'd spent a year with him testing and I knew how he functioned. Yes, he was hard but he was clean. Me and him were doing like 212mph on the grass. He'd stick me, I'd stick him but we knew what was going on between us. There were no issues of closing the door or not opening the door.'

Is that almost like a telepathy?

'I think maybe you get to a point where it is like a secondary consciousness. You are so fully in tune with what's going on with yourself that you are also in tune with what's going on around you. From that you create the situation where you understand, and that is something drivers do.'

In my book *Ayrton Senna: As Time Goes By* (Haynes, 1999) there was a delightful photograph of Senna and Alboreto sharing a joke. In 2000 Alboreto, driving for Audi at Le Mans, recalled the incident. 'This is exactly the picture that I have in my house and I have it there because I remember the discussion that we had and how relaxed we were. I was with the Footwork which was Porsche in this moment [1991]. It was a very bad car and he asked me why I continued when I was on the last row for all the season. I said "because I love the driving!" Then I asked him "ah, you are two times World Champion, why do you continue when you could stay in Brazil?" And I answered it: "for the same reason as me, because you love the driving!" And he was laughing and I was laughing.'

Is it possible to be friends with other drivers?

'No. Sorry. But you can have respect for somebody, and for many reasons. Friends is something different. Respect comes from the action that you and all the other drivers do: drive. Ayrton was bad in some moments and very bad in others. As a human being he was very strong and very good so in that I had a lot of respect for him.'

But you did not have any real enemies.

'You cannot have enemies in sport. You can have people maybe you don't like, yes, but real enemies no.'

I've never heard anybody say they didn't like you.

'Maybe you haven't spoken to the right people! Maybe I was too tough in some moments at the beginning of my career especially with Ayrton, and maybe you don't know that. We had a very, very big fight for nothing. For example in Zeltweg. That was because he had pushed me out in Hockenheim with no reason. It was at the start of the race, I was second, he was first, he was in the Lotus and I was in the Ferrari and it was the exit of the *Ostkurve*. Coming out of the chicane he missed a gear and I was in the tow and I passed him. When I was alongside he pushed me onto the grass. I don't lift off, he don't lift off, boom, boom, but the worst thing was I had no space to come back on. He was so close to me, and he don't brake and I cannot brake because you don't brake on grass or you spin.

'So I was there looking and then in the end slowly, slowly he give me a space, but I lift off, I lost the position and we do the race. He blew up the engine and I finished third or fourth. After the race I came to him and I said "look, Ayrton, this was not a good thing to do after the start. Next race will be Hungary – too slow – so I'll see you in Zeltweg [Austrian Grand Prix], when it will be another quick one."

'So Hungary was good: I don't see him and he don't see me, and then we arrive in Zeltweg. Free practice I saw him around, I waited for him and into the top speed I put my wheels into his rear wheels. He was looking at me. He cannot move, I cannot move, but I was in the advantage position – we were in the *Porsche kurve* – and he was really really scared. I did that first day, second day and in the warm-up. And he came along with [Marco] Piccinini, the head of Ferrari, and he said "are you crazy?" I said "I promised you: you did that in Hockenheim, I do this in Zeltweg, so stay away from me. Until you say sorry for Hockenheim, every time I see you I push you in the grass." He went "um, um, um. Sooner or later somebody will be killed." I said "yes, but maybe it will not be me." I really was mad about that.

'In the race I started third and he was fourth and we did the race no trouble. I was in front, he was behind no problem, and then I blew up an engine. So going up on the hill – remember the old Zeltweg – I was stopping and he was behind me. I was looking for him and when he tried to pass me I braked and he flew over and he crashed into the barrier. I pushed him out, just like that. For something like that they can take my licence and throw away, but I really did do it to him like this. And then I said sorry I didn't see him ...

'After this they call us to Ferrari. It was a very, very bad moment. Mr. Ferrari called us into the office – nobody knows this – and said "now you two have to stop these things because you are a Ferrari driver and I want Ayrton to be a Ferrari driver one day and I do not want you to kill each other." I said, "yes, but he started it." Ayrton said "no, he started it." After a few things it was a big deal, we shake the hands and that's the story over but it was really, really tough for those three or four races, really so bad.'

After that they competed against each other hard but with the nastiness removed. 'We had fought for years and we had a big fight going to the airport sometimes in the rental cars ...' Which is a different thing although, if you want the truth of it, much more frightening than the race. One time a couple of colleagues and I were halted at traffic lights leaving Imola in just such a rental car. Stefan Johansson espied us in his and drew abreast, stopped, looked over and smirked. The unspoken understanding – the etiquette – was that we wouldn't jump the red light and neither would he, but by God he had his engine howling in preparation. As the red flicked off, his car burst forward and vanished into the distance.

It was this same Johansson who had become embroiled with British driver Johnny Dumfries. I had quoted Dumfries at length in a book on Gerhard Berger, *The Human Face of Formula 1*, and perhaps that is worth reproducing here.

'Berger did me up once, he did me up like a kipper at Brands Hatch because I'd blocked him some time before. I was going on to the straight at Hawthorns, two or three cars in front of me and I went for the gap. He pulled over into the space intentionally and I really had to take evasive action. At the drivers' briefing the next day he came up to me and said, "I screwed your qualifying lap yesterday, didn't I?" I said, "yes, you did." He said, "well, you know why I did it, don't you?" I said, "yes, I do, it's no problem." So we sorted it out and that was the end of it. Berger is like that.

'I had a thing with Johansson, it got silly, it got out of control, we were really screwing each other up in qualifying and it was probably exacerbated by the fact that I had an accident with him in Canada, but that's part of the edge Formula 1 has over other formulas, that vindictive side. It's an aspect of what makes Formula 1 what it is. It hones everyone, gets everyone hyped up, and they end up becoming much more competitive, wiser. When I reached Formula 1 Berger said to me "it takes a year to learn this" and it proved good advice. He was right.'

Today Johansson can't remember the feuding with Dumfries and insists 'I made a point of letting drivers through on their fast laps – gave them plenty of room into the corners – so that they would remember and let me through if they ever met me on my fast lap. I always seemed to be having problems with Philippe Streiff but I don't think that was deliberate on his part so I didn't go and sort it out with him. The point is that if you go slightly off, and take the edge off your tyres doing it, that's the lap gone.

'Arnoux went round screwing everybody but he got screwed all the time as well. It's not easy to sort out because of the distance between drivers. Arnoux was a team-mate for a year so I spoke to him during that time but, other than that, not a word. If you do sit down – as Michele and Ayrton did – you find it was nothing very much and you end up the best of pals. You will always have traffic of course, but that's not the same thing.'

Palmer's experience with Martin Brundle confirms what Johansson has just said. 'The first big feud I had was with Brundle when we were at San Marino. He accused me of holding him up and we had a ruck in the paddock afterwards. He reckoned he could have gone quicker and I was holding him up when he came to lap me and I wouldn't let him by. I said "you had the line, you were three seconds quicker than me, you should have got yourself by." That was in 1984. By 1985–1986 we were pretty good mates, actually …'

It's always tempting to remember these 'incidents' and forget the sublime laps where man and machine achieved something approaching the ultimate harmony. The three leading exponents of this art in the modern era have been Prost, Senna and Schumacher. Here are three sublime laps.[2]

Prost, Spa, second qualifying, 14 September 1985
Lauda, partnering Prost at McLaren, crashed on the Friday morning injuring his wrist and withdrew from the meeting. Thus Lauda's race engineer, Steve Nichols, was now free to go down to *Eau Rouge* for second qualifying. He found a good vantage point which proved to be out of earshot of the loudspeakers. He watched as the drivers went through and up the hill.

The driver who impressed him was Mansell, the Williams 'twitching this way and that, his arms a blur, a shower of sparks from under the car.' Mansell was on his way to 1:57.465.

Nichols watched as Prost came through on a warm-up lap, smooth and slow because he wasn't stretching the car. Nichols waited for Prost to burst by on the fast lap but instead he came smoothly and slowly through again. Nichols immediately deduced that Prost had had a problem and was on another warm-up lap, 'neat and tidy, no fuss.' Nichols waited and Prost came smoothly and slowly through a third time, obviously, Nichols deduced, on a slowing down lap. He walked back up to the pits to see what the problem had been. That second lap had been 1:55.306 – pole.

Senna, Monaco, second qualifying, 14 May 1988

Senna had just joined McLaren from Lotus and this was his third Grand Prix meeting for them (Prost had won Brazil, Senna disqualified; Senna had won Imola from Prost). In first qualifying Senna was much quicker (1:26.464 against Prost's 1:28.375) and now, on the Saturday, prepared to deliver the blow. It came 25 minutes into the session.

Prost made a sustained run of six laps, moving from 1:27.938 to 1:27.520. Senna was into a sustained run too, striking out 1:27.014 on his third lap and then, as if a terrible force seized him, moving into a sequence of fast lap, regain breath, fast lap which – as he would confess – took him into a different physical and mental dimension.

Regain breath:	1:39.378
Fast lap:	1:25.592
Regain breath:	1:32.078
Fast lap:	1:24.439

'I suddenly realised I was no longer driving the car consciously.'

Regain breath: 1:37.323

As he moved into the climactic lap, the whole circuit became a 'tunnel' and he found more and more speed on the other side of his limit, and then even more.

Fast lap: 1:23.998

Now he suddenly realised that this had taken him to a strange, frightening place which he did not understand ('beyond my conscious understanding') and he slowed immediately, returned to the pits. He hinted at how the laps of the sequence had merged so that he couldn't 'separate them in my mind' and in fact had no idea whether he'd even come upon traffic or not; and this from a man who habitually remembered every instant of every lap.

Prost needed 25 laps to get down to 1:25.425, which was 1.427 seconds slower. Perhaps the best way to emphasise the extent of the blow is by giving you the margins between pole and the next man in the three years before: 0.672 in 1987, 0.420 in 1986, 0.086 in 1985. As Watson says, Senna threw Prost away in 1988 and the world was never the same again.

Schumacher, Sepang, qualifying, 16 October 1999

Schumacher crashed and broke his leg on the first lap at Silverstone in July and there were rumours that he had been forced into the Malaysian Grand Prix too soon – he was needed by Ferrari to help Irvine towards the championship. Too soon? Schumacher banished that and reasserted his domination of Formula 1.

He set an early target time of 1:40.830 and neither Häkkinen nor Coulthard in the McLarens could reach it. Nor could Irvine. With a quarter of an hour of the session left Häkkinen did

1:40.866 placing himself between the Ferraris. Schumacher responded with a sweeping gesture. He did a 1:39.688, 0.947 seconds quicker than Irvine and the natural order was restored.

'I expected we would be strong here,' Schumacher said, 'but to be one second ahead is surprising. The car allows me to drive like I want to drive.'

Such words had been ominous for every other Grand Prix driver for a generation and Schumacher knew that better than anybody.

NOTES

1. Of all the millions of laps driven at Grand Prix meetings this can claim to be the most meaningless – and mysterious. In any qualifying, provided you cross the line before the chequered flag falls to signal the end of the session, you are entitled to complete your lap. The obvious implication is that McCarthy crossed the line and did a lap in 27.565 seconds, a thought which – when I pointed it out – made him roar with laughter. 'I always said I was quicker than Senna. What did he do?'

    'One minute 16.267 seconds.'

    So how did McCarthy get the time which clearly could not have been a lap? (The 27.565 was recorded by the official timekeepers Olivetti/TAG Heuer and is in their records but elsewhere – Autosport, Autocourse – appears as 'no time'.) 'I haven't a clue,' McCarthy says. 'The FIA were sympathetic to my efforts that season and maybe they gave it to me as a consolation prize!'

    Maurice Hamilton, wise in the by-ways of Formula 1, was initially puzzled – you either complete a lap or you don't – but there is an explanation which he has worked out. The timing beam in the pit lane records the instant when a car goes out on to the track. McCarthy went out with 0:27.565 seconds of the session remaining and was travelling round to begin his lap. On his way he went through the first and second timing points and then the clocks froze because the session finished. Or not, as the case may be …

2. I am indebted to Autosport, Autocourse, Grand Prix People by Gerald Donaldson (MRP), the Ferrari press service and Olivetti-Longines timing in reconstructing these three laps.

Chapter 9

NOT REALLY A PROBLEM

'I have to say sorry, but driving a Formula 1 car is better than sex.'
Do you want me to rewind the tape and erase that?
'Yes, and it's not for print, either. The interview is now terminated!'
– Martin Donnelly

Brian Hart, a driver who became a celebrated engine manu-facturer, is one of the guardians of motorsport's purity. He understands the commerce – few better – but sees that as a conduit to racing, not an end in itself. We were discussing this chapter. 'If you're going to get into the crashes they won't like it, you know.' Of necessity, each driver has found mental mechanisms for accepting that the crash might – will – happen, and then found mechanisms for excluding that thought.

The crash is enacted in public but remains essentially a private matter between a driver's mind and body, both prisoners of the car, and the car itself. Another driver may be involved but it remains private between them. The spectator and the journalist know only as much as their imagination will grant them; the driver knows all about it in excruciating slo-mo as the orderly world breaks out of control. Who are we to intrude unless the drivers freely grant us access? I respect every driver – even René Arnoux who once used a very naughty French verb when I inquired how he was, even Nigel Mansell who once poured abuse on me across an engine at Spa and a dinner table in Mexico City.[1] Any man who forces a Formula 1 car to its limits on a regular basis is nothing less than brave.

Niki Lauda can strip life to enduring simplicities. He said that if anyone looking at his seared face after the crash at the Nürburgring in 1976 feels anything, that's their problem. No concern of his. He had ruthlessly excluded it from his thought processes.

Johnny Herbert almost lost a foot in the 1988 multi-car accident at Brands Hatch and put on a bravado performance for his mum. Lauda doesn't talk much about his crash: I'd guess that it probably hasn't interested him for years. Herbert talks about his crash because, as a philosophy, he'll answer whatever you ask. Other drivers talk too. Once upon a time I was having lunch with Mika Häkkinen and, although not overtly discussing his near-fatal crash in Adelaide in 1995, we were on the general theme of accidents. He spoke in a completely dispassionate way about how they will happen, and hoped his next accident wouldn't be a big one.

In the interviews for this book, the drivers all showed the same fatalism: not a passive acceptance but an active, coherent philosophy that – given the highly stressed state of both man and machine and the circumstances of racing – whatever you do, whatever precautions are taken, there will sometimes be crashes. Interestingly, they never once mentioned their bravery, ability to withstand enormous impacts, or fast reactions. For the most part the drivers discussed their accidents in a semi-detached way as if it had happened to them and yet to somebody else. These men are not careless of their bodies – they protect them mightily – but the inevitable does not intimidate them.

John Watson (Marlboro McLaren),
Italian Grand Prix, Monza, 13 September 1981, lap 20. Age: 36.

'When, and only when, something external comes into the programme – something suddenly different – it makes you look around, look down at the instruments, whatever. It's not just racing drivers who have this. Fighter pilots and, to some degree, soldiers possess this same sort of sixth sense. You live on it to survive.

'Looking at the circumstances of tragedy – a large number of people die in ferry crossings or plane crashes – the survivors are sometimes exercising these mechanisms. That's either because of their job, or because something they've experienced in life has enabled them to deal with the catastrophe better than other people. The public aren't capable of dealing with the danger, and the stress which goes with that danger, because they are not trained to. A racing driver is. It has evolved in him: maybe he starts off on a push bike or a motor bike, then into karts, then into racing cars, so it is a self-educating process concentrated over years.'

David Coulthard had a plane crash and was suddenly in a life-threatening situation. A few days later he raced in Barcelona.

'I was asked in a radio interview before Spain if I thought Coulthard would be affected and I said "no, he won't" because sudden life-threatening situations are what he spends his career experiencing and coping with. It's another day at the office. I then went on to qualify my comment by saying that if I'd still been driving I'd have been affected more, and I am sure David would have been affected more, by the fatality of Ayrton Senna. David had an accident and he walked out of it. I think the psychological effect on a lot of drivers – and David

235

came in as a consequence of Ayrton's fatality – was what I had when Jim Clark died in 1968. It made me appreciate that if someone like Jim Clark can be killed in a racing car then we all can be killed in a racing car.'

Watson was also confronted by something dangerous and unexpected in civilian life not long ago. 'I was at my parents' home and it was broken into by three men. I pulled back the curtains and two guys were at the window trying to get in. I thought they'd run away but they smashed the window and came in. The third guy was by then in downstairs.

'I was naked. Well, I had boxer shorts on. A naked man is very, very vulnerable.

'So in my situation how did I react? What I was doing was trying to strip my "competitors" naked, trying to make them feel vulnerable. I felt in extreme danger because these two guys smashed the window in and the glass came all over me. I was in Belfast. I didn't know if they were para military. I thought: assassination, murder. All those things went through my mind. I had to react. My mother and sister were downstairs. I left the room shouting "call the police, call the police, two men have broken in upstairs." They didn't understand what was going on but luckily my sister was by the phone, dialled 999, and was able to get part of a message over. Then these guys were in the room ripping the phone out of her hands.

'The police turned up but they thought they were coming to a domestic dispute. I am lying face down on the floor, my mother was sitting in a chair. Two of the three guys were standing there and one of them was thinking on his feet, fast. He had the presence of mind to say "ah come on dad, it's all right, it's all over now". He walked out the front door. To cut a long story short, an hour later he was recognised.'

Do you think you reacted like a racing driver?

'I gave myself time and space, that was what I effectively did. I didn't stand there and take them on because I didn't know if they had a gun. I assumed that they were armed – one of the guys had a plastic bag and there was something in it, maybe a gun or a knife. My immediate reaction was to vacate that space: the bedroom. I couldn't make the 999 phone call from there because I was compromised. I needed my mother or sister to make the call. I didn't know whether there was going to be a murder or not – I'd never had to deal with that. I've thought about this subsequently and asked myself if I did the right thing. Should I have stood my ground and tackled two guys who could have been UDA or IRA assassination squads? On balance what I did led to the best outcome possible.'

Were you thinking logically and did it seem to happen slowly?

'The total time was probably not that long but it seemed longer because it's a bit like having an accident. You watch an accident and it happens in milliseconds, but when it's happening to you it goes on and on and on. Although you are operating in real time, you sense that you are operating at half speed so that everything you experience is not perceived as being in real time.

'You are rationalising all the time. It's a bit like playing chess. You're looking at every move and asking "is this the right move? Which move can I make to ease the situation or win it?" Suddenly – like the incident in Belfast – you're in a very loaded situation and you don't have very many options. You're asking yourself what the right thing to do is and I thought that was 1) to get out of the bedroom, 2) warn my mother and sister, 3) try and get help as quickly as possible.'

Tell me about Monza and your crash.

'Hit the barrier, big fireball, all that sort of thing. It was three cars.'

Watson vividly remembers those cars as Nelson Piquet (Brabham), Alan Jones (Williams) and himself[2] as they came through the Lesmo corners. 'Jones was racing with Piquet but I felt I was quicker than these two cars ahead. At the second Lesmo I ran up close to the back of Jones and in doing so lost a bit of front downforce. Instead of coming out of the throttle to check that, I thought – my confidence was high – "no, I'm going to stay in it" because I wanted to get the run on him in that corner. "I'm going to make a move on him in the next chicane." We were doing 130, 140mph in the corner.

'I ran over the kerb and two wheels straddled it. At that point the cars were running fairly low – the two wheels on the left-hand side went off the track onto gravel and the bottom of the car came into contact with the kerb, and that rotated it into a long, looping spin. I thought "this is going to hurt." I just sat there, put my head down and *smack*: had the bang, car spun a bit more, came to a stop. The speed at the point of impact was probably 80, 90mph. That's still a big impact.

'The public don't understand because they don't know, they have no means of telling. They crash at 90mph and they're dead, because normally what happens when you crash is that you stop, whereas the most important thing is to dissipate energy before you stop. The flaw of road cars is they are not designed to have high-speed accidents in: they deform too much and too quickly. Some are better than others but ultimately it's to do with the weight of the car, the kinetic energy, the speed – all those factors.

'I remember sitting in the car looking down and there was no gear lever, the gear lever had gone. I looked up and I saw an engine sliding across the race track. I thought "bloody hell, whose engine is that? Somebody behind me has gone off and crashed and they must be dead." The engine was sliding across the track as [Michele] Alboreto [Tyrrell] came past and Alboreto just caught the engine: he spun off a hundred yards further up the track. I got out of the car and thought "[expletive], that was my engine." I found the gearbox ripped away from the engine and wedged in the armco barrier. I imagined the car was damaged but not that damaged.

'I got back to the pits and OK, I'd had a bang, whiplash, but I didn't know there had been a flash fire, oil and fuel vapour, boom, a fireball. I had been travelling away from it. All the spectator saw was this huge fireball but I didn't even know about it until later that night when I watched it on the TV.

'It had looked like another Ronnie Peterson[3]. I got back to the pits and everybody was saying "bloody hell, we thought you were dead" and I said "no, I'm not." Other teams came down and I said "I'm fine, what's the fuss?" I apologised to my people. "Sorry about the car, guys, it's a bit of a mess." Then six or seven hours later, very much alive and uninjured, I was watching it on television and it was like watching a film.'

Did you connect with it?

'No. And that's not self-preservation, that's pragmatism. After the race I went to Monte Carlo and stayed a couple of days, then on the following Wednesday or Thursday I drove at Donington. That was the first day Niki [Lauda] was driving a McLaren in preparation for making his comeback. I got into the car and I did the quickest time I'd ever done at Donington in that car. The crash had had no effect whatsoever on me.'

How can that be?

'I don't know. I think it's just a function of the confidence that you have. You trust yourself. It was my mistake, I made an error and I acknowledge that. Monza was down to me. I should have backed off, I shouldn't have been so anxious but, you know, I'm a racing driver and I want to get on, I want to win.'

But mechanical failure can imperil you too, not just your own error.

'You have to trust the team. Certainly in the 1970s car failures contributed to a lot of fatalities. There is no question about that. In the 1980s, and when Ron Dennis and John Barnard came to McLaren, they brought a new standard of engineering into Formula 1. Forget about what Colin Chapman did.[4] Chapman was an innovator, a conceptual designer. He was not a stress engineer, he made cars that were too fragile and then beefed them up.'

Chapman remains a controversial figure for several reasons, and his relationship with drivers says a great deal about how they think, so a little diversion is in order here. I'd been discussing with Mario Andretti the rewards of mastering speed.

Taking one of Chapman's Lotuses right to the edge, and arguably making it do what no other human being could, has got to be fulfilling.

'Well, indeed. That's any car, but the Chapman Lotuses – was I ever concerned about something breaking? You're damn right, and I talked to him plenty of times. I wanted to live. I wanted to live to do another one.

'I was very open about that. I'd seen what happened to Clark and Rindt, which I thought were wasted lives. Chapman played it so close. I refused to sacrifice 2lb or 3lb [car weight] for safety. I refused – I refused – titanium brake pedals. In my car I had to have steel brake pedals and things like that.'

Chapman would have gone for the lighter material straight away.

'He did. They had to make special steel pedals for me because I would not allow titanium and in the end, as fate would have it, that's what paralysed Clay Regazzoni.[5] The titanium brake pedal broke for him at Long Beach.'

You have come across the Atlantic to a fabled genius, Chapman, and you have to be strong enough in your mind to say 'Colin, I'm not having this.'

'Indeed. I think I arrived with Colin from a position of strength in the sense that I am sure he knew that I could do the job, because otherwise we would never have got together. I had supreme confidence because I felt if Colin was coming back – his performances were peaks and valleys but if you were on the upswing and at the point where he was renewed in his excitement you knew you had a damned good chance of becoming World Champion. That's exactly what I felt. But at the same time I also felt he had enough respect for me that he would listen when I was adamant about certain things.'

Pursuing this theme of safety, Watson points out that 'John Barnard made a full carbon fibre chassis car and I was the first person to race that.[6] Believe me, I had severe reservations about it because carbon fibre was a material which at that particular time had never been utilised as a full chassis: parts of chassis, panels here and bits there, but never the whole. I was thinking "this thing's going to go to dust in an accident" but there had been enough accidents in 1981, with Andrea de Cesaris particularly, so I had full faith, but also my faith was in Barnard.

'He's probably never really been acknowledged for his

contribution to safety. He used the material in a manner which was unique. At the time I had the accident I had every faith in the car but I didn't even think it was going to be a big accident. I thought it would glance off the barrier and take a wing or corner off the car and that would be it. The chassis saved my life, or certainly saved me from serious injury. The FIA had begun to show more concern about regulations and fuel lines so a lot of work was going into the safety and design of cars. John took it a step further in his understanding of the material.

'The chassis I had that accident in went back to Hercules[7] in Salt Lake City, Nevada. It was a very valuable part of their motor racing involvement in terms of sales, because they would use it as an illustration to help them convince the military that these lightweight materials were safe to use in military hardware, particularly for helicopters.'

You have spoken about Monza and the dangers. Now compare that with, say, Senna at Suzuka in 1990 when he made a conscious decision to go flat out for the first corner and if he crashed into Alain Prost, too bad.

'Clearly there was revenge for their crash at Suzuka in 1989 and in taking Prost out he was walking away with the World Championship. As a driver, I never thought like that and was never in the position to think like that. Had I been, I suspect I would have been dethroned, as it were. By 1990 Formula 1 was becoming a major global television product whereas in the 1970s and 1980s it was not. Balestre[8] would have just thrown me out had it been me doing it to Keke Rosberg.'

Contrast Senna with what Brian Hart claims: that after a certain age the racing driver does not go to the absolute limit – he stays 12 inches clear of that 'for the wife and kids.'

'Brian might be referring to the days when he was racing in

the 1960s, into the early 1970s, and I don't think it's so true today. When he raced it was very, very much more dangerous. The natural instinct which a driver had for survival was infinitely greater. Today there is not the same necessity.'

You once told me you would never get married while you were an active driver because it wasn't fair.

'What I said was to do with kids. I didn't want to have responsibility, to have to commit myself to a relationship at that age – I wanted to be free. Eddie Irvine has a similar principle, but it's different for different people. What I considered critical was what I had seen happening around me. When a driver is killed he is out of it, his worries have stopped, but what is left for the wife and, in particular, for the kids? The kids don't ask to be brought into this life …'

Mika Häkkinen's wife Erja has just had a son. That's got to be in Mika's mind, hasn't it?

'No, I don't think it's in the mind of drivers today, largely because of the degree to which safety has improved. Everything is infinitely better than it was when I started in the 1970s and you have to say that the possibility of a fatality, in percentage terms, is very low.'

Jonathan Palmer (Tyrrell),
Belgian Grand Prix, Spa, 17 May 1987, lap two. Age: 30.

'I bisected my team-mate's car. I thought I was going to hit him. Kill him, rather. I was coming over the brow to be confronted with the whole track covered in smoke from left to right. I braked as hard as I could and went piling into the smoke. It was on the exit of *Eau Rouge*, doing 150mph. The last I saw of Philippe Streiff [the team-mate] he was ahead of me by about a second and a half.'

The exact positionings are not absolutely clear but it seems that they were running in this order: Streiff, Alex Caffi (Osella), Palmer, Philippe Alliot (Lola).

Streiff 'went down into *Eau Rouge*, up over the brow and disappeared. Second and a half later, up over the brow I go to see nothing but smoke. The whole track was smoke. Clearly Streiff had gone off. That was the only logical thing that could have happened. He'd lost it at the top of the hill but I hadn't seen him lose it. I was hard on the brakes but no way I was going to stop. It would have been 100 metres away: next thing I was on it. I locked up into the smoke and just then I thought – and it was a pretty scary moment – "your team-mate is in there somewhere." And I hit him. My car stopped and I saw his car in two halves. I thought "I've killed him."'

You couldn't get out and run towards him to help because other cars would have been coming along, and they were blind also.

'Yeah. Yellow flags everywhere, the race was stopped. Before long I realised he was fine and I was fine.'

And here is the difference between them and us. Palmer and Streiff returned to the pits while the wreckage was cleared away and you'd think they'd want to go somewhere quiet to recover. No, no. Palmer says that 'what really cheesed me off more than anything else was that it was his turn to have the spare, and he caused the bloody accident! I was extremely hacked off.' Streiff took the re-start and finished ninth but four laps behind the winner, Prost. Much ado about nothing, really, except life and death.

Philippe Streiff (Tyrrell),
Belgian Grand Prix, Spa, 17 May 1987, lap two. Age: 31.
'Second lap so the car was full of fuel, Eau Rouge. I lost control in the left-hander at the top and I don't know why. It was

difficult to find out, because the car was so damaged, whether there had been a rupture of the suspension. The rear of the car hit the barrier on the right and then hit the barrier on the left after it had crossed the track. Then it came to the middle of the track.'

Caffi got through. Palmer was then confronted by the screen of smoke while Alliot, arriving later, was able to stop to try and help.

Does such an accident happen fast or slowly in your mind?

'Very slowly. I can still clearly remember losing control of the car and thinking "ah-ah-ah, I am going to hit the barrier." I remember hitting the barrier at maybe 300kmh and then the other one. I remember the engine coming away and losing the four wheels, I remember coming to rest right in the middle.'

You are sitting there helpless: the others can't see you.

'That's just luck. It can happen the other way: look at Riccardo Paletti at Montreal[9] or more happily Häkkinen in Australia. I didn't see anything because there was too much smoke. I was content that the car had come to a halt, I wasn't hurt and I could get out of it. I did not think of the other cars.'

Palmer said he thought he'd killed you.

'Ah, he said that? I can't remember how fast the cars were going through.'

For a normal person, to have the sort of experience you and Palmer had would give us severe delayed shock but for you it was a question of the spare car.

'I went to the medical centre, the re-start was in half an hour, I had the spare and I had to drive again. I had the check-up, everything OK, so they let me go to the grid. Ken Tyrrell said "the spare car is OK for you?" and I replied "yes." I was calm. And I finished the race. Afterwards I returned to Paris.'

This involved driving his Mercedes at 250kmh (155mph) from Spa to Paris in around two hours and on the Belgian autoroute, towards Valenciennes, he was picked up by radar. He told the police where he'd just been and about the accident and they told him to clear off, which is how he got to Paris to celebrate with Alliot in a nice bar in a nice *arrondissement* – celebrate escaping *Eau Rouge* and a hefty fine in Belgian francs. Streiff was in top form. Only when he got into bed did he notice he'd been bruised.

Julian Bailey (Tyrrell),
Mexican Grand Prix, 28 May 1988, second qualifying. Age: 27.
'You try not to think about the danger. I had a very bad experience when I first started racing. I was 18 and I spent three months in Norwich & Norfolk Hospital so I was quite aware of the danger. I rolled.'

Your fault?

'No. The car in front of me had a mechanical problem. I don't actually remember – this is what people told me. It veered into me as I was going past. It had a radiator stuck up its wheels and as I went past it clipped my car. I went over the barrier into the crowd and, when the car rolled, my arm came out and I was lucky actually to keep it. I broke my leg, I had to have skin grafts and all sorts of things. My elbow was ... well, it broke that way and came out. So, as I say, the danger aspect I learnt about early on.'

How do you get over that?

'I was laying in hospital and I thought to myself "I've only just started really and I know I'm good enough to beat these blokes. This can't be my career over. I've got a lot left to prove, I'll get on with it." I remember the first test I did after coming out of hospital and I was quicker than I had been before. I don't know why. I think that was more determination than anything else.'

But what is the mechanism which allows that? You've a permanent reminder of what can happen via your right arm.

'Yes. I can't carry a suitcase because I can't lock my arm. I always remember the doctor telling me that and it's amazing how many times I've remembered it at airports. He said "the only problem you will have is, because you can't straighten your arm, you can't carry something like a suitcase." And you know what it's like in Formula 1 where you're always travelling, always carrying something.'

Have you ever felt fear in a car?

'… No. I don't think you feel fear, I think you feel … well, you're just looking for a way out. That's the first thing. "How can I get out of this? What's the best option?" I don't know how quickly you think this, but you do. You look. You might be going backwards and you think "if I lift off the brakes now I might be able miss this." You've an instinct to try to escape.

'You have to be very aware of what's around you although there are lots of cases where you have no control. The momentum is going to take it to wherever it's going to go and there's nothing you can do about it.'

What goes through your mind?

'Well, you just think [expletive] and turn away from it. You wait and see how it works out. I remember screaming in the car, and I have only done that once in my life. It was in Mexico in the Tyrrell. You know the Peralta curve?[10] Came down to it, turned in and the car went straight on. I did it overtaking Senna. He was on a slow lap. I thought "I want to make this lap, I've got to get past him." He knew I was there because his finger came out of the cockpit indicating "go round the outside of me." I ran a little bit wide, it was dusty and I went off.

'I remember going over the top thinking "this is going to hurt." I could see it coming and there was nothing I could do about it. It was a head-on and I hit it so [expletive] hard – it was a barrier, a bank. I remember screaming because I thought I'd smash my legs to bits. I went under the cockpit and my head hit the cockpit. When I got up I thought "I'm all right and I can't believe it."

'The next day I couldn't move my head. I had ripped all the muscles in my neck. I remember laying in bed and I had to pick my head up with my hands.'

What sort of speed would you have been doing?

'I don't know, but I tell you it's the one time I remember it coming towards me and thinking ...'

Johnny Herbert (Reynard),
FIA Formula 3000, round 7, Brands Hatch, 21 August 1988. Age: 24.
Herbert led but a crash halted the race on lap 21. He was slow away at the re-start and, as the cars crested the rise behind the paddock to go out into the country, something happened at 150mph. Nobody is sure what but it seems certain that the cars of Herbert and Gregor Foitek touched. They speared off and on again, and the cavalcade behind them crashed and thrashed in wild, terrifying destruction. Nine cars were reduced to something approaching debris. Herbert's feet were so badly mangled that amputation was possible.

'I can remember my crash in terms of when it started, I still have a vision of when the car started to turn. I was very aware.'
Did it happen slowly?
'Pretty much.'

Were you thinking in the mayhem across and back up the track 'he's done this, he's doing that?'

'I wasn't thinking anything like that. The first thing, I had my eyes closed. Bang, crash, the car stopped and I then opened my eyes. I looked down and saw a big hole in the front of the car and all I could see was my knees. Instantly I thought "from the knees down they've gone." I put my head back and I was going [to the medical people] "knock me out, knock me out, knock me out." I didn't want to know. I had no pain. The body has something in it 20 times more powerful than morphine and it can deaden it. It's like a shut-down. As far as I have been told, the body has that. If you cut yourself you feel it and you see it and you get the pain but something on this scale, no. I remember at the hospital it ached, it was horrible and it hurt but at the time I don't remember any pain whatsoever.'

Was there any doubt about continuing racing if you were physically able?

'No. I was going to go back and I was going to be as quick as I had been. There was no worry about going back. Speed didn't scare me. Well, it's not as if it didn't scare me but it was something that I loved to do, I still wanted to achieve the goal I had set myself and I hadn't done that. If I'd tried as hard as I could to get back into it and I had the chance to do it, then great, I'd take that chance and I'd do the best I could. If I simply couldn't do it – I'd lost a foot or the foot wouldn't move or something – at least I'd have tried my best. Then I'd have done something else.'

What would you have done?

'No idea. Peter Collins[11] used to come to the hospital once a week, twice a week and my feet were all bandaged. "How you doing, how you doing?" and I'd say "Yes, I should be up soon. My foot's moving" and it would move just a tiny bit. He must have thought I was an absolute bloody nutcase.'

I think he understood.

'Not like my mum. My mum just didn't understand at all. It frightened her, and that's understandable, frightened her to death that I thought like I did and wanted to do it again.'

Did the feet affect you psychologically over your career?

'Before the crash I thought I was invincible. I could drive any car anywhere in any conditions and I'd win. I believed that in a very, very big way. Afterwards I didn't have that any more. I had the competitive sense, and the will, and the skill but I never had that invincibility. The only guy I see now who's got that is Michael Schumacher. Prost used to have it, more so Ayrton. There's one person every now and again.'

But Schumacher had that crash at Silverstone.

'Michael's never had a crash! It was a big impact and he broke a leg. I wish I'd broken my leg rather than what I had at Brands. A leg heals no problem. He still hasn't had what I would class as a life-threatening crash. The guy who doesn't get any recognition, or as much recognition as he should do, is Mika Häkkinen. Mika had a monumental crash at Adelaide, he was in a coma, he had facial scars from it and he still has it a tiny bit with his mouth.'

Prost once said that you're never quite the same after your first big accident because, whatever they tell you, you know it could happen again.

'Before it, I never thought it would happen to me. And after it I never thought it would happen to me again. It could but I always thought it wouldn't.'

Martin Donnelly (Lotus),
Spanish Grand Prix, Jerez, 28 September 1990, first qualifying.
Age: 27.

'I read a headline about Johnny Herbert at the end of the 2000 season saying he was carried into Formula 1 and he was carried out. Why does he want to go and race Champ cars in the States? He doesn't need the money. You look at the accident Mark Blundell had in Rio. He's lucky he can still walk. Johnny's weakness is already there.'[12]

You honestly thought you weren't going to die in a racing car, that it couldn't happen to you?

'Yes, because I had belief in my own ability. I never got into a car and thought I was going to have an accident.'

But it can be the car going wrong, not you.

'If you are going to get into a car and think "have the mechanics tightened the wheel nuts, have the mechanics checked this or that?" and if you start thinking of accidents, you are not justifying the money the team is spending. If you've got those questions in your mind, you may think you're doing a good job but you are not driving the car ten-tenths.'

How is it possible to live without going down the checklist?

'Because driving is your job just as other people around you have theirs and are employed at different levels. You've got a number one mechanic, a number two mechanic, and a chief mechanic. They've got areas which they work in, which is their job.'

But it's your life.

'It is my life, yes, but hang on. When you sign a contract, there's nobody holding a gun to your head or any driver's head, nobody saying "you have to drive that car." We do it out of free choice. The driver gets fantastic money, no end of PR, everybody wants a piece of them – be it the press, the media, the sponsors, the family, the friends, everyone. And it's fantastic. And did I mention the girls? Yes, there are the dolly birds. But nobody – and I want to make this point – nobody forces a driver to drive a car against his will. We all have our choice and it is a very simple one: getting into the car or not getting into it and stepping away.'

I'd like you to talk about the pleasure of it.

'That's just winning, isn't it? Everybody's ego is as big as the man next door's. It's all about egos. His ego is bigger than mine and mine is bigger than his.'

You have used the analogy that the next race is like an injection for the addict.

'Yeah. If a driver gets into a car and says he's not nervous, then he's going to have an accident. You need to be 110% focused in what you are doing, and the best way I can describe the buzz is if I said to you "right, we're going to go down to a bridge and I'm going to tie a cord round your ankle, make you stand up on that girder and jump off it." You're standing up on that girder and you'll be wetting yourself, your heart will be trying to jump out of your chest. *That* is what it is like driving a Formula 1 car quickly. There is no other experience in life to replace it. The only way you can describe the buzz of driving a Formula 1 car, or any racing car, quickly is in terms of that high bridge and someone saying "if you jump off, you're going to be OK."'

This is a serious question. It has been compared to sex.

'I have to say sorry: driving a Formula 1 car is better than sex.'

Do you want me to rewind the tape and erase that?

'Yes, and it's not for print, either. The interview is now terminated! Driving a car, be it Formula 1 or 3000 or a sports car, if you are driving it quickly and being successful it is the same feeling, yes it is – same no matter what you drive.'

And so we moved towards Jerez and one of the most devastating accidents a human being has survived. I met Donnelly at his workshop at Snetterton and we went to lunch at a pleasant pub, *The Red Lion* at Caston in deepest Norfolk, run by his long-time friend Ed Devlin, who used to run the café frequented by drivers. What developed was a dialogue.

Devlin: We'd been away with Martin for the Spanish Grand Prix weekend.

Donnelly: I was in Portugal the weekend before. You went down in the middle of the week and met up on the Thursday.

Devlin: We went round the track on Thursday morning on mopeds. We had never been to the circuit before, you see, and we had the ladies on the back. The sun was shining on the Friday, we got to the circuit and all was good in the world. We were guests of Lotus Formula 1 team, just tucking into a nice steak and Martin said 'go out the back for qualifying, it's really quick.' We stood out the back and all I remember saying is 'he's coming now, he's on a flyer' because you could see he was quick. 'Here he comes.'

Donnelly: It was qualifying tyres and easy flat.

Devlin: You were building up to maximum speed, you were probably doing 160mph ...

Donnelly: Yeah, 160.

Devlin: Then my God, that was it – the most horrific thing. Something broke on that car. It went down like a sledge. If you imagine seeing your best mate hit a wall and it was just like a car exploding. From lifting off, when he obviously realised something was wrong, until he hit the wall, was 1.9 seconds. It hit the wall, the shockwave coming back through the car met the engine still coming forward and it popped him out like a champagne cork. The whole car exploded. It's a terrible thing to say, but I couldn't see his legs, I thought his legs had been ripped off him. I was so upset I ran to the fence to try and get to him.

Donnelly: Roberto Moreno …

Devlin: … Little Roberto Moreno [driving a Euro Brun] had failed to pre-qualify in the morning and he didn't want to talk immediately after that so I said "I'll speak to you later." During qualifying, he was standing there near me. When Martin crashed he got hold of me and held me – and he's only tiny. He said "he's all right." I said "no, no he's dead." He said "no, he'll be OK." Then I think Derek Warwick came and they let Warwick through the fence because obviously he was Martin's team-mate at Lotus. Then they took Martin to the medical centre and we went back there and the only driver that came apart from Derek Warwick was Senna. He put his arm round me because I knew him from when he was at Snetterton and we used to feed him at the café. He said "he's going to be OK, Ed." When I got outside, Moreno was sat on the wall and I said "he's still alive" and he said "no". He'd said what he'd said to me, when it happened, to calm me down. And then Senna went out and put it on pole.

How do you feel, Martin, about us discussing it in this slightly jovial sort of way? It's your life.

Donnelly: … I don't remember anything about it. When I see pictures of the accident, yes, it's me … it's me with my helmet on. There was an hour and half's warm-up, I'd done my first lap and … I remember vaguely things happening on the Thursday. I don't remember going round on the scooters, I do remember getting in the hire car, a big Citroën, and that's it. So it's easy to talk about it. I remember some press articles and people saying "we read you can't remember the accident and we're qualified hypnotherapists, we can help you remember." I said "well, give me your number and if I can't sleep in my bed at night I'll ring you, but other than that I'm happy not to remember."

So what did you feel when you returned to the circuit courtesy of a magazine called Rambo?

Donnelly: We went to the corner so they could take some pictures but it wasn't me because I don't remember it happening at all. I woke up in hospital. Talk about amnesia. Yes, it's sentimental because it's the place where my career ended as a professional racing driver. You can feel hard about that, hard done by, but compare what I had with what Senna had. Senna was three times World Champion, rode on the crest of the world and had umpteen businesses but he didn't even get to talk about it. What use is it to him now? That drove the final nail in the coffin for me and laid it to rest. Why should I be bitter and twisted because somebody else or something else had taken my livelihood away from me when it wasn't my fault? And I tried for a year and a half to get back to it, going to Willy Dungl for 15 weeks, and physiotherapy and all this, and nothing worked. Hey, but Senna …

You woke up in hospital, what, in Spain?

Donnelly: No, it was in London.

So you're not aware of anything until you're back in London?

Donnelly: I can honestly say to you that I remember nothing until after Christmas of 1990. It was only then that things started to register. Maurice Hamilton,[13] all the boys, came into hospital to see me afterwards, brought me tee-shirts and press packs and all the rest of it from the Jordan car launch. I was sitting there and we were cracking jokes and it was fine, you know. Two days afterwards I said to my ex-wife Diane 'where's all this stuff come from? Where did I get these press packs?' Couldn't remember Maurice being there. Couldn't remember anything about it. I might as well not have been there.

You must have realised when you came round in hospital that you were in a hell of a state.

Donnelly: No, because your mind doesn't work like that. I was still high on drugs. OK, I'd broken bones. Bones heal. The only problem I had was that all my internal organs had gone into shock so my kidneys, lungs, everything inside had just 'switched off.' Sid Watkins[14] knew this. He knew it was important to get me back to London.

Devlin: Prof was God to me that day of the crash. He flew Martin to hospital and I drove in with the girls. We got to Seville, it's huge, and we saw the sign 'hospital' so we parked the car there. It made the Norfolk & Norwich look like a cottage hospital. It was absolutely massive. It took us an hour to find where he was. Sid had gone in with the Spanish doctors. He came out and he said "they want to operate straight away" because they were afraid of massive haemorrhaging in his legs. They went in to operate about six o'clock. Sid had flown back for qualifying but returned and went into that operating theatre at six o'clock. He emerged at one o'clock in the morning: seven hours it was. And he was absolutely magic, came and sat with us, put our minds at rest. He said "I have to compliment the Spanish surgeons on their technique. They are using stuff we are only just starting to use, they've done a brilliant job, straightened his legs out and put on what they call external pins ..."

Donnelly: [deadpan] ... strong fixators ...

Devlin: ... external pins so they could adjust them up to keep tightening the bones together. It looks like scaffolding. At one o'clock, when Sid emerged, he said "the next few days are going to be critical because of the blood clots and the massive swelling in his legs." They allowed us to go in and see him and, in fairness, he had his legs covered, he looked OK, he had a little mark on his chin and a mark on his collar bone. My car had been broken into and I got back to the hotel about half three in the morning.

Donnelly: He's unlucky, too!

Devlin: Next morning Sid came up again in the afternoon, saw us and had a chat. He said "look, I've got to get him back. His body will go into shock and when it goes into shock we won't be able to move him ..."

Donnelly: ... move me ...

Devlin: Sid then made arrangements, flew him back Tuesday and by Thursday his body had gone into shock. Everything packed up, his heart, lungs, the lot. They had him wired up to a brain scan to make sure there was still some brain activity because he was in a coma.

Donnelly: Derek Warwick came in to see me and he collapsed! Diane, the ex-wife, was trying to let him know I was not a pretty sight, all these tubes, blah-blah-blah ...

Devlin: I said 'you are going to be in for a bit of a shock, Derek.' This was a while later. He said 'I don't really like hospitals.' I said 'well, he looks horrific,' and he did. He was wired up and there were the tubes. Derek came in, I caught him and took him out. He said 'I'm sorry, I can't believe it's Martin.'

This accident was the nightmare, the driver become passenger. How do you rationalise that in your mind?

Donnelly: No Formula 1 team owner or mechanic or engineer will give you a guarantee that you are in a car that's not going to break. It's slanderous if they say you won't get hurt and you do.

And you wanted to get back in. Was that something to aim for, something to pull towards?

Donnelly: I ... I think it started the far side of Christmas – March time – when I went to Dungl's. I didn't realise at that stage just how bad my injury, i.e. my leg, was. I thought: Niki Lauda had a tragic accident at the Nürburgring, six weeks later he's back in the car. OK, Gerhard Berger, Imola, burnt hands, only missed a race blah-blah, then he was back in a car again. I get to Willy Dungl's so he can wave his magic wand, heal me, and I'll be back in time for the start of the season.

There was never any doubt in your mind that you wanted to do this again, even though you knew you'd been so lucky it was not true?

Donnelly: No, definitely not.

Devlin: I don't think that even appeared as a question. He never once said it. You and I might find that strange, I know, but drivers, that's in them, that's what they want to do – drive. From the first moment he started speaking he started looking at dates to see which race he was going to be at.

Donnelly: It was 'how many races am I going to miss?'

Devlin: It was 'how long is it going to take before I can start qualifying?'

You have said that you can't really remember your Formula 1 career, which covered 13 Grands Prix. Is that because of the crash?

Donnelly: I think so. People who know me – my mother, for example – have said that my memory and my attention span are a lot worse since the accident. My memory's terrible. There are other things I do remember, but people's names: terrible.

Ayrton went to the scene. Why do you think he did that?

Donnelly: [sighs, no answer]

Devlin: Ayrton had a very analytical mind, he wanted to go and, I would think, convince himself there was not an inherent problem in the track. He wanted to work out in his mind what had happened, why it happened.

Donnelly: Was there a drivers' safety thing involved then?

There wasn't. It re-formed after Ayrton's death.

Donnelly: Um … Sid had to go all round the circuit to get to me. He could see I was asphyxiated. He got tubes into my nose and down my throat to get me oxygen and Ayrton was leaning over his shoulder watching Sid more or less reviving me because if I had been 30 seconds to a minute later I'd be six feet under. They cleared the circuit up, qualifying resumed. Ayrton got in his car, went out and set the fastest lap ever round Jerez even though 20 minutes beforehand he had seen me struggling for my life. He was able to pull his visor down and blank that out of his mind. Then he went to the Press Conference, as he had to do, and then he went to the medical centre to see if I was all right. Sid told me that Ayrton had quizzed him about why he had done things in a certain way, why he had not taken the helmet off first of all, why he had put the tubes up my nose, and Sid was in awe of Ayrton: what he had just done on the track and then that he had to know why Sid had done things in a certain order.

Can you understand how he was able to go through a very traumatic experience, then eradicate that from his mind?

Donnelly: To an extent but not fully. Also there was the second day of qualifying, because my accident was on the Friday. Senna had second qualifying on the Saturday so he didn't have to go out and do that lap.

You spoke to him at the British Grand Prix.

Donnelly: I knew him when he was at Van Diemen. At Silverstone in the early 1990s [Donnelly now a team owner] one of my drivers had a girlfriend who was in awe of Senna. He was her hero. I said 'look, if you want me to, I'll organise for us to go down to McLaren hospitality and we'll meet Ayrton.' She was … oh, gone. So we got to the McLaren motorhome and he was at the far end of the awning doing an interview with some journalists. We sat there and he came over and he sat down and said 'how are you?' He said something along the lines of I was very lucky to be alive, it was good to see me, glad I was there and that he had met me. We had a picture taken of him and the girl together, and he was getting her to laugh. And she was making the noises that young girls do. He and I had a normal conversation and I could tell that he was genuinely pleased I was there.

You had this objective that you were going to drive a Formula 1 car again?

Donnelly: I was convinced I was going to and what gave me determination was this. When I was at Dungl's doing my recuperation and trying to get better – not realising the full extent of the problems – Julian Bailey drove a couple of races alongside Häkkinen at Lotus. Häkkinen was to be my number two. I'd known Julian from a few years back since he'd been my Formula 3 team-mate, and that gave me the impetus to work twice as hard to get off the crutches and back into the car. I got to the stage where Willy Dungl said 'I can do no more for you until you go back to England and have an operation' – my thigh muscle was stuck to my femur. I came back to England, went to the British Grand Prix and held a press conference. The story was 'when can we expect you back?' and I said 'well, I have an operation in three or four days time and I hope to be back in the car after that.' I had the operation and the leg was then bending about 85 degrees. I had a CPM machine – Constant Passive Movement – and it bends your leg for you all the time. You lie on your back and your leg doesn't get stiff.

I went back to the hospital to have the stitches taken out. I said 'look, give me a general anaesthetic' because when you feel pain your muscle tightens and you start to get more pain. These two doctors actually broke the bone on my shin pushing it, because the bone was still so soft. One of the doctors came to my bedroom that night and said 'Martin, I looked after the

West Ham football team, they are professional football players, and I am telling you now in my official capacity that you and Grand Prix racing won't happen. It's finished.' Floods of tears came down my face because I'd been through umpteen operations, I'd been to Dungl's, I'd done physiotherapy every day for over four hours for a year ...

Did you accept it?

Donnelly: No, no, because I believed that even though he was a specialist in his field of medicine and even though he was a far cleverer guy than me, I was determined. Mind over matter. If I worked on it there must be somebody else, somebody in America – the man who looked after the IndyCar drivers – I could go and speak to. He'd dealt with massive accidents, people shattered, and they were back driving racing cars again. Maybe he might have an answer for me. But time passed and you can't sit on your behind dreaming for ever. I gave up my education at Queens' University doing mechanical engineering because my sponsor wanted me to go racing full time. I had no qualifications to fall back on, my best qualification was motor racing. I'd worked with some of the best people in the sport and so I decided to start a racing car team.

Derek Warwick, partnering Donnelly at Jerez.
'I was allowed through onto the track when Martin had his accident. I had finished my laps, come into the pits and I think I was out of the car. All of a sudden there was a deathly hush which always happens when there is a big accident. For some unknown reason the whole circuit gets this vibration. (Brian Hart was in the next pit to Lotus. 'There was that horrible silence, like there was with Pironi at Hockenheim in 1982. Nobody dare say anything because you don't know.') Then it

became obvious that Martin had had an accident. I ran out to the back and straight onto the circuit because I always feel that I can do more than a lot of people around. I was the first one to Martin, or one of the first. I was there long before The Prof [who had to go the whole way round in the medical car].

'All I remember doing was giving him some space. One of the drivers – I don't know whether it was Piquet or who – had already driven his car sideways to protect Martin, so that no car could hit him. By that time there was a lot of press and cameramen and all sorts of people. I remember pushing them away to give Martin room to breathe because by this stage, when I got to him, the guy was dead for sure. It was only The Prof that brought him back to life.'

You honestly thought he was dead?

'Not I thought: he was. But you respond to the situation. You make sure people are away from him, you give him space, you make sure there is a space for The Prof to come through. You do all the things that are unnatural but very natural at the time.'

Were you thinking coldly and clearly?

'I think you do, because the level that we drivers are on you do see things much more clearly than other people and you think more clearly than people ever, ever, ever will. Time slows and you are doing things in slow motion. Not everybody has this slowing down ability, because a lot of people panic, but some do. They understand what's needed in order to make that person survive.'

Is that part of being a driver?

'I think it is: it's the strong mind and vision in which we see things, the clarity during high pressure situations. A good way of looking at it – and this is what makes some Grand Prix drivers better than others, and makes some of them absolute legends, like Schumacher, Prost, Senna – is that they can take more in. They are able to work in their environment easier than the rest of us. The capacity of Ayrton Senna was obviously only 100% but he just needed 95% of that to drive his car at 100% so he always had 5% left to look at the tyres, the strategy, the overtaking – everything you need to be able to do to be exceptional.'

You said you were sure Martin was dead.

'There were several things which I remember all around that time, first when The Prof arrived. Normally The Prof is very gentle and very exact. In this particular instance he was violent. He realised that he'd lost Martin and he realised that he had to work quickly. It was quite brutal the way he made sure that Martin lived. Normally if there's broken bones the crash helmet comes off very, very slowly and you are moved very, very slowly. He did everything within two seconds. He'd taken the helmet off, he'd got his hand down his throat, he'd cleared his airways, he'd straightened the body out, all within two seconds – because he knew the guy was gone. That will stick in my mind for ever. Then when they eventually took Martin away I went back to soothe Diane and make sure she was OK and then I went to the hospital on the circuit with her. There were cuts and bruises on every part of Martin's body and they were still working on him. Diane and I were the only two allowed in there.

'The big decision for me, because the car had broken again – broken at Monza and here – was whether to drive in the race, so there was a lot of soul-searching, a lot of crying, a lot of talking with my family and friends that were there. When I arrived at the circuit on the Sunday morning I had decided not to drive because I thought it was far too dangerous, but when I got to the garage I realised that the guys had worked all night and done a conversion to the front of the car which I was happy with. The pressure on me from me was enormous. It wasn't just not letting the mechanics down – and that was very, very important – but Lotus were going through an extremely troubled time and I believe that had I not driven that day they'd probably have gone bust there and then. It was almost as if there was a weight on my shoulders to carry the team forward. And that's what we did.'

Was there any external pressure on you?

'No, none.'

Derek Warwick (Lotus),
Italian Grand Prix, Monza, 9 September 1990, first lap. Age: 36.

'I was coming round Parabolica [the horseshoe onto the start-finish straight] and I think I was too close to the car in front. I'm not sure but I believe the front left-hand side collapsed on me – the suspension – and the car started to go towards the wall. I had no steering, the car just going straight. The ironical thing about that is there's what some people might believe is a myth: in a very dangerous situation your life flashes before you. I can honestly say it did. In my subconscious there was something going on that made me believe I was going to have a big accident and hurt myself, and there were very, very small visions of my brother, my wife, my children, my mum, just lots of absolute millisecond pictures of people very close to me.

'And of course: I hit the wall, the thing went upside down, ripped off the left side of the car, and this is where I say to you that things slow down for certain people. As I'm going upside down and going along the track and there were sparks and all sorts of things going, I remember exactly what I did. One is lifting my head off the tarmac because I'm thinking "this hurts" – it wore the side of my crash helmet away. The next is turn off the engine. The next is fire. That's all I kept on thinking. I had 220 litres of fuel in the car and I could see the sparks. I was frightened of fire so I turned off the engine, turned off all the pumps and the next thing I did was took off the steering wheel. I knew that as soon as that car had stopped I was out of there.'

This is when you're upside down and your helmet had just stopped being ground down by the track surface.

'Absolutely, at like 100mph or whatever it was, but you understood what was going on in the car and I was getting ready to get out of it.'

You did and you trotted across the track to get in the spare for the re-start.

'Well, you know it's funny. I got out of the car and there were still safety cars and all sorts of things going by me. I turned round and looked and thought "this car is finished, destroyed. Right, OK, they will stop this race so I have 15 minutes to get back into the pits and into the spare car." If I did that I knew I could take up my grid position for the re-start. All this I had sussed within, I don't know, probably 30 seconds of looking at the car. I started to run back to the pits because the accident happened opposite the pit lane entrance. There was an Italian TV camera guy running beside me crying with emotion as I'm running down the pit lane. The crowd were roaring all around me in approval. When I got into the pits all the mechanics had come to the front of the garages and they were clapping. At the time it was just something that was going on but when I look back now it was a pretty special moment.

'I remember getting to my garage. First of all I went into the wrong garage – Arrows – because of years of driving with them, so obviously I wasn't completely aware. Then I went into the Lotus pit and I was screaming at them that I wanted "set 9, set 9" – being my next best tyres so I still understood what were my best tyres, understood what fuel I wanted in the car. I didn't understand why they wanted my helmet, I thought they wanted me not to race and I wouldn't take it off. In fact it was because they'd realised the helmet was finished and they wanted me to wear another one. I got into the car and all the cameramen were there. One of them was focused on my helmet and my face and my eyes, which were open like great big saucers. I didn't blink and I was just staring out of the front of the car. Now that to me was not somebody who understood exactly what he was doing. Deep down I think I should never have been allowed to race.'

That's extraordinary.

'Yes ... yes, it is.'

Were you perfectly calm?

'Yes, until a few months afterwards when I looked at a video of the whole thing ...'

Mark Blundell (PacWest Reynard-Ford),
PPG IndyCar World Series, Rio, 17 March 1996, lap eleven.
Age: 30.

'The racing over there is a lot harder than it is in Formula 1. You can count on the fingers of one hand how many overtaking moves you remember from a whole season in Formula 1, and that's the equivalent to turn one in any IndyCar race. When people ask me "how many cars have you overtaken at 200mph plus?" I go "well, how many days have you got for me to tell you?" You say that to a Formula 1 driver, he puts his hand on his heart and goes "mmmm, once at Monza, once at Hockenheim – oh, there was that one at Spa." That's over the last ten years.

'There is a lot of trust and a lot of respect for each other in whatever you drive at that level, but in the States there's more of a social aspect to it too, because there is a little bit more time. Although that time has been reducing even during the last five years I've been in it, everybody mixes a little bit more and has fun and games, which you never see in Formula 1.'

Does that suit your temperament?

'I have enjoyed that side of it, staying at the track and hanging out with a few of the guys. Might be after qualifying: six of us having a bit of a barbecue and playing a game of football. To me that was great. I can only presume that's how it used to be 20 years ago. But it's not Formula 1. Everything in Formula 1 is at a different level. There is nothing else in motorsport that touches Formula 1.'

Most motorists have never done 110mph in their lives once, and you're now going to have a crash at – what was the speed of that first one in IndyCars?

'200. Head on. No brakes.'

Talk us through.

'Every driver has some big crashes and on the law of averages you are going to. Things go wrong. That crash was the most scary, the one point in my whole career that I thought this is it, I'm going to die. I really did think my number was up. You know, you just know, that if you hit this wall at this speed it is not meant to be.

'It was very early on in the race. I was coming through the field quite strongly and I was directly behind my team-mate Mauricio Gugelmin. I came into the last corner – turn four – and hit the brakes. At that point I was doing 210, well, 209mph.[15] So I hit the brake pedal and the pedal went straight to the bulkhead: full down. Whatever brakes there were had a little bit of an effect, knocked about 10mph off the speed. I was then approaching the wall at 200. My instant reaction: "this is not good. This is bad. You are heading for a concrete wall at 200." At first I tried to position my car to hit Mauricio. I wanted to hit him before I hit the wall and I aimed to hit him. This was just to reduce the speed. I'd much prefer to hit him at this speed than the concrete wall, because he's going to give. I'm going to move him but he's going to take some speed off me.'

How far were you from the wall when you hit the brakes?

'I was at the braking point for turn four which was only 30, 40 yards, maybe a little bit more. You have to see it on video: it's like a bullet. I tried to hit him, took my car across the grass and missed him by ... two inches. He felt the back of his car get loose because he felt the draught as I went by. He could see in his mirrors someone going across him. My immediate thought was "that didn't work."

'I turned the steering wheel because I wanted to spin – friction, trying to knock the speed off. You read about strange things like kids lifting cars because their dad's trapped underneath. I am sure I did that because I bent the steering wheel, which you can't do, but I couldn't get it into a spin. The velocity and the force were way too much.

'Just before I went into the wall I crossed my arms over my chest and thought "this is it, I'm dead." To this day I can remember the noise and the impact. A huge thing. The noise was the most deafening thud you've ever heard, like getting a claw hammer and hitting it on concrete so you get a ring and a bang, then multiplying that sound by a factor of a hundred.'

Were your eyes shut?

'Wide open. It never knocked me out.'

Were you not tempted to shut them?

'No. All I was thinking was "this is it". They estimated that I had a 120G impact and they heard the noise down the pit lane. A photographer behind the wall leapt. The chief designer was nearly physically sick.'

There has to be a moment when you think 'but I'm still alive'.

'That moment was when everything had come to rest. I'd been knocked about and basically I started touching myself. I couldn't feel any sense of touch. I didn't have any sensitivity but I could feel solids. My legs were still there.'

What had happened to the sensitivity?

'It was the impact. The base of my lungs hit my ribs and all the cartilage muscle got ripped off the sternum. My internals got [smacks palms together, doesn't finish sentence]. Your body is just not made to do that. I have the remains of my car in my garage in England. I asked them to give it to me because I wanted it as a kind of reminder, a reality check.'

What do you think when you look at it now?

'"You're probably the luckiest feller around" and, touch wood, I hope to remain like that. You speak to so many people, especially over there, and they say how I got out of it they'll never know.'

If you'd made a mistake and could analyse that, it's a problem solved. But you can never get back in a car without thinking this could happen again. And you'd been at Imola in 1994 ...

'The fact is that it was a mechanical failure. I got out and tried to walk but I crashed to the ground because I had a broken foot and stuff like that [he crawled away on all fours]. My first reaction when they got me on a stretcher was to tell the team that the car had broken because they had to tell Gugelmin. That was on my mind because I was so aware of what had happened, brakes gone. His car did the same thing five laps later and he was lucky he got brake-tested[16] by Emerson Fittipaldi in the middle of the straight. He rode up to the wall and took the speed off that way, otherwise he would have been in a similar situation.

'To me what was tough was that I'd never had a broken bone in my childhood, my motocross career, my racing career. Then I'd gone to America to start racing there, second race I had the biggest crash I'd ever had – nearly killed myself – all because of a failure. I began to think: have I done the right thing? Why has this happened?

'Within seven weeks of that accident I was back in a car again, testing for the first time on a super speedway – a two-mile oval at Michigan. I'd had hardly any testing as it was because my deal had been done so late and I'd gone straight into the 230mph environment. At Michigan I went out, came back in and I said "you've got to give me a break, I must go and think about this." I had to resolve one fact: whether the fire was still burning or just smouldering. I went away and I said to myself "this is still what I want to do." I finished the rest of the day testing and that was that, the end of it.

'I'd spent those seven weeks every day, day in, day out, thinking "yes or no, yes or no?" and the only way to find out was to get back in. It's like falling off a bike when you're a kid. The first thing you must do is get back on. I had never experienced that before, going through the process of sitting there for several weeks before I could get back on the bike. It was all tough to deal with.'

Jarno Trulli (Jordan),
United States Grand Prix, Indianapolis, 24 September 2000, lap 12.
Age: 26.
How important is the driver?

'It's difficult for me to say. If you don't have a good car you don't win races, but sometimes teams say "you don't have a good driver, you don't win races" so it is difficult. What I do think is that the driver is part of a package and it's important to have the right package.'

You have said that you'll be speaking English even with your Italian engineer. Maybe you want to become more English. In 2000 you were more Italian.

'I was very polite! I had several accidents and I think when you have an accident it doesn't matter who caused it. I was very, very quiet until the last one. I had had so many accidents that the last one was just, you know, the one that made all the water come from the glass. It was really impossible. So I regret about the last one in Indianapolis.'

In Belgium, Trulli was hit by Button and complained that Button had been 'too aggressive.' At Monza, Frentzen – slip-streaming the Ferrari of Barrichello – ran into Trulli [this was the accident which killed a marshal]. At Indianapolis, Trulli was in collision with Button again. Trulli, extremely angry, said then: 'Button really is an idiot at the moment. He tried to outbrake me, and hit me. It's not the first time he's done that and I think he needs to cool down.'

Reflecting, Trulli would say: 'That was really hard for me: three consecutive races, three retirements – Monza I didn't even do a lap, Spa it was three laps. But I still think I was polite. I accept that it can happen. In Monza I accepted it but the third time ...'

Eddie Jordan was so dissatisfied by the team's performance in 2000 that he cancelled the Christmas party. Did Trulli go to Jenson Button's instead?

'I have nothing at all against Jenson. I have said it many times, and probably I was one of the few drivers of the opinion last season to accept him. I am positive with him because I think he can do a good job and at the end of the day he did do a very good job. He proved that to other drivers.'

Surprising how magnanimous drivers can be, and surprising how many of them are good men and true, in spite of the hunt.

Juan Pablo Montoya (Williams),
Brazilian Grand Prix, Interlagos, 1 April 2001, lap 38. Age: 25.

The Williams team hadn't won a race since 1997 but now their Colombian driver, Montoya, chased Michael Schumacher at the beginning of the race after the safety car pulled off (Häkkinen had stalled on the grid). Montoya went to the inside at the end of the pit lane straight and forced Schumacher wide in the S after that, then going through. It seemed in that instant that a new generation was announcing itself.

What did you feel when you passed Michael Schumacher in Brazil?

'Initially I was surprised because I was a long way back when we got to the braking. I said to myself "just give it a try" and it worked, it was good. I thought he should be a lot quicker than me and he would try to re-pass fairly soon. I paced myself, a decent pace but I wasn't pushing really hard, I was trying to do clean running and take care of the tyres because we were on one stint: a long way. I didn't want to try to get in front of Michael Schumacher and kill the tyres after ten laps. After I settled in I started pushing harder to see how fast he could run and I started pulling away from him. I couldn't believe it, I went "wow, I am going faster!"'

Montoya, leading, was making a further announcement: 'this is my rightful place, I can handle it easily and I'll be here again and again.' Unfortunately Jos Verstappen (Arrows) ran into the back of him after moving out of the way to let him through.

You must have felt an enormous amount of frustration.

'No, that is racing. It is the same as if there's a technical problem with the car. If this happens, I am not going to kick the car and everybody in the team. That is where you have got to learn to be on top of your game. I was so happy with the job I had done that, although being put out of the race was disappointing, it was another step forward for me. If I had won ten raccs I would be livid if that happened. I would go ballistic, believe me, and going ballistic was something I used to do.

'I remember when I got out of the car I could hear the fans screaming and I lifted my hand and waved to them and they went crazy. I felt really good because I knew I had done a good job. I didn't cock it up, I didn't spoil it and I didn't do anything silly.'

NOTES

1. The Arnoux 'incident' was on the Friday of 1983's deciding race in South Africa. Arnoux's Ferrari stopped on the circuit and Arnoux got out. Marshals, moving it to safety, pushed it over his foot. He returned, sat in the pit with his foot in a bucket of cold water and all I did was ask him how he was. The Mexico 'event' was at Murray Walker's birthday party in a pleasant restaurant in the city centre. Mansell got the squitters and I didn't. Montezuma's revenge!

2. To get a better picture of the crash, I turned up the relevant issue of *Autosport* and discovered that their report (by Nigel Roebuck, an accurate observer) said: 'Then, on lap 20, came real drama. Watson had closed right up on Piquet and [Didier] Pironi [Ferrari], looking set to challenge them. But at the exit of the second Lesmo – flat in fourth, remember – John hooked his outside wheels onto the kerbing.'

   Whether Watson was following Jones or Pironi one autumn day in 1981 is not crucial to humanity's future but it niggled me and I knew it would niggle him because, most unusually, his memory seemed to have betrayed him. We discussed this at a Jordan launch and he was sure it hadn't been a Ferrari. I faxed him the race report and lap chart and we discussed it again. He was puzzled, not convinced and said he'd get a video of the 1981 season to watch the crash.

He did that but, of course, the video was an edited compilation. It does show that Watson wasn't following Jones: might have been Pironi or Piquet. Memory is capricious. 'That's why people go into the witness box and swear on stacks of Bibles that something is true when it isn't.'

All leading drivers carry a mental attribute through their lives: attention to detail. The easy option, just letting it go, is invariably the wrong option. Watson had to know.

3. The death of Peterson at Monza has already been covered.

4. Colin Chapman has been dead these many years and cannot defend himself. His reputation, however, is drawn into two distinct dimensions: the genius who saw simple solutions to complex problems, but a man who took big chances.

5. Clay Regazzoni's Ensign crashed very violently during the United States (West) Grand Prix of 1980 from what was reported as complete brake failure.

6. Carbon fibre: as Watson says 'in the 1970s cars were made out of tin and there was an inadequate understanding of stress analysis.'

7. The Hercules Corporation, based in Salt Lake City, made a carbon fibre mould for McLaren in 1980 and continued to make them.

8. Jean-Marie Balestre, an autocratic Frenchman, was President of FISA, the sporting arm of the governing body, the FIA.

9. Riccardo Paletti (Osella), an Italian, was killed at the start of the 1982 Canadian Grand Prix.

10. This corner, which is known everywhere as Peralta, is a long horseshoe right onto the pit straight. Jo Ramirez of McLaren, a Mexican, once told me: 'When they named it, they called it Peraltada, which means the shape of a pear in Spanish. I started to see that in England everybody called it Peralta but I never got round to mentioning it to people.' It was bumpy and Ayrton Senna crashed and rolled the McLaren here in 1991.

11. Peter Collins, then running the Benetton Formula 1 team, was an active supporter of Herbert.

12. What Herbert said was 'I went into Formula 1 in a wheelchair and I came out of Formula 1 in a wheelchair.' During our interview, Herbert was mildly indignant about people suggesting that he shouldn't go to

America because of the risk of injury to his legs. Last year [2000], he pointed out, Grand Prix cars raced at the dreaded Indianapolis of concrete walls and he found no problem whatever in staying away from them. Hmmm.

13. Hamilton is an Ulsterman and so no doubt feels a kinship with any driver from the Province.

14. Professor Sid Watkins is the most respected figure in Formula 1, full stop. Many are the tales told but my favourite is taken from his book *Triumph and Tragedy in Formula One*. A driver is being transported to hospital and they are putting him onto the helicopter. He calls out plaintively 'don't leave me, Prof!' You cannot say how many lives of brave young men Watkins has saved but Donnelly must be amongst the goodly number. One of the reasons The Prof is so popular is that, despite his seniority in all matters medical, he retains a benign approachability and earthy humour. In the official video review of the 2000 season (Duke Video) he's asked about Coulthard driving so soon after his plane crash – 'must the race driver be mentally very special?' Only The Prof could counter with 'well, they have no brain, so it's very simple …!'

15. This seemingly trivial difference between 210mph and 209 shows the exact dimensions which drivers think in.

16. The 'brake test' is a motor racing expression covering a way of demonstrating displeasure. If one driver has been upset by another he pulls in front and brakes hard, forcing the other to brake hard too.

THE PRICE

Chapter 10

DARKNESS

*'Now when I look back, I find the whole Imola weekend quite
strange. I had a friend with me there, and afterwards he said "it
looked a little bit as if you didn't care that they died." I said "no,
that's wrong." I was completely confused in my head. I didn't
know what to think any more. I didn't know whether
I should start to cry or say "no, no" or what.'*
– Karl Wendlinger

We will come to it, this nightfall that cannot be avoided,
with gentle steps. We will not deify or diminish but only
try to see it as it was and them as they were.

I am standing beside a row of graves in the cemetery of the
Maxglan church to the west of Salzburg. Rudolf Ratzenberger
has brought me here. A winter's sun, low and sharp, makes the
rows of ornate headstones into shadows: they seem like sentries
guarding the past. He points out his son Roland's grave and says
that a Japanese team Roland once drove for sent over rare
granite for the headstone. This makes him proud. He wonders
aloud what transporting a chunk of granite from Japan must
have cost and, in a nuance of a moment, hides his pride. They
airmailed it, you see.

He fusses up and down the path by the graves and the
shadows lengthen as the sun goes down.

Outside the churchyard there's a small, white, curved war
memorial with the names of Salzburgers fallen in the two World

Wars engraved in alphabetical columns. Rudolf traces up and down them until he finds the Ratzenberger he is looking for, an uncle who died in combat.

This uncle had to go: nobody made Roland.

Oh yes, yes, correct, Rudolf Ratzenberger says, but my son lived into his 70s.

I say that Roland was 32 when the Simtek car hit the wall at Imola.

Oh yes, yes, correct, Rudolf Ratzenberger says, but in the motor racing Roland filled every day of his life so full that it would have taken a normal man at least 70 years to do the same. My son, he concludes, had a long and fulfilling life, but not on your timescale.[1]

In 1978 Mario Andretti partnered Ronnie Peterson at Lotus, and when he reached the hospital the day after the Italian Grand Prix at Monza to be told that Peterson had died he said 'unfortunately, motor racing is also this.'

In all your years of it, right from the beginning all the way to here, does the racing driver think in a different way from ordinary people?

'I've been looking at that question and I don't know how to answer it because I've never been anything but a racing driver in my adult life,' Andretti says. 'How do we think? How do people that are very goal-orientated think?'

Almost nobody I know does something that might kill them tomorrow.

'Yes, but we don't look at it that way. I don't think our sport is that dangerous. Probably it used to be. I always looked at it as a calculated risk. Why did I ever expose myself, why was I willing to take that risk, what was the ultimate reason? The incredible satisfaction that we derive from a win, a positive result. I valued that to the point that it justified the risk.

'If it's not that important to you, why would you do it? You can say "OK, it's the money" but that's not what starts you there, that's not what really gets you there in the beginning. There is a rush, something that stimulates you. That's been the case with me for sure. I didn't have to sit in a corner and start motivating myself, that was automatic. I was energised immediately at the thought that in the next day or the next hour I'm going to be in that racing car and doing my thing. As long as you had that electricity, that force, it's a natural thing you keep looking forward to, you don't need to justify it to anyone in any particular way. In my case, I never felt that anything else that I have ever done in my life could have satisfied me like I was satisfied doing my job as a racing driver.'

Is it better than sex?

'Better than sex? It's ... different!'

That's not a flippant question because in many ways the qualifying lap is a kind of sexual experience and maybe sex is the only thing you can equate it to.

'It's something that you'll have to have in the next minute and will only last a minute and seconds, and it's a high that I don't think you can describe unless you experience it. You couldn't ever describe it adequately. You reach to the ultimate of everything and you allow all your senses to participate. Sometimes you get a pay-back and sometimes you don't but if you're lucky enough, if you're intense enough, you should get one and that's why you do that thing.

'I pride myself on being a particularly good qualifier because I have a record to prove it. I know what I am talking about as far as really, really reaching – I have always, always, always gone faster in qualifying than I had ever done during any practice or anything else. There are drivers that are quick in practice and cannot duplicate it and for some reason or other, looking at my record, I was always quicker qualifying even to the point that I surprised myself sometimes. Yes, because I never would know where it would go, where it would lead: not that I was going in there hell for bent and what will come out will come out – I always tried to stay in control. But I think I was pressing that envelope to the point that only that moment could take me to.'

In your mind you must have known you were doing that.

'My whole sight was for that, I always looked forward to that. Time and again I was deriving results from it, it was not an elusive thing.'

But it's got to be beyond results, hasn't it? It's got to be the ultimate fulfilment of being alive.

'But I never felt that I was defying death.'

Jonathan Palmer explains how he came to terms with the danger. 'It's not really a problem. You just have to compartmentalise things very firmly and I suppose as a character I'm quite good at doing just that. If I have a problem in a certain area I will be able to blank it off and deal with that another time. I think you have to do it on that basis when these things happen. You look at it and you think "what do we learn from that? What should happen?" Then it's like a little room in the house: you brick it up and you have to do that.

'I suppose of my era there weren't many of us who came through and didn't know someone who got killed. We tended to know them: Winkelhock, Bellof, Jo Gartner at Le Mans[2], so it was a part of the environment you grew up in. Today's drivers don't really have that so much. The cars are so much safer now that it's very rare anybody actually gets hurt.'

That rarity was broken, of course, at the 1994 San Marino

Grand Prix although, as was constantly recited like an incant-ation, no driver had died in a Formula 1 accident since 1986 (Elio de Angelis, testing at Paul Ricard) and no driver had died in a race since 1982 (Riccardo Paletti, Canadian Grand Prix).

Mark Blundell was at Imola driving a Tyrrell.

You must have gone past Senna's accident.

'… Being a racing driver, it's a choice. There is nobody behind me with a stick, hitting me over the top of the head and saying "you've got to get in the car." It's my desire to drive it. Forget the money, forget everything else, it's my choice to do it, and it's the other guys' choice as well. When I get to the point where I don't want to do it, that's it, that's done.'

In the same way with PacWest, if you'd said you were walking away no power on earth could have made you get back in.

'Nope. Nothing at all.'

What does the driving give you that is not available in any other way? A plumber does not say 'yes, some of my friends have been killed, one or two are maimed and in wheelchairs, but I still feel so strongly about it that I have got to be a plumber.'

'Nobody likes to see anybody else hurt or killed but it is an associated risk with what we're in. That may be where the gladia-torial element comes in – and in some way when you see people react, especially drivers, sometimes you could say they're a bit cold, but it's the switch, the ability to switch it off.'

Contrast that with the joy and fulfilment when you get the lap right at, say, Spa.

'Like any track, it's the reward from you, the car and the track and nobody else but you. That's the great thing I love about racing. When I was a kid I played team sports like football, rugby, and I'd always get so frustrated with the other players if they didn't do what I wanted to do. Although I am totally dependent on mechanics and engineers and the team, come the moment of the proving, it's on my shoulders. So when you get a lap right it's an immense personal reward. You know everything has come together and you've got a very accurate reflection of it: you've just done a one minute 05 or whatever, and it puts you there on the grid. More than that, everybody knows what that time in that car in that weather really means: the guy has just brought that car round there in one 05 – impressive. I guess you thrive on that. Everybody has an ego.'

Let's narrow this to Eau Rouge.[3] You gun the car down into it, it's steeper than it looks and then you come over the top. Do you say to yourself 'that was great'?

'You do, but that buzz is not immediate because your concentration level and focus is on putting the whole lap together. Maybe you start to reflect on it when you are getting back to the pits or you are in the pit but I don't register the instant reward because the lap is not over. I'm not finished, I'm still working, I'm still doing my job. That's the feel. Some people may have enough mental capacity to come out of a corner and reflect on it there and then. I don't. When I've finished the run – tyres gone, whatever – then I can say "well, I ballsed up on that, if only I'd not done that." There's a perfect round of golf out there and nobody's ever going to play it but you strive for it every time although golf is a little bit different in that each shot is independent whereas ours is a continuous flow, corner after corner.'

Have you ever driven beyond your limit?

'Yes, and I have driven beyond the car's limit on occasions. Sometimes I got away with it, sometimes I got bitten. I think, again, that's all about levels and experiences and knowledge and understanding. The classic for me was with Ligier at Silverstone in 1993 when it was wet [in the untimed Friday morning session]. You look at those laps.[4] I was all pumped up, British driver, British Grand Prix. I was always competitive in the rain, always had been and was then. I was the fastest guy. I went quicker and quicker and quicker, and I got more confidence from it but I lost sight of the car's limits and my limits in the conditions. I stuck the thing in the bridge coming through the old Abbey. I was trying to take the kink flat in the wet. We can all joke about it now, but if you looked at my speed trap figures, my speeds in the wet were not far off what some guys were doing in the dry – which was crazy.'

Was that a conscious decision or was it something which built up and took you over?

'A little bit of both. It built up because I was on a roll and you are seeing "P1" in the session on your lap board and I got overwhelmed by it. The control factor went and I lost that little edge of understanding my limits. That could have been any driver. You can even examine what I did and say that maybe it was a lack of concentration, or that maybe you were too complacent with the whole situation because it was all going your way. I went beyond my limit and beyond what was available to me as well, and then I got woken up ... quickly. I slapped the guard rail. You think "let me analyse that, let me find out what happened: well, you went over the limit and you've just paid for it." What I'm happy about is that I can understand this. What is the limit? The old micro-processor in your brain tells you.'

You were partnering Mika Häkkinen when he had his crash in Adelaide.[5]

'It's the inbuilt switch again but it's ever so difficult to activate it when you're physically and mentally involved in the environment where it has happened. If it's happened outside that environment, outside that little hub of people you are with all year round, that's different. But when you have maybe been chin-chatting to him half an hour before, it hits home. In the case of Mika, you had no understanding of what state he was in and there were also some issues of what went wrong. That meant you were having to carry that as well and it was tough to cope with.'

Was there any doubt in your mind that you'd race?

'There was some discussion and I was asked whether I wanted to. I said I did. We were pretty certain it was a puncture and my feeling was that if it'd been Mika, and the situation was reversed, he'd have raced because that's what's built in us. We are all aware of the dangers, we all understand, we all know it's part of the job even if it's not the part you want to be involved with.'

Nigel Mansell made an unfortunate return to Grand Prix racing with McLaren in 1995 and withdrew after the Spanish Grand Prix in May. Blundell came in and completed the season before going to IndyCar racing.

'I'd gone back to McLaren to test again [after spending 1994 at Tyrrell] so was already in the process of the Formula 1 driver going back to test for a big team rather than race with a small team. I was ahead of the game at that point because in effect it immediately turned into a Grand Prix drive. And I'll tell you something. If I hadn't had a couple of failures mechanically I would have finished ahead of Häkkinen in the championship. I brought home the bacon for them a number of times in difficult circumstances and situations.'

How did you feel getting into a car that Mansell wasn't happy with?

'I didn't have an issue with it. To me it was a golden opportunity and the circumstances and the politics behind it were just something that I could shut myself off from. I didn't worry.'

I'm thinking about your body, the fit in the cockpit.

'Hmmm … That's a risk. You know that's a risk. On the back of the ticket when you walk into a Grand Prix circuit it says THIS IS DANGEROUS. A driver takes that on board. If you are going to worry about that side of it I suggest you get out. There's a separation, an in-built trust of those guys working on the car. They are at the top of their professions and you have to believe that what they put together functions.

'The danger is always at the back of your mind, sitting there but under control.'

Do you get nervous in life generally?

'In some areas, yes. I think everybody gets nervous, especially in anything sport related.'

Would you be more nervous doing a live TV interview than driving a race?

'Probably not now because as the years go on, and your experience goes on, you start to understand how to take nervous energy – or adrenalin rush – and turn it from a negative into a positive. Imagine you're experiencing a physical feeling because something is happening: you're having a fight, say. You get the adrenalin rush, you get a high, an instant low afterwards and that hurts the nervous system. What you want to do is accommodate it by smoothing it out. You don't get rid of it, you thrive on it. Imagine now we're talking about a race. At the start you've got all those nerves pent up to do the first lap. You're draining with energy and mental awareness so you want to try and flatten this curve out.

'I've learnt to do it. I'm not saying I don't get nervous. I do. Anybody who says they don't is a liar, but I think you can control it more. That's with sport in general. Imagine golf and a big putt. You see the young guy coming up, you see the pressure going on him and he folds. The old, experienced guy says "ah, in it goes." He's still nervous but he's been through it and he's learned.'

Johnny Herbert was at Imola in 1994, driving a Lotus.

How do you cope?

'Well, the only way I coped with it was I knew the danger, Ayrton knew the danger, and that helped.'

But you went past it.

'I know, but … you know the danger is there. At the time we didn't know [the extent of Senna's crash], we found out afterwards.'

At six o'clock that night. How do you cope with it then?

'Only that same thought: I know the risk is there and it could happen to me. I am comfortable with that. It was a horrible thing that happened the day before and Roland was in his very early days in Formula 1 – he was a great guy as well, like Ayrton was – but that risk was always there.'

You didn't have any problem getting back in the car?

'No. I know Gerhard [Berger] said that was it, finish, but I just couldn't duck it because of that. In some respects it was flukey – what happened to Roland and the way it happened, and then Ayrton.'

Karl Wendlinger was at Imola, driving a Sauber.

Do you think racing drivers are different from other people?

'No, I think professional sportsmen are different. If you are a downhill ski racer or a first division footballer or a Formula 1 driver – or in other categories – all these people in their minds and in their thinking, in their living, they are different from other people.'

Thinking about somebody like the Austrian ski racer Franz Klammer[6]: his brother was paralysed and in a wheelchair so Franz knew what could happen but it didn't stop him.

'He didn't stop, no.'

And you know what can happen.

'I had a bad accident and a bad injury and I didn't stop. There was not even once the question of stopping. The only question was when I could start again. You have so much confidence in yourself. Take Klammer: his brother is in a wheelchair but I think Franz never thought about it or connected it to himself because he believed he was the best and nothing could happen to him.

'As a racing driver I am on the edge, but for everybody the edge is different. My limit is different to Schumacher's limit and to Frentzen's limit and to Olivier Beretta – who was my team-mate for the last two years [in the FIA GT Championship]. So, which limit is the highest? I believe my limit is the limit – it's impossible to go faster and do anything better, but other drivers have a different way of racing at the limit.'

What happens when you believe you are the best and you meet someone like Schumacher and you understand you are not the best? Can you accept that?

'When somebody is faster I can accept this because I always have to decide why. If he's in a different car maybe the car's faster. If he's in the same car, like in long distance races, and he's faster I accept it only for a short period because I want to change this.'

In 1994 we go Brazil, then Japan, then Imola.

'The Imola circuit I like very much. I was quite confident to be competitive because in testing I was faster than Heinz-Harald. First qualifying on Friday I couldn't fix my car from the handling side but that was not a problem because Saturday morning the car was good. Saturday afternoon we didn't drive because of the accident to Roland Ratzenberger.'

Did you know him?

'A little bit because, how can I say it, in age we were quite different – he was older – and we never raced together in any category, but of course he was Austrian and we talked to each other. "How are you?" and so on.'

How did you take his crash?

'Now when I look back I find the whole Imola weekend quite strange. I had a friend with me there, and my father was there on the Saturday. Afterwards my friend said to me "it looked a little bit as if you didn't care that they died, the both of them." I said "no, that's wrong." I was completely confused in my head. I didn't know what to think any more. I didn't know whether I should start to cry or say "no, no," or what.

'The confusion I had in my head was because of these accidents but I showed it to people in a strange way. For example, I could not show my feelings about this to anybody. Other drivers were crying when they heard about Senna, and people were crying, and were in a bad mood. I was also in a bad mood but I could not show this to anybody. From the outside I looked as if I had everything in hand but inside my brain and my body the feelings were so strong that I didn't feel I could show them.'

Then you've got two weeks.

'I went testing on the Tuesday after Imola. Originally it was planned to test in Imola but of course not any more so we went to Paul Ricard. Heinz-Harald said he could not because of the accident and I said "oh, no problem." This again looked to other people like I didn't care about accidents or anything but it wasn't like that. I said I could test because right after the Imola weekend I decided I would continue motor racing, and if I was to continue I also had to go testing, so if the test is two days after Imola or two weeks after Imola doesn't matter for me.'

Was it a difficult decision to continue?

'For me there was never any question. I went to Ricard, two days, and then we came back to Monaco for the Grand Prix. I was living in Monaco then. I remember the Wednesday in the paddock. I even remember that we had a photo shoot for a sponsor. Normally on the last day before the race weekend begins you have meetings with the whole technical staff. You speak to your race engineer. "What do you think about this, what do you think about that?" I can't remember anything from it, not one single meeting or whatever happened. The last thing I know is watching television the evening before. Thursday morning I had the accident.'

There is a way that the brain automatically closes to protect you.

'This is what the doctor – or the neurological professor – in Innsbruck, where I was after Nice, explained to me. This is the self-protection mechanism of the body and he said normally the memories would never come back because they are not there. For me, the whole day is gone – not even breakfast on the Thursday morning – and, even on the day before, anything which has something to do with the racing I can't remember either. For example, from 1993 I know exactly where the motorhome was parked, I know where the car was in the pit, I know everything. From 1994 I don't even know where the motorhome was.'

When did you realise how bad the crash had been?

'... There was the time in Nice, the coma and everything, then they woke me up and I was there with open eyes for I think five days. I don't know anything about it because I was still on the drugs. They decided to wake me up the first time after six days and then they thought it was too early. Then they decided to wake me up the second time after ten or twelve days and this was a very difficult time again. They found again it was too early and also – I didn't ask exactly afterwards but they told me a little bit about it – the problem was that one part of the brain is swollen and this part tried to move when they woke me. If it moves a little bit too far to the back you're dead, huh? Then it was very difficult again for one or two days. Then we had to wait again and they saw it improved and after 19 days they woke me up the third time.

'It worked, but of course I can't remember anything of this because I was lying in the bed looking at the wall for 24 hours a day, or sleeping, or I didn't know who I was, who my parents were, what my name was. I was in a bad but normal condition for people with such an injury.

'They told my parents "OK, now it's this and this and this, and it will be more and more and he becomes normal again." Then I was taken to Innsbruck and there I can't remember the first ten days. I can't even remember going to Innsbruck. I was woken in the plane and I was already speaking normally to my girlfriend, now my wife. She was in the medical plane with me and I was making jokes with her, but I remember nothing. There was not one single day which I remember: it was part by part, slowly, slowly. I do remember everything was fine. No problem. What is the drama, huh? I didn't understand the drama.

'My parents and my girlfriend got the word from the doctors that slowly but surely they had to explain to me what had happened. "You had a bad accident in a car, but no problem, no problem." Then I'd say "what accident?" Then I said to them "OK" and they asked "should we show you pictures from the newspapers?" I said "yes, bring everything." I had no pain and when I was woken I never had a headache or anything like that. I just recognised that I could not stand up alone, because I had been laying so long that I had muscle wastage. Also the balance was not there and I'd fall down, so in the beginning they had to put me in a wheelchair in the hospital.

'I realised that it must have been very bad but, and here I was very lucky, every day was a step forward. Every day I was less tired, every day I was speaking more, every day I was joking more with my friends. Every day I ate more, every day I had these therapy programmes for one hour and every day it was easier and better. I never had to fight against it being good one day and not so good the next. It was easy.'

What did you say when they showed you the photographs?

'Well, nothing, just "why did this happen?" and they said "we don't know, nobody knows." The last three weeks in the hospital I could go home at the weekends. They showed me a videotape of the accident but from that you cannot see why it started.'

It was a bad accident but not spectacular, in the sense that accidents can be.

'The thing is that although I was lucky to survive, if the angle of impact had been different nothing would have happened. I'd have got out and used the spare car in the afternoon.'

You now have to ask yourself the question you asked after Imola: am I going to continue?

'There was not even a question about it because the doctors said to my people "don't talk to him about whether he wants to continue or not" and I said "[expletive], I need to go out there on the track." Gerhard Berger brought this guy – the boss of the hospital in Innsbruck – down to Nice with his plane. This guy looked at the scanner pictures and said to my people "I tell you, when we can start the therapy we can start the recovery. He's out of physical condition: minimum one year before he can live his own life again without help. I don't want to be too optimistic so I'm telling you the truth." After six or seven weeks in Innsbruck he said "OK, now everything is fine I can release you!"

'In September I did the first test in Formula 1 – already, so everything was very fast, a lot faster than expected. Afterwards I thought my strong head – no, my goal to achieve – was important: to get me out of the hospital as fast as possible, to get myself fit again as fast as possible, to drive a Formula 1 car again. This helped a lot. It was in my mind: I want this. The doctor said a lot of people in hospital wait and see how it continues: if it's two weeks earlier than expected or two weeks later doesn't matter. It mattered to me.'

So now you get back in the car.

'Paul Ricard. I felt easy and happy about it. I was happy to start the engine again and go out along the pit lane, never any fear, no, no, nothing. I was just happy to be driving the car again, like normal, like I'd got out of the car the day before and I was getting in again. It went a little bit like this: I did about ten laps in the dry and it started to rain. I finished the day driving in the rain and everything was fine, no question. Then they said to me "OK, now you must do a test in Barcelona in a couple of weeks."

'We went there and it was impossible for me to drive because my physical condition was not yet good enough. The Sauber car was very bad over bumps and Barcelona is not smooth – a lot of waves. I had extreme pains in my neck and this was also from the impact of the accident. When you bend your neck too much in an accident you pull the muscles and they were still too weak.

'I went back to Willy Dungl in Austria to make more therapy to cure the problem and then they said "OK, now the next test is at the beginning of December at Barcelona. If you want to have the chance of a contract for 1995 you have to be fast there." I said "yes, but what do you mean by fast? I haven't really driven for several months." They said "Frentzen will drive the same car as you: morning Frentzen, afternoon you, the next day the opposite and you have to do the same time as Frentzen. Then maybe you'll get the contract." I said "maybe that's impossible because he's driving all the year long." I decided to try and enjoy it: if it works it works and if it doesn't it doesn't. This made me so strong at this test and I was [expletive] fast. I did nearly the same times as Frentzen. I got the contract and in 1995 nothing worked again. Mentally-wise I was very bad. I had no concentration, I had no fun anymore in driving racing cars and I was in a bad position. I asked the doctor in Innsbruck who'd taken care of me and he said it was a normal reaction to the sort of brain injury I'd had. It takes a while to become stable and you do have good days and bad days, these ups and downs. In 1995 I could not bring the performance to Formula 1 any more.'

But you accepted that.

'I always made one excuse because against Heinz-Harald I had a disadvantage. I was carrying about 20 kilos more than he was, so the car was too heavy. They put all the light parts on the number 1 car and I was around 15 kilos heavier by body weight against Heinz-Harald, so it amounted to about 20 kilos, and you know 20 kilos in these modern times is a lot. Of course it was not the only reason but if I had been at the same weight level then maybe the difference would have been only half a second to one second in qualifying and nobody would have said "ah, Wendlinger is not able to drive Formula 1 any more." And maybe after a few races I could fight against him again or maybe come close to him again. I have always said my mental condition was not good, and together with the weight this made the difference. I accepted it was finished.'

Did you sit down with your wife and say 'let's talk about this?'

'No. It was not necessary. They said to me after Barcelona "OK, you are now the test driver and by testing you can find your performance and maybe come back to the team again." This was in May. The first day of testing I did in July at Nogaro in France and the second I did two days of testing in Mugello in October and honestly when I saw that I could not do the times in the testing I accepted already that this would be the finish of Formula 1 for me. The Mugello test was very good, I was very fast, consistently fast, and they told me "OK, come to Suzuka." I was to drive the last two races, but Suzuka was not good. I had the weight disadvantage, I had to drive against Heinz-Harald who'd been a Formula 3000 driver in Japan and together this made it bad again. Adelaide in the morning session I had an accident, I crashed the wall and then I knew it was finished.'

Were you able to do that – walk away?

'Yep. I didn't care about it any more because, believe me, the 1995 season was not very easy. There were not only my problems but there was a lot of pressure and slowly but surely I got the impression that the team didn't care. I never looked back at Formula 1 with tears in my eyes. Not at all. To me it's a normal way of life. It happens, for sure there is a reason and you have to accept that.'

After the race at Adelaide did you tell them?

'The whole weekend was strange. I had the impact Friday morning, I did the qualifying on Friday afternoon. The thing was, Sauber told me half an hour before I went in the car Sunday lunchtime after the warm-up. I was sitting with my wife putting my things on and he said to me "I have to tell you one thing, we will not give you any contract for next year."'

Sauber also wondered about how much pain Wendlinger was in, because it might cause trouble with the FIA. Wendlinger drove eight laps and retired – 'eight laps with this pain that I had to cry in the car, going over all these bumps and so on, and I came in and that was it. I changed my clothes and left. I went back to my hotel.'

Dinner in the evening. 'This was the final "konsequenz" and I did not care about finishing my Formula 1 career.'

Your final thought?

'I look back now on the positive moments ... huh?'

Philippe Streiff was at Imola and we will come to that soon enough. Born near Grenoble, Streiff became passionate about motorsport early and reached Grand Prix racing in 1984, driving in sequence for Renault, Ligier, Tyrrell and in 1988 the small French team AGS. Streiff intended to help AGS become a big team. He was testing at the Jacarepagua circuit, Rio, in March 1989 and, as it seems, clipped a kerb at high speed. The AGS, pitched into the air, hit a barrier upside down and hard enough to tear off the rollover bar. The car was brutalised and so was Streiff, although nobody knew that immediately. If they had, if he'd been taken to hospital in a special stretcher for back injuries, if he'd been operated on earlier ...

We are sitting in the lounge of his house in the Parisian suburb of Reuil-Malmaison and his assistant Gilles is feeding him. Streiff, in a wheelchair, remains a handsome man, the torso broad and strong but his arms become slender and his hands virtual flippers. His legs are lifeless.

A television documentary had been made about his life and Streiff wanted me to watch a video of it. His secretary Chantal put the tape into the player and he instructed me how to work the remote control. There he was, fit and smiling as he lowered his legs into a cockpit – 'Tyrrell,' he says. This cuts to amateurish footage, shot from the distance, of the AGS going along a straight at Jacarepagua and this in turn cuts to even grainier footage of the AGS exploding against the barrier.

He made me rewind it twice to see it more clearly. Watching it did not seem to touch him at all. I asked him what he thought.

'It's a tape of my career which lasts 20 minutes.'

Yes, but what are you thinking?

'I'm 45 now, I'm a long way away from my career as a Formula 1 driver.'

What he means is that his first life ended at Jacarepagua and his second life (as he calls it) began some three years later when Ayrton Senna said 'I like your crazy idea about a karting championship.' (Actually, Streiff alters the number of lives he's lived to three: before the accident, the agony of recovery – 'the worst of them' – and the life he leads now.)

In between, he collaborated with a book on his life story[7] although such was his inner turmoil that he is not sure about the book now. He wonders aloud, for example, about the final chapter 'Croire en l'Avenir' [Believe in the future] because he doesn't think he did believe in the future then. The book is so honest that twice I was in tears. Some extracts:

'For myself, I find that the accident is the worst thing that can happen to a human being.'

He was flown from Brazil to a hospital in Paris and there his two young sons came to see him.

'They looked at me with large, serious eyes. I was very moved. We exchanged a few tender and soothing words ... in leaving, they asked "tell us, mother, why doesn't father take us in his arms like he used to?" The question was terrible, unforeseeable and touching. She explained that it was necessary to wait a little longer but she promised them that I loved them as I had done before.'

In his despair he wrote of suicide although, of course, he was physically incapable of that and wrote of the hours in hospital.

'What good was it being cared for? What good all this medical décor all round me – these machines keeping me alive, these nurses, these doctors, these specialists? Yes, what good all of it? I understood I was in an artificial condition. Illusory. The whole world was tricking me but I, at least, wasn't tricking myself. That was forbidden to me.'

In his despair he felt such guilt that he wondered if his family would have been more fortunate if he'd died at Jacarepagua.

'At least it would have been over in one blow and I wouldn't cause anyone any more trouble. I strongly held it against myself that I had put my family in peril, principally Renée [his wife] and our two sons, in the name of my passion for racing and all the advantages I'd enjoyed from it.'

The full extent to which Streiff has recovered mentally emerged during my interview in 2001.

If your elder son wants to drive ...?

'I let him drive. He has seen me with my handicap and if he still wants to do it that is his decision.'

Streiff confessed that certain moments had been almost unbearably poignant, even as he began to reassemble his mind and recover. For example, on one son's sixth birthday they were driven to a toy shop in a taxi but he – Streiff – was unable to get out so the boy went in alone. He chose his present and asked the sales assistant if he could take it out to show his dad, and show him the price, and would come back with dad's credit card. 'For me it was a big problem to be unable to do anything. Now it's different. I go everywhere in my wheelchair.'

The second life began when Streiff organised a celebrity karting event at Bercy, Paris, in late 1993, inviting Prost and Senna to compete. Prost said yes and Elf sponsored it. Both, of course, karted in their youth but at this stage had barely exchanged even a grunt for years. Their enmity ran that deep.

Streiff went to the Italian Grand Prix at Monza, put it to Senna and Senna said yes. However, complications subsequently arose. Senna was leaving McLaren for Williams so which sponsors' livery and logos could, or should, he wear at Bercy? Worse, some few days before the event Senna was due in Paris for a FIA hearing (over his rumpus with Irvine in Australia), making it unlikely he'd stay for the event or go back to Brazil and then return to Paris for it.

'My life began again 19 December 1993. Senna returned it to me with the karting.'

They became friends and Streiff was at Imola with him in

1994. 'I was with him the Thursday before when he went to Padova to present his first business project [a sophisticated bicycle] under his logo 'Driven to Perfection'. I was with Ayrton one hour before his death. Senna and Barrichello had a little lunch at 11.30 at the Williams motorhome and I was there. Senna tried not to race on the Sunday, he tried to stop the weekend. Not possible. Look at his face one hour before getting in the car [shows photo of Senna looking emptied]. Destroyed, I would say. His thoughts were not there but somewhere else. A premonition?

'I saw the accident. I was in the Larrousse pit. I saw Ayrton crash and it was all so long and I saw the ambulance coming back. I saw Erik Comas [the Larrousse driver] come back with tears in his eyes because he'd seen Ayrton dead or very, very seriously hurt. He said to Gerard Larrousse "I will not start again" and he did not. You know what I did? I said to my nurse and my assistant "we are going back to Paris." Eight hours in the car and I learnt from the radio – we were between Milan and Turin – that he was dead.'

What did you feel then about your passion?

'I said "it's crazy to do such a thing as motor racing" but it didn't kill the passion. However for a month afterwards I couldn't eat properly and I had to go to hospital. I had skin problems, many other problems because of Ayrton's death.'

Streiff pauses. 'Twelve years after my accident people still don't understand why I am around Formula 1 and involved in karting.' (He and Ecclestone are organising a world series and Streiff runs a circuit in Paris where kids as young as six learn to drive. Maybe only 1% will have racing careers, he says, but they'll all have learnt such control that they'll know what to do later on in saloon cars in dangerous situations.)

Why are you still in it?

'I have the passion.'

At the 2001 Australian Grand Prix a marshal, Graham Beveridge, died when a wheel hit him. Jacques Villeneuve's BAR had collided with Ralf Schumacher's Williams – the wheel came from the BAR. It was a freak accident because, as one report said, the wheel was 38cm (14.9in) wide and it went through a 40cm (15.7in) hole in the safety fence. The fact that a marshal had been killed during the Italian Grand Prix the previous September heightened the sense that, almost whatever precautions anyone took, a rogue sequence of events could produce the ultimate tragedy.

The aftermath of Beveridge's death caused a great deal of soul searching in the Formula 1 community. However, before the next race – Malaysia, two weeks later – Villeneuve told Bob McKenzie of the London *Daily Express*: 'It was a freak accident. I am very sad the marshal was killed but it is like walking down a street and a pot falls on your head. Getting back into a car will not be a problem. I have raced for too many years, I have crashed before. It is part of what I do. I still have a good feeling from driving. If I did not I would have stopped a while ago. I started racing because I like being on the edge. If that feeling died I would not be racing for long after that.'

It is this slightly fatalistic philosophy which confounds outsiders: living their lives as cocooned as possible from danger, they cannot comprehend how intelligent people need risk despite seeing what its consequences can be.

Throughout the history of motor racing there has been a drive for increased safety. Jackie Stewart began the modern campaign after he crashed at Spa in 1966, was taken to a farmyard barn and then, on the way to hospital, the ambulance got lost. Many years later the farmer explained that each year he invited friends to watch the race – the farmhouse butted on to the road, which was the old circuit. He and his guests watched the first few laps from inside the house because, as he said, when the cars were still bunched it was very dangerous even for spectators. Only when the cars had thinned into a procession did his party venture outside.

John Watson's career began in 1973, the year that Stewart's ended. Despite Stewart's efforts, motor racing remained dangerous in a way which would be completely unacceptable today. (Watson had been watching *Equinox*, a British television programme about drivers, which said that in the early 1970s a racing driver had a life expectancy of less than that of an RAF fighter pilot in the Battle of Britain. He murmurs to himself 'bloody hell!')

I recently heard Stewart saying that he was known – I can't remember if he used the phrase – as the undertaker. When a driver was killed he would go to their room to pack all their stuff and he knew how to get the bodies back home.

'He would have learned that from Louis Stanley, I suspect.'[8]

Yet Stewart still kept getting back in the car.

'Sure,' Watson said. 'I never had the unfortunate task of going to a driver's room and doing the packing up. Part of this was done because in some cases – and I know one driver who sadly lost his life – the driver wasn't alone in his room. There was a girlfriend with him and he was married. That brought an element of sensitivity: you didn't want the poor wife having to come and do it. I didn't know that Jackie did it particularly, although he had a great sense of responsibility and duty. I think a lot of that would have been because he saw things through

Louis Stanley's eyes. As much as Stanley was mocked at times – he was a slightly Dickensian figure and an easy target – he was also responsible for a great deal of the GPDA[9] medical unit and all those things.'

Stewart was insulted when he started on safety. As if being burnt to death or mangled is somehow macho.

'Well, let me put it this way. It's a bit like the bullfighter syndrome. If you go into an arena with a bull it's a fairly loaded kind of context. This thing weighs almost 50 times more than you do, is extremely agile and very quick on its feet. This thing's got two massive horns. All you've got is a cape and a small sword. If you get hurt or killed you've lost because you made a mistake or you misinterpreted something – and racing was the same. There was an implied risk of fatality. I accepted that when I raced. It was brought home to me when Jim Clark was killed. That really was a moment in my life. Talk about Kennedy dying, for me it was Jim Clark. I remember hearing it on the radio driving home in an MGB coming up the hill out of Holywood [outside Belfast]. I felt like I'd seen a ghost. I can feel it now. It was just a moment … when I couldn't believe it.'

Did that make you think I don't want to do this?

'No, it didn't do that, it made me think "don't ever, ever underestimate the potential of danger." In a way, you are teasing fate but it's very intoxicating, exhilarating, wonderful. It's like walking on a tightrope – no, walking on the edge of the tightrope, not walking in the centre of it. The nearer the edge you get, the more tense the excitement is – and the greater the danger is. The two things go hand in hand. People who lead safe, boring lives have never lived. People who get involved in crime, for example, who thrive on danger, on adrenalin, they are exciting people. Why would anybody want to have been with Reggie Kray and all that? Because there was excitement, because there was danger. The Holy Joes who've never done anything in their lives which is physically dangerous don't understand. They'll almost be snide about it. I can look at Oxford academics lecturing. They are very clever people and probably interesting people but they've never done a thing in their lives other than read books and lecture people.'

But at some stage you have to accommodate this danger.

'The first time I had to ... I'm just trying to think ... the first time when I was actually competing was 1974 and Peter Revson died in testing in South Africa ... No, I'll tell you the first time, the 1973 US Grand Prix. Bernie [Ecclestone] entered three cars[10] and I was in the third car. In Saturday morning practice François Cevert was killed. It was a very high-speed accident, car just fell apart and he was unpleasantly ... he was mutilated, let's put it that way. Jody Scheckter [to be World Champion in 1979] saw it all and that affected Jody a great deal. It was a seminal moment in his life.

'Suddenly there was this silence, the death silence, and you're into respect for a colleague. François was a very nice man. I knew him a little bit and I'd talked to him and he was just one of those people who was a lovely guy. And suddenly he's dead.[11] Anyway, after a couple of hours the circuit was cleared up, the barriers replaced and qualifying continued. I was sitting there and Bernie said "what are you doing?" I said "I'm in the race and it's not right to go out, is it?"[12] He said "let me tell you something. What's happened has happened, it's history now, François is not with us, he's dead. Up until that milli milli second when he had his accident he was doing the thing he wanted more than anything else and enjoying it at a level which only you guys understand. So don't feel you have to sit here out of respect for him. It's got nothing to do with that. You're a racing driver, he's a racing driver, he's dead, that's sad, go out and do your job." I used that for the rest of my career and still do in a way. Certainly in a motor racing context, if you wanted to call it a mantra it was my mantra.'

And it's not cynical, just true.

'It's a balance, it's recognition. This is what Bernie is very good at: seeing what you have to see. He doesn't get distracted, he cuts straight to the issue and, as I say, I still use what he said. A young kid, an Irish driver, was killed at Oulton Park: 18 years old, the light of his parents' eyes and not really a teenager but still their child.[13] He had the potential to go on and possibly be a Grand Prix driver but his life was taken from him because he was racing with other kids and they were going for bust. You become extremely hard in a racing context, at times too much. You don't give the other guy room to breathe, and you can pinch somebody to the point that it leads to an accident.'

Watson was not discussing Oulton or apportioning blame.

'After the accident I thought "I've got to write to his parents and express my condolences." I used the analogy of Cevert to help them understand, while they have lost their son and they are now suffering the grief and sadness of that, don't feel sorry for your son because, up to the point of the accident he was having the most phenomenal experience of being alive.

'This may be off-theme, but I'd like to add that what upset me about Ratzenberger's death – and, all else aside, Roland was a nice young man – was the way it was all brushed under the carpet.'

It is difficult to judge this, because Senna was killed the

following day and the long shadow of that masked everything else. Ratzenberger was, despite his age, a newcomer. With the Simtek team he had failed to qualify for Brazil and finished eleventh in the Pacific Grand Prix. Imola was only his third meeting. To imagine the impact of his death if Senna had not died is impossible. But one may wonder whether the rush for greater safety which, post-Imola, suddenly became an absolute imperative, would have been instigated if only Ratzenberger had died. Immediately after his crash – that is to say the 24 hours before Senna died – there was no such rush.

Four years earlier, at Donington on 22 April 1990, Allan McNish was driving in the opening round of the Formula 3000 International Championship. Aged 20, he was one of the outstanding young drivers of his generation and clearly would be within reach of a Formula 1 drive soon. And it all went wrong, not just the crash which killed a spectator on the fourth lap but much else besides.

You have said that the going wrong was a convergence of factors. Was Donington one?

'Obviously … because I think, whether anybody likes to admit it or not, that you can get over these things physically quicker than you can get over them mentally. Physically I was fine. Mentally I think it took me quite a long time just to settle it all down. I couldn't say it takes one year or a specific period. The curious aspect was that if other factors hadn't followed on the back of it, this wouldn't necessarily have been an issue. It had an influence, although I was on pole and won the next race with fastest lap, which was three weeks later. Therefore I can, I think, quite easily say that I hadn't lost any speed and hadn't lost any racing ability.'

Does anybody know what actually happened?

'I can remember everything up to it but I can't remember after that because I was unconscious. I remember a couple of little snippets but nothing at all really, which I think is your brain putting itself on Pause because it doesn't want to remember. When you go to racing you know it is dangerous. That's the reason you have insurance. You do know and you do understand, even if you don't like to think about it. You accept that things can happen every time you get in the car. What is not necessarily acceptable from the driver's point of view is that somebody outside of the car can be injured. That's why the situation where the marshal was killed during the 2000 Italian Grand Prix was probably sadder and more traumatic [for Michael Schumacher]. There's no differentiation in life, but when drivers are injured or killed they know what they are getting into. You saw Schumacher in tears afterwards at Monza and I can understand why. You are putting your own self at a calculated risk but you don't think that you're putting others at risk.'

At Donington, McNish was in collision with Emanuele Naspetti. McNish's car was pitched into a series of rolls and – torn in pieces – went into a public area by an underpass. A spectator died and two marshals were hurt.

How were you told?

'I think in the medical centre at the circuit, but I don't definitely know. I knew they were injured but I think it was only when I got to hospital I realised …

'The first thing I had to do was sit down and look at it. OK, I was involved in an incident where Emanuele Naspetti and I collided on a straight and then, because of that, my car speared off and broke and went into the crowd. Effectively when two cars touch you have no control and I had absolutely zero control of what was going on after that. Therefore I had to understand that, once we had touched, I was a passenger and not in any way able to change the direction of what happened. It still does not alter the fact that I was involved, and it still does not alter the fact it was very, very hard to understand this, very hard to accept and very hard to go to the funeral.'

Did you go?

'Yes … The hardest thing about it all was having – and this is no offence to the media – journalists calling up at different times of the day and night asking me to watch videos of the crash. I found them completely insensitive. The motoring press all understood the situation and they had to report on it but they stood their distance afterwards. I really did appreciate that. For the rest of the press obviously it was a bit of a story. It was making something that was very private very public, not only for me but for the family.'

Once you get something in your mind it can expand itself in a way that is very difficult to control. It feeds on itself. Was it like this or could you apply the philosophy that there was nothing you could do?

'I could certainly apply it to the accident. I couldn't necessarily apply it to the results of the accident.'

Was it difficult living with yourself?

'No … no … no. That's one thing I can say, that it wasn't difficult to live with myself because I understood that I didn't actually have any control over what happened … I didn't … sit down and see myself as the 100% sole reason that this gentleman was dead. You do think about it, you do think "well, what if this, what if that?" but it doesn't change anything.'

Was it difficult to get back in the car?

'Yes, because I didn't know what it was going to be like. That was the hardest bit of that part of it. I had tested in France four days before the next race I competed in. I wasn't allowed to race for three weeks because Sid Watkins did a little bit of a medical and said "look, you have to keep out because you have bumped your brain a bit." I saw him again, he gave me the OK and I went to France. All the trip to France I really was very nervous about what it was going to be like because I didn't know. I hadn't got a clue.

'I got in the car and once I got to the end of the pit lane it was OK.'

Back in the office.

'Back in the office, back to what I did best, what I knew, what I could control. Then obviously there was a tension. I didn't necessarily … think about the accident but you tend to … you always think about the results of them. You can never forget it, you can only understand it, never ever forget it. I don't know if Emanuele will ever forget it, and the marshals, and …

'In racing terms, I ran on. That season was very good to me: I ended up fourth in the championship with two wins and overall very happy. I was 21 at the end of the year.'

Presumably you had said to yourself 'if I get back in the car and it doesn't really work, I will stop.'

'I said to myself "you will have to think about it." Look, at any time in your career if you get back in the car and you are nervous about driving, if you don't feel comfortable driving, you are not going to be quick. In fact you are going to be uncompetitive and you are going to be dangerous to yourself. Therefore you have got to be very, very hard with yourself in those circumstances. I was fortunate that it did not apply: when I got in the car and drove out I was OK. I think it affected my confidence. I was driving just on talent, not necessarily with the back-up of the confidence.'

And now we come to Oulton Park on 21 July 1991. That day Paul Warwick, 22, was leading the fifth round of the British Formula 3000 Championship. Something seems to have failed on his car at about 150mph and he was thrown out, fatally. He was popular and he was talented. He had been actively supported by his brother Derek, and the Warwicks – dad, uncle Stan – were close-knit but, more, they were the sort of people who form the backbone of this country. Derek faced the aftermath of Oulton Park as an open, brave man would do.

In our interview of January 2001 we were covering quite different terrain and the conversation turned, almost by itself.

You've had tragedy very close to home. You've had your crashes, you've lost your chums like Elio, but the joy of it seems to be something normal people can't experience. What is that?

'I don't know. I think that first of all we have to remember that Derek Warwick is a soft, caring, home-loving, can't-bear-to-see-people-or-animals-hurt sort of man. Can't bear cruelty. A very normal person, a very emotional person. But there was a certain thing in my life – Formula 1 – where I was clinical, quite hard but probably not hard enough. I could take away all the problems, all the tragedy, all the disasters that were going on around me and give 100%. When Paul died, that was probably the biggest single thing that could affect anybody and, you know, within two weeks I was back into a car and driving faster than I have ever driven before. When Villeneuve was killed, when de Angelis was killed, you just get back into the car and you do your job. So that is a very cold, calculating person, which is not the normal person.'

Was that Derek Warwick a bit of a stranger to you?

'He's only a stranger now when I look back. He was not a stranger at the time.'

Was it quite normal to make the switch?

'Quite normal, yes. It was quite a natural switch as well. But now when I look back he was not always somebody I knew because he would do anything in order to stay in motor racing. You've got to remember that I wasn't one of the fortunate ones. I didn't drive the best cars, I didn't have this thing pushing me on called success, called winning, called top teams. I always ... had to fight for every single thing. Even Renault was a struggle. When I look back now, a lot of people will say that I wasn't hard enough. I think I was bloody hard to have survived 147 Grands Prix and not win one. To have survived and stayed there you had to give something special and I always gave something.'

The shadow which Senna cast stretched to Martin Donnelly, and in a particularly poignant way. We were discussing the importance to him of driving a Formula 1 car again, and that he achieved it at Silverstone in a Jordan.

'I got back in and it gave me great satisfaction. My biggest fear that day – the world's press there, more photographers and TV cameras than you can believe – was stalling the car three or four times in the pit lane and people saying "Donnelly can't do it." For me to get back in the Formula 1 car and drive pretty hard down Stowe Straight – flat chat – was something. There was so much fog that you couldn't see the trees but I knew the circuit. It was two and a half years since I had driven a Formula 1 car but I said to myself "no it's not, it's two weeks." It felt like two weeks. I wasn't afraid of the car, wasn't afraid of a wheel coming off. I spun because the oil was coming out onto the tyres but I kept going and eventually the engine blew up – one of the oil seals wasn't fitted properly – but I knew I got it and I wanted it even more.'

Brian Hart was at this test because Jordan were running his engines. 'It was on the Grand Prix circuit and a fairly cold winter's day. I don't believe we did an installation lap because it was Martin. There was this problem with the oil pipe but I think Martin would have stopped anyway. Seeing him get out – how awkward it was – we all looked at each other and thought: oh. What I do remember is that you could see his face and it was all fired up because he'd proved that he could do it. However, it was pretty obvious to me physically he probably wouldn't be able to co-ordinate at the level you have to – maybe even for a lap, never mind a Grand Prix – at racing speed. Simply doing it is quite different to the speed you need to compete. The whole exercise was for Martin to prove that he could drive one again and he did that.'

Maurice Hamilton says that it was 'never publicly' stated that Donnelly wouldn't drive a Grand Prix again and clearly Eddie Jordan did it for Donnelly himself. This was not a serious test of a potential driver but much more important: giving a brave man his dignity back.

Now Donnelly:

Had you accepted by then that this was a symbolic moment of self-fulfilment but your career was over?

'It was a way of me sticking two fingers up to all those medical guys who'd said "you'll never drive a Formula 1 car again." I only finally accepted my career was over when Ayrton died. I felt cheated, I felt hard done by, and my mate Damon was on the scene and one of the main guys, Johnny was there, and Alesi was at Ferrari – all the guys I had come up with. It became difficult, not when you watched the race but on the podium afterwards with one of them on it, and you were thinking "I should be up there." Very hard to accept that. But the day of Ayrton's accident at Imola I thought "hey, hang on, I'm married, I've got a family, I've got my boy, I've got my team and I see no reasons now to be bitter. So what if you can't race in an F1 car? There's more to life than that." And time can be the biggest healer.'

And so we take the last gentle step into the darkness. The first interview I did for this book was with Michele Alboreto at Le Mans when he talked about the photograph of him and Senna smiling. Alboreto was a lovely fellow, unspoilt, always slightly tanned, his face consumed by a huge grin. His eyes sparkled. This was a man who was very much alive.

One time at the French Grand Prix he was at a table where I was chatting to another driver and, in the conversation, I said I was driving on to Italy for my holidays. Alboreto said 'hey, go and stay at my place in Portofino. I'll get the keys.' I felt I didn't know him well enough to accept. And by the way, Portofino is the most chic, most expensive (and beautiful) little resort in Italy ...

At Le Mans, after the race, there he was in the Audi hospitality area doing what he'd always done, which was talking happily to anyone who came along. During the race he'd overtaken someone – a proper, crisp, calculated move – and I said I knew he'd do it instantly and like that. 'How did you know?' he wondered. 'Because,' I said, 'I've been watching you do it for 20 years!' 'Yes,' he said, 'you have!' and there it was, the grin and the sparkle. I never saw him again.[14]

At 5.30 on the afternoon of 25 April 2001 Alboreto was testing the Audi R8 for that year's Le Mans at the little known Lausitzring circuit in eastern Germany. On a straight, the car somersaulted and he was killed. Nobody knew why this had happened. Everybody knew he left a wife and two daughters.

As Mario Andretti said, unfortunately motor racing is also this.

NOTES

1. Ratzenberger crashed 18 minutes into second qualifying on the Saturday of Imola. His Simtek hit a concrete wall at 200mph. He was taken to the Maggiore Hospital in Bologna and died there.

2. Manfred Winkelhock (Germany) was killed driving a Porsche at Mosport, Canada, in 1985; Stefan Bellof (Germany) was killed in a Porsche at *Eau Rouge* in 1985. Jo Gartner (Austria) was killed in the Le Mans 24 hour race in 1986.

3. *Eau Rouge* is much more than a legendary corner: downhill, flicking left-right, then up the hill and left over the brow. The corner is actually part of a normal Belgian road and open to traffic so if you're ever near it, go along to drive it. You will be astonished by how a television camera flattens it. *Eau Rouge* is steep.

4. Blundell did an exploratory lap then worked up to a 2m 23.630s (touching 273kmh/ 170mph – with only two other drivers faster, by fractions) then crashed.

5. Mika Häkkinen crashed at Adelaide in first qualifying for the 1995 Australian Grand Prix. Two doctors, Jerome Cockings and Stephen Lewis, were positioned close by, reached him in 15 seconds and saved his life.

6. Klammer, a hugely heroic figure in Austria, won the downhill gold medal at the 1976 Innbruck Winter Olympics and was for a time the best downhill skier the world had ever seen.

7. *Drapeau Rouge* (Solar, Paris, 1992) with Gilles Gaignault, Renaud de Laborderie and François-Xavier Magny.

8. Louis T. Stanley wrote books on motorsport, took pictures of it, ran the BRM team and advocated a Grand Prix Medical Service.

9. The Grand Prix Drivers' Association was active in the late 1960s. It faded away and was reformed after Imola 1994.

10. Ecclestone's three cars were for Carlos Reutemann, Wilson Fittipaldi and Watson.

11. Cevert was in a Tyrrell and the team, like Brabham, had three cars entered. Stewart and Chris Amon were in the other two and both

withdrew from the race. Stewart announced his retirement a week later.

12. Watson qualified on the twelfth row of the grid.

13. The driver was Neil Shanahan, who had been outstanding in Irish Formula Ford 1600.

14. This book was essentially completed before Alboreto died. Out of respect, I have decided to leave previous references to him as written.

Chapter 11

THE BEST WAY TO TRAVEL

*'It's a very fragile environment and it's a very vulnerable
environment. You sort of lurch from year to year hoping you'll
manage to talk yourself into a better drive the next year,
but there's no security at all'*
– Jonathan Palmer

Always there are endings and beginnings. Grand Prix racing
is steadily evolving but the central core – man and machine
against other men and machines – remains a constant that spans
generations, continents and nationalities. We've already heard
Niki Lauda dismissing flags and anthems as dangerous
distractions to winning the World Championship.

*Do you need competition in your life? Lauda Air were
competing with Austrian Airlines …*

'Looks like it, looks like it! I have always been in a
competitive situation and I think it starts when you decide to
be a racing driver. It's in your blood and never goes away.'

That seems to speak for every driver.

The Toyota launch was more than a well-ordered extrava-
ganza at Paul Ricard in the spring of 2001: it was a significant
part of the endless regeneration. Toyota was the first major
manufacturer since Renault in 1977 to present a car and engine
made by themselves.

Around 500 people gathered to witness this – media, VIPs
and staff. Ecclestone and Mosley flew in to the landing

strip at the circuit. Coffee and croissants were served under canopies along the pit lane, a carpet underfoot; in the vast shimmering conference room there was a stage for the unveiling, promotional videos on a giant screen and triumphant music. Banks of photographers and television crews craned to see. Young ladies in uniform, prim as air hostesses used to be, steered the guests effortlessly here and there. Be-suited people purred into mobile phones. Lunch, including Japanese delicacies, would be served in what was the Press Room when the French Grand Prix ran here.

Towards the end of the question-and-answer session someone wondered when Toyota would announce their other driver for the entry into Grand Prix racing in 2001 – Salo had long been confirmed, of course. Ove Andersson, President of Toyota Motorsport, said that unless something disastrous happened, McNish would be the second driver. McNish, visibly delighted, spoke as if he'd come to the end of a long, long journey and, in a sense, his life had been vindicated. Maybe Harvey Postlethwaite was wrong about everyone exiting Formula 1 through the back door. After all, McNish had just come in through it.

There remained to be clarified what definition disastrous might carry. 'If I'm four or five seconds slower than Mika Salo, I suppose,' McNish said. He never did amplify the words because he didn't need to. No driver, none of them, believes that given an equal chance it could ever happen, and the reason is simple, so simple it's laughable.

Their minds won't let them.

So McNish joined the endless regeneration, and the Formula 1 career which seemed to have ended so long ago was beginning again. He remembers the dark days, especially when he tested for a drive with the PacWest team in IndyCar racing. 'That proved to be one of the hardest times. Before I went out they said "look, the fastest man gets the job." I was quickest in every single way you could look at it, and they gave it to Mark [Blundell]. They said "Mark's got a name in Formula 1" and I could understand that – but don't tell me the deal beforehand and then change it. I came back from that thinking "what the hell do I have to do? What do I actually have to do to prove to somebody I am good enough for the job?" The hard part was not having a belief in myself – a few times, yes, you questioned whether you were good enough, whether you could do it. If you have the belief, why don't other people?'

McNish's delight must be balanced against the main weight of interviews in this book, including the one he gave. I had become concerned that the material was unbalanced because the drivers seemed to be speaking much more about disappointments than delight. In some of the interviews I deliberately steered the conversation from, if I may put it this way, the darkness to the light. I shouldn't have. The drivers were describing F1 as it is. For many – however much they love it, and they do – it's a daily grind beset with problems large and small occasionally relieved by the delight. In many essential ways the driver is living very much like everybody else and it is only in the extreme moments that he becomes different.

Julian Bailey is one of the few Grand Prix drivers I've ever met who is slightly introspective, shy, almost withdrawn – he doesn't come to you, you go to him – and as a consequence he's been mistaken for stand-offish. Just the opposite. He is also honest enough to discuss his weaknesses, which is also rare.

'I look at my record in Grands Prix, and I don't know how

many I did, but I got a point [sixth, Imola, 1991], and I've seen people do 30 or 40 and not get a point so I'm not disgusted with it. It just didn't work out.'

You dedicated your life to motor racing, you reached the top but didn't make it at the top. Do you feel a failure in that sense?

'It was not successful, was it – but it was a lot more successful than most people in motorsport. The main thing I've done is make a living out of it. I'd like to go back and do it again, yes.'

The analogy with Darwinism can be pushed too far, and the insistence on the survival of the fittest has caused plenty of trouble in other spheres, but the hunt is merciless, and sometimes to the strong as well as the weak. Only one driver wins a Grand Prix. All the others, however they quantify it to themselves, lost.

Mark Blundell, who did get the PacWest drive, is quiet but not shy.

Did you ever have any self-doubts?

'Some about coping with Formula 1 when I was coming up through the ranks but to this day I have not doubted my own ability, and I've been through as hard a time as anybody in the last few years with the accidents in America – which were beyond my control because they were car failures. It's tough to sit there day after day after day and ask yourself whether you still want to do it, whether you feel you are good enough. On this point, still, I have no doubts in my own ability.

'What does chip at you is not having had the right opportunities in your career and the frustrations which go with that. You look at some of the people around you and reflect.

You say to yourself: OK, the cookie crumbles, and you're the crumb which broke off and they're the big bit. You could be bitter about it because you haven't quite got the break you feel you deserve, but I can still sit back in years to come and say to my grandchildren ...'

What he can say is that, at a specific time, he was among the 20-odd best drivers in the world, and the world watched him doing it. This is no mean thing.

Derek Warwick is open, genuine and radiates a bonhomie which has made him popular for a couple of decades. We were talking about the beautiful laps when everything comes right.

'They're the easiest, they really are. I remember driving the Jaguar, driving the Peugeot, driving the Toleman at the end of 1983, driving the Renault in 1984. They were easy times for me because I was in the best cars. Dead easy. The problem is when you've got a different sort of car. I remember when I hurt my back in 1989 and I tried to qualify at Silverstone.[1] I put the most incredible lap together that you ever could in a Grand Prix car and I qualified nineteenth!' The car was [expletive] and we were always running at the back of the grid.'

There is no escape from the limits of the car.

'There isn't. I'm sure that had I been driving whatever was fastest at that time I would have been on pole by a second and a half with the same lap.'

Does that give you a private feeling of satisfaction?

'At the time it did because I knew nobody could have done any better in that car, and that's why I was always quicker than my team-mate. But now I look back and there is a twinge of sadness: the fact that the bit of talent I had was never shown – or never recognised by the journoes, the teams, the television, the fans and so on. They just saw this old car pounding round at the back of the grid and they didn't know what we were going through.'

But the people who know do understand.

'The trouble is history doesn't show it and that's why I say there is a twinge of sadness ...'

These are the two themes that run through the book: you measure yourself against your team-mate first – and you cannot afford any self-doubt.

An absence of self-doubt does not, however, guarantee anything. Perry McCarthy says trenchantly that 'very few people can win in top level motor racing because it's not a level playing field. I made some mistakes. The time for me in Grands Prix is certainly gone and I sometimes think I am not cut out to be a Formula 1 driver. It's easy for me to self-criticise because having no kind of stability leads you to doing rash things on and off the track – but you are fighting, it is total panic and you cannot be the considered, calculating person in that environment. It's certainly made me pretty different from most people, and that might be an attribute.'

This approach is in complete contrast to that of John Watson who preferred everything to be quietly ordered and even liked Bognor Regis, a genteel resort, although his career began and ended before Grand Prix racing became the vast industry it is today.

'I arrived in Bognor in 1971. Most of my childhood had been spent growing up beside the sea in Northern Ireland and I liked being near water. In 1970 when I started Formula 2 I was living in London, just bedding down in a flat shared by journalist friends. I hated London and felt lonely. This was the first time I'd been away from home and I was lost.

'In 1971 I'd found a mechanic and a workshop at Bognor. I'd friends down there and "could I come and stay for a couple of weeks until I get somewhere to live?" I ended up staying in their house for three bloody years! Bognor was fantastic and I bought my own house. Apart from being by the sea, I realised that when you get into Formula 1 and you're travelling to Grands Prix you want to have the tranquillity and balance of a very rural life, which is pretty much what I'd had growing up.

'In contrast to what I loved at a Grand Prix – which was the pressure, the intensity, the glamour, the excitement – I used Bognor as a healing process. I'd come back from a race, get into the house, shut the door and that was it. On the Monday morning before the next race I'd resume the process of preparation and continue it up to the point when I departed.

'It worked for me, and I was very fortunate in that I had reality at my doorstep. I wasn't going off to Monte Carlo, I wasn't jumping on to some fantastic boat, I was leading what I thought was as normal a life as possible in the context of being a Grand Prix driver. I was controlling the balance by where I lived and I had normal inputs, normal people around me, normal neighbours. The only thing I did that was different to them was every fortnight go off and drive a Grand Prix car. I enjoyed that contrast.'

If you'd been on $5 million a year would that have increased the appeal of Monte Carlo?

'You have to look at it pragmatically. In the 1970s, even proportionately the money was much lower than it is today. If I suddenly had to deal with a $5 million salary and face the prospect of giving 40% of it to the tax man I'd certainly think about it – but that's me now, at 54 years of age. If I imagine how I was at 24, I couldn't have lived in Monte Carlo. I would have been out of my depth.'

Here are a couple of examples of interviews shifted from darkness to light, both at Monaco in the spring of 2001.

Karl Wendlinger drove 41 Grands Prix with seven finishes in the points (three 4th places).

What was the best moment?

'There were several. In 1992, we arrived at Kyalami with the March and everybody said "we are very sorry that you are in that car because you cannot qualify" and I was seventh on the grid! This was a good moment. Then in 1993 with the Sauber, Imola qualifying [fifth], then the race and it was a good fight. It was raining in the beginning then half-wet, half-dry but I couldn't finish' – he'd been as high as fourth but the engine failed.

Johnny Herbert drove 161 races and won three of them, Britain and Italy in 1995, and the European at the Nürburgring in 1999.

Which one are you going to look back on and say that was the one?

'I think Nürburgring. Silverstone was good, I was in a good position but the way I decided with the tyres and everything else at the Nürburgring was great. I made that race winnable.'

Since we were at Monaco (in an Italian restaurant which, for directions, Herbert had quite naturally said was near *Portier*) I wondered about the start of the Grand Prix just over there. If you ever happen to be passing through the Principality you can, of course, drive a lap in your road car and, if you do, the distance from the grid to Ste Devote seems very short, just as

Ste Devote itself seems very narrow as it twists to the right and up the hill.

What about the start of the race? How do you cope with being on the grid?

'It was never a big deal because I'd done it for so long, I guess, and it just became routine. At the beginning you wanted to stay as cool as possible and I used to get into the car as late as I could. Then I'd do the out-lap and stay in the car. Some do, some don't. Latterly I'd get out. I wanted to stay as relaxed as I could, not get worked up about it because that's when the muscles start contracting and stiffening up – and if you weren't relaxed your concentration would wander away. You'd never be quite in contact with the lights when they go off.'

So you're on the grid here …

'It's just moving up to the electronic line that they've got, then you sit there and wait for everything to happen. When the lights start to go on you go into gear. It happens very quickly. To me, I never found it was like an hour. As soon as the lights go off you're away, that's it, no nerves any more. The nerves are always before.'

And what do you see going into Ste Devote?

'Small gaps. It's instinctive. When I see a gap I'm going for that. I'm not worried about anybody else. I never think "what happens if …?" That may never happen anyway. All you can do is deal with it as it happens. You cannot plan a start and anybody who says you can is wrong. Somebody may stall – or they may not. It may be that nobody stalls. It may be that all five in front of you stall. There might be eight crashes, there might be no crashes.'

So you're in Ste Devote …

'You're trying to gain as much as you can.'

But you've got this shoal of cars going in.

'Because it's such a short distance from the start, there's no real [gestures jockeying cars] ... it's not wide enough.

'There's no weaving about – the weaving about is actually off the line. By the time you get into third gear it's all happened. Then it strings out.'

When do you start to think consciously again?

'I think the consciousness is there all the time. I never used to emerge from any "zone" or distant "mode" and switch to something else. When the lights went on I was in one mode and when they went off I was in race mode. That's when I changed, not half way up the hill after *Ste Devote* or half way round the lap. Maybe other guys do that.'

Is it possible to sustain concentration, say here, for a whole race?

'Yes.'

What does concentration mean?

'You're just fixated.'

Are you aware of what all the others are doing?

'Yes, you should be aware of everything. The ultimate racer should know exactly what's going on. I don't think all of them do. There are guys who make big, big mistakes in races. When I won at the Nürburgring, Ralf Schumacher should have won but he got a puncture and Fisichella should have won but he spun off the track and he'd already been off three times. I didn't go off once.

'The only way I can explain it is to compare it with soccer. Imagine a player coming towards goal with the ball, he reaches the six-yard box and thinks he's done well. He kicks it but hits the post. The equivalent is me almost losing my life if I make a mistake like that. During the match the player will pass the ball but it goes to the other side. That's the equivalent of me wiping a wheel off on a normal track but here even more so. We're in trouble if we make small mistakes and it's concentration which helps you avoid them. The soccer players make a lot and they don't have the ball for an hour and a half. If you total how long they do have the ball at their feet it's not long – and half of that they lose it.'

Years before, at Estoril, I'd chatted with Herbert about how a driver regards other sports, for example tennis. The tennis player faces a soft ball on (mostly) a soft surface and if something goes wrong – he makes a mistake, he's outplayed – he loses 15 points. No tennis player has faced having his feet amputated. The danger does separate the Grand Prix driver from you and me and every Agassi who's ever been.

The Grand Prix driver is a star at the very centre of something important – and never more so than at Monaco, itself at the very centre of a firmament of wealth. The centre is the precious place which, one uncertain day, the driver will have to leave. He may, in one capacity or another, get something else near it in his life but not as one of the 22 going up the hill from *Ste Devote* with the world watching.

Some, like Lauda, leave but keep returning, constantly regenerating themselves in their own series of ends and beginnings. This is how he saw the spring of 2001 and Jaguar. 'You have to have the baseline to start off with. You have to move in a very consequent [German usage: step by step!] way to fulfil your targets. It took Ferrari 21 years to win a championship and I hope it will not take us that long. We have a car now which exists, very few people here [at the announcement of Lauda's appointment] had anything to do with it – it was in hand – so then you start running this car and you analyse it, and then you start making changes to it to make it quicker. This is the year when we have to stick with what we've got. The next year will see the next small step – because these are small steps – to improve it. Really where things should get much better, which is the normal plan in this kind of approach, is the third year. This is what we are aiming for.'

Lauda was no longer capable of being at the centre and, typically, knew that better than anybody.

'I had the opportunity to drive a couple of times in a double-seater car with some VIPs in the back, so basically I know how these modern cars work now because I was interested to compare my times and what it is today. It is completely the opposite. I think it's very simple to operate the car today. It is difficult to go quick, which is always the same problem – but the gearbox and other things, it has never been as simple as it is now. The speed and the limit of the car: these can only be achieved by a race driver who is dedicated to doing the job, is totally fit and really driving to the limit. Today I don't think I would be able to drive as quick as the others.'

Some, like Gerhard Berger, discover truths in their leaving (the driving) and staying (as a senior executive with BMW). 'I'm more a team person than I used to be. As a driver one is very egocentric. If anything goes wrong, you tend to pin the blame on others and on the technology. If things go really well, you find yourself being patted on the back as the driver. Today I look at the team as a whole and see each individual as an important cog in the machinery.'

Some postpone the leaving as long as possible. When Herbert lost his position with Jaguar he became an Arrows test driver which, of course, might even give him a chance to drive for them if a vacancy suddenly arose. Some move into the (supposedly) more sedate world of sportscars, but no form of racing is ever sedate. One source suggested that when Michele Alboreto's Audi sportscar crashed in Germany it went five metres into the air and travelled 100 metres before landing.

Some drivers are pragmatic and, however reluctantly, accept the inevitable. Eric Bernard drove 45 Grands Prix between 1989 and 1994, gaining ten points.

'You have to have a certain amount of philosophy. I believe that if you have the chance to get into Formula 1 with a first rank team, favourable things will happen and you will have a great career in front of you. If, unfortunately and for whatever reason, you don't have that chance – which was my case, because I was in a second or third rank team – things are much more difficult. You won't have a good car and you won't get good results. I'm not ashamed because each season I scored points and I did get on a podium [third, Germany 1994] and I was sixth at Monaco [1990].'

Is it difficult to live with being in a second rank car?

'Yes, but you don't have the choice. If you did, everybody would sign for McLaren or Williams! Without the choice you're battling against drivers in similar circumstances.'

But you do have a choice – to say 'that's it, it's not worth it.'

'It's the choice I made in 1995.'

You spend seasons nurturing hope against reality.

'It's always difficult but as a driver you say to yourself there will be something better tomorrow, so you do the best job you can with whatever you have got.'

But when it is tomorrow?

'It's not easy. And one day you say "that's it, I'm stopping."'

Bernard uttered this shorn of emotion, as a statement. The French use the word logical a great deal in conversation as an argument-clincher and, I suspect, Bernard surveyed his career – its grind and its fleeting delights – logically and saw that, if it was going anywhere it would have been getting there by now, and he accepted that.

Some solve the problem of leaving by grafting their new world onto motor racing, albeit away from the centre. Palmer created Formula Palmer Audi and got himself into corporate hospitality. He left his Grand Prix career without any trace of self-delusion but, more than that, he explains the camaraderie born from shared experience. These strangers, drawn from so many places and so merciless in the hunt as fit, hungry young men, move into a kind of gentility when they are no longer assaulting the hill at *Ste Devote*.

'If you're competing you can't say a lot and never let down your guard. I'd never say anything to expose a weakness. Martin [Brundle] and I used to go on holidays and things together but even so neither of us would ever let our guard down, really. You might have the odd "oh, the car's this or that" but you'd make sure you didn't give too much ground when you resumed at the next race. Having gone through the years like that, it's quite nice for it not to matter any more.

'My over-riding thought is that if I'd got in the same car I would not have matched Berger and Senna.'

You're the first driver I've ever heard say anything like that.

'I'm not surprised. I think far too many drivers – and it's understandable when they're competing, but it lasts into their retirement – are still trying to convince themselves and everybody else that if they'd got the right car they would have won the World Championship. Well, they probably wouldn't.

Alesi came to Tyrrell, he was quicker than me and I knew it myself. End of story. Nothing to be ashamed about.

'I think I probably used my capabilities – my talent – as much as anyone could have done, and that is all you can expect of anyone. If you look at it the other way, all you do is kid yourself and end up being a slightly chippy and disappointed person. It's a question of being intelligent and making logical judgements about what's around you. Ultimately the most fundamental thing is how talented you are at your job. If I'd been as quick as Alesi I'd have beaten him, but I wasn't.

'You see a very different outlook when they've been there five years: money is the biggest factor. It's a very fragile environment and it's a very vulnerable environment. You sort of lurch from year to year hoping you'll manage to talk yourself and drive yourself into a better drive the next year, but there's no security at all. When I was racing I'd be earning a few hundred thousand pounds a year – I never earned millions – but even so it was a lot of money in your twenties, and a good lifestyle. However, you face the prospect of having virtually nothing the year after. When you go from that level, the next step down was that you'd be scratching a living in sportscars for maybe fifty thousand. The big difference is that now I am building for the future. Every year I build my business and it is worth more, whereas in motor racing you get to a point where you start to be worth less.

'It's so much more comfortable working hard and knowing that you are building security. Another aspect is that you are able to do things day-in day-out which benefit your prospects in what you're doing. In motor racing you really can't do that. Simplistically, you get in the car once every two weeks and it doesn't matter what you've done in between. What matters is what happens in the one-hour qualifying session on a Saturday afternoon and what happens in that one and a half hour race. There's a limit to what you can do with the car and what you can influence with the car. Ultimately the team don't want you hanging around.

'At the end of a Grand Prix the team want to get some concise but good information, they want you to go away and they want to see you back in a couple of weeks. They'll do what the budget allows, and what technical ability allows, to try to improve things. Then you jump back in it and go and do what you can with it for another weekend. It's terribly frustrating. There is a limit to how much you can go to the gym even if you're keen, which I wasn't. In business you're testing every day.'

What sort of a relationship did you have with other drivers?

'When you are racing, you tend to think of drivers with a greater range of respect or otherwise, depending on how they go: he's not very good, he's slow. Your whole world is based around that. With ageing and a few years into retirement, the results people got at the races tend to blur, and what you get is mutual respect for everybody. If Nigel Mansell was to walk in here now or Derek Warwick – or Martin Brundle, although we're very good friends – or Johnny Dumfries, there would be a bond and a respect that, regardless of the results, we achieved what we did. We got to Formula 1 and we weren't an embarrassment. We'd been in a world of competition and very high stress, and there's something quite nice about it actually being over.'

Balance Bernard's pragmatism, and Palmer's pragmatism for that matter, with the other approach which is distilled into the seldom dormant volcano of Jean Alesi. To him, Grand Prix is a wonderful full attack.

You are passionate.

'You know, my life in racing is only because I love to drive. Formula 1 was not really what I was looking for because in my mind before, when my career began at 16, I believed it was too complicated to be a Formula 1 driver. You need to have support from a sponsor, political help because it's so difficult to get in – so I was not thinking at all about Formula 1. I just enjoyed the races, in karting, in Formula Renault and then in Formula 3. But because I won all the categories I competed in, suddenly I was at the door of Formula 1. For me the first day of Formula 1 was such a surprise! [We've already seen Eddie Jordan's machiavellian machinations to get Donnelly into Arrows and Alesi into Tyrrell for the 1989 French Grand Prix.] I was so excited. And I am still the same. I love so much to drive and to do what I am doing.'

Is that from your father?

'Probably, because he had a garage to repair cars so I grew up in this atmosphere. He was a racing driver but in rallies. Since my birth I have been in the middle of racing cars and that's where I get this passion from.'

Is that passion Sicilian?

'I don't know, because from the south of Italy, or the south generally, we have this passion for life. We enjoy everything. Maybe that helped me as well: the way I have been educated with my Sicilian family!'

Jackie Stewart says 'do not have feelings in a car, distrust emotion.'

'I think he's right because when you have a passion you forget the job. You just enjoy it. On one side that's nice but on the other side for the team sometimes it's not good!'

And sometimes for your career it's not good.

'Exactly.'

Because it's full attack.

'Exactly.'

Maybe sometimes 90%, then you finish second or third but you're not Jean Alesi any more.

'Exactly. But I never changed, you know.'

Do you want to change?

'Not at all.'

Monza in 1994. You were leading, your first win in sight after all those years of trying and the Ferrari broke down. The whole world wanted you to win. Somebody told me that your brother was there and you were so angry you drove from Monza to Avignon in about 35 minutes …

'Let's say: I finished my Grand Prix going home …'

What did your brother say?

'He was not saying anything. He was next to me and we were just … flying.'

Canada in 1995 when you finally did win.

'When I was second behind Schumacher, suddenly I saw the crowd exploding. Everybody was jumping up and down and I realised something was happening. I came past the pits and saw on my board P1 and I understood I was first. Something had happened to Schumacher – in fact he had to change his electronic steering-wheel. When I saw P1 I started to cry. I understood it was *the* day. I was not able to see the road any more because my eyes were full of water. For a moment I had to be tough with myself and say "OK, stop this and try to finish the race." For four or five seconds it was very difficult to concentrate. Then in my mind I switched off and I was not thinking of P1, P2 or anything. I was driving slowly – no, not slowly, repeatedly – to finish the race.

'On the last lap, at each corner I was saying to myself "that's another one." On the last corner I say "OK, even if the car stops I am able to push it over the line and finish first." Everybody was happy and that's true because that night I stayed in the city of Montreal and everybody was so excited. You know I finished second 16 times and I think I had a problem on my car seven times when I was leading the race – so for me the victory was not just to have the trophy but to see the people made me crazy, you know!'

But on that last lap you were able to stop the emotion and the passion. You drove like Schumacher – then you became Alesi again and the whole world became Alesi.

'Yes! You know, many times when I am talking to people they say "do you regret not having been with Williams?" I always say "no." For sure the results would have been better but the way I live, the way I grew up, Ferrari was the right choice for me – the only choice. When I left, it was as if I quit Formula 1. Same thing.'

One year at Monza you were going round on a scooter and Schumacher had a bodyguard.

'Yes, yes.'

You don't need to say any more.

'Yes. Yes!'[2]

It may be that trying to husband the drivers into compartments is impossible because the sport is so broad in its appeal and execution that anybody from anywhere can play provided they are able to cope with it. Not long ago we had Piquet the Latin, Senna the Latin, Prost the Gallic and Mansell the Anglo-Saxon, all at the front of the grid …

I know when I finally knew they were different.

Philippe Streiff cannot feed himself, cannot lift a bottle of mineral water to his lips, cannot turn the pages of this book. He is prisoner of a wheelchair. When he offered to drive me to the station I was curious. When he assured me that the journey in from the suburbs of Paris, where we were, through the rush hour to the Gare du Nord could be done easily in the time available I was even more curious.

The Matra people-carrier looked normal from the outside and I was directed to the front passenger seat. This had a steering wheel and two foot pedals. 'Don't,' Streiff's secretary Chantal warned, 'touch the steering wheel.' She and Gilles, Streiff's assistant, lifted him into the driver's seat. No steering wheel and no pedals there. They strapped his right hand to a joystick on the central console and, using only that, he worked the Matra up the curving, sloped drive and out into the traffic. Everything after that is a rush towards and away from reality.

We are on a three-lane highway, the traffic heavy, and immediately we are doing 60mph, dancing from lane to lane, from gap to gap, racing towards a bus lane and bursting through a red light to get to it. 'I like bus lanes,' he says. Even at this speed he can position the Matra with astonishing precision, the hand which was so useless a moment ago now capable of the utmost sensitivity.

'You're not frightened?' he wonders absently, and when I say I truly am he grins.

'Good!'

'You have learnt nothing,' I say. 'Nothing!' He grins again, taking that as praise.

Gilles, in the back, sits impassive and silent. He's seen all this before. Streiff guns the engine harder and we're way over the 60. He abuses any driver in his way, even the startled and incredulous, and simultaneously when he does stop at traffic lights I hold the bottle of mineral water to his mouth ('pit stop – refuelling!' he says) and I have to tap numbers into the mobile phone mounted so he can speak into it and in a gap in a telephone conversation he explains how he was following Elio de Angelis that day at Ricard and saw the crash and the fire which killed him. Streiff had stopped at the scene and others did too, but there was nothing you could do.

His son had been born the week before and now suddenly de Angelis was dead. 'For the first time in my life I thought about Formula 1 and why I was doing it. It was very hard to go to the next race.'

We approach a tunnel and I wonder how he can put the lights on. He does this by slapping his left hand against a button in the door. Evidently there is an electrical fault because the lights come on but the Matra bucks as if it's struck the tunnel wall and I'm thinking 'this is it.' The notion amuses him. We approach a roundabout with heavy traffic clogging it and he rams the Matra through, push-elbow-push. 'If the police stop us, I'll tell them you were driving!' The grin. I have the steering wheel and what policeman is going to believe Streiff could conceivably be driving the Matra himself?

He cuts up a hapless little man in a white car and the man flashes and flashes his headlights in rage. 'It's all right – he's recognised me!'

Occasionally, as if to amuse himself, he pulls out into oncoming traffic. 'I like to intimidate them. You know, like Formula 1 drivers do.' At the precise moment when you're ready to howl from a deep place he dances the Matra back, and he's grinning again. He does not like to be overtaken, incidentally, by motor bikes. Well, he doesn't like to be overtaken by anything. At one supreme moment he pulls into a bus lane and we are going up it the wrong way. He turns and – grins.

We get lost and he runs a red light so drastically that even Gilles howls 'stop!' because traffic is hammering hard across us. If at this moment I had regained the power of speech I'd have howled 'stop!' myself. Streiff does not stop, of course, although I have my right foot rammed so hard on an imaginary brake pedal that I get agonising cramp, the arch of the foot locked solid.

The look of a woman on a pedestrian crossing will stay with me for years. She felt our draught.

We're in a side street and he says 'regardez les putes!' These are ladies of African appearance wearing mini-mini-skirts and standing equidistant, like sentries marking out the kingdom of instant sex. I wonder what he thinks about all that but there are things you don't ask a man paralysed from the waist down. At the Gare du Nord I get good and clear of the Matra while he sits there grinning. I stumble into the crowd and it is only later that I realise I hadn't asked him how he works the brakes, and later still that I wonder if he has brakes.

Behind the rush of impressions is something fundamental. At home, in the wheelchair, Streiff is a slightly irascible man because, I suspect, even a full decade after Jacarepagua, March 1989, he finds dependence on others very difficult. His mind works at racing speed. He is uninterested in self-pity and spends his days creating projects like the world karting, but he remains forever a prisoner of the wheelchair and his hands which can't even turn pages.

In the Matra the dependence ceases. He is free to go where he wants and how he wants. It is more important than that though. He becomes physically the man he was before the crash as well as mentally. He can do whatever he could do then, except with the minor nuance that it is done in a different way.

It remains fascinating to me that the act of driving fast can give so much, take so much away and give even more back again.

Perhaps this, too, is simple, so simple it's laughable. The driver needs the act to be alive and everything else is strictly for other people, which is why they are not like you and me, however humdrum much of their lives must be.

Someone (doubtless an Anglo-Saxon) coined a phrase – *thinking is the best way to travel* – which might sum up everything in this book, and there's an elegant simplicity to that. But I prefer Philippe Streiff's philosophy of driving, and of life itself.

'Passion is always right.'

NOTES

1. Warwick hurt his back karting, which allowed Donnelly to take his place for the French Grand Prix. Warwick returned for the British. Senna had pole with 1:09.099 while Warwick wrung 1:12.208 from the Arrows.

2. My interview with Alesi was arranged by his manager, Mr. Miyakawa. 'Ring him in Geneva on Monday,' he said, and gave me an orthodox number with the Swiss prefix 41. I rang it and Alesi said he was in the middle of Easter Monday lunch with his family and could I ring him at Avignon in an hour and a half? I know Alesi drives fast but to finish his

lunch and then cover some 300 kilometres (186 miles) in 90 minutes seemed pushing it. Anyway I rang the Avignon number and there he was. It defied credulity. How the hell did you do that? 'I've been here all the time,' he said. 'The Swiss number is my mobile!'

CHAPTER 12

TIMELINE

'It is a huge jump between anything else in motorsport and Formula 1: the Media attention, the technology that's involved. Driving a Formula 1 car was a surprise – how quick it was, how much downforce it had, how difficult it was.'

– Ralph Firman

They are not like you and me. That theme has arched over the whole of our story from Sir Jackie Stewart having lunch at the Grosvenor House to Philippe Streiff reshaping the Parisian rush hour by himself. They, and all the drivers in between, are united by the passion Streiff has expressed so strongly. They express it in different ways, as you would expect, because they are fiercely independent and ambitious men drawn from every continent and every background. But the message transcends everything.

'It's like a cure for everything. It doesn't matter what problems you have – financial, in your personal life – and it doesn't matter if you feel really ill. All that goes away and only you sitting in this protective cell, this cockpit, remains. I have never felt anything like this in any other way and only driving at the limit gives it to you.'

You cannot deduce the nationality of the speaker or his background. It was a Swede, Stefan Johansson, who is a resident of the United States and he was speaking to me at Le Mans, France, where he partnered an American and a Briton in the 24-hour race. He was also speaking for the collective, from the gentlemanly 1950s through Stewart's 1960s, Niki Lauda's 1970s, the relative safety of the 1980s and Schumacher's 1990s all the way to here.

In a very real sense motorsport – and particularly Grand Prix racing – is locked into a never-ending process of reinventing itself, day by day. The possibilities of technology permit this and the imperatives of competition guarantee it. Each driver makes his own accommodation with this but their impulses and imperatives all live within the unity. *None* of these men, I repeat, are like you and me.

I know when I first knew. It was a warm, dry August afternoon in 1982 and Lauda's red and white McLaren came screaming along the start-finish straight towards turn one. He had already done several laps in qualifying, the best at an average of 217kmh (134mph). Ordinary motorists never reach such a speed, never mind average it across 6.7km (4.2m) through corners, chicanes and a tricky final section of loops.

Approaching turn one Lauda positioned the McLaren on the racing line over to the left. Without warning the car broke free. Spinning in a wild contortion it tore through catch fencing and battered into the tyre wall like a hammer. Always, you look for the driver to move because that signifies life. Lauda moved. He rose from the cockpit, stepped clear of the car and, without even giving it a cursory glance to see what might have gone wrong, ran away. These drivers, I told myself, are ordinary. Instinctively they get away from danger as fast as they can. Lauda of the fire-consumed face – consequence of an accident six years before – was heading back towards the normal, safe world.

But he did not of course think like that at all. He was running towards the pits because there was just enough time left to get in the spare car and maybe improve on the 217kmh. He'd already banished the accident to memory, if indeed he'd remember it at all. Years later he wrote a book about his McLaren years and made no mention of it: nothing.

I mentioned this anecdote to a couple of drivers who were initially bemused by it. *Of course he went to get the spare car*, they said, *what else would he have been doing?*

Lauda was World Champion three times and, before Senna, one of the very few drivers famous beyond the confines of Formula 1 (Stewart was another). To demonstrate the full extent of the unity, I want to move far from such elevated drivers and concentrate on someone much more modest. Nigel Mihell had two quite different ambitions: to be the first black Formula 1 driver and to win the South African Grand Prix when apartheid still ruled. He wasn't South African but that didn't matter a damn. He ponders what that might have felt like, for himself and for a lot of black people in a lot of places. He settles on a single word: sweet.

You'd better believe it.

Mihell remembers when *he* first knew that racing drivers were different – Mallory Park in 1995. He was 'skint' and driving an elderly single-seater helped by 'a guy called Ian Roley who ran a company in club racing. I was straight out of karts, I was going to be the next best thing blah blah blah blah.'

The first hint, that Mallory day, was 'when I saw this guy walking round the garages – Latin guy, very purposeful.' Mihell didn't know his name and it turned out that he was driving for Paul Stewart Racing, then arguably the leading team in Formula 3, in a Vauxhall Lotus.

'We went out on the circuit. Admittedly it was my first time, but I was going round getting quicker and getting quicker.

About my third session out I thought *right, I've got to try and follow this Vauxhall Lotus*. I knew they were 2-litre cars and I was in a 2-litre. I thought he would be quicker but I might just be able to learn a bit by following so I tried that.

'Down the straight and turning into the corner wasn't too much of an issue. I was watching as he pulled away from me, which I could have dealt with if it seemed like it was on rails, but what was killing me in the head was that the back was sliding out as it pulled away. His back was at such an angle that I could see his nearside front wheel turning into it. I could watch him opposite-locking the car all the way round the corner *and he was still pulling away from me* – which left me a little depressed.

'I came back into the pits and they were looking at the times. I said "bloody hell" but Ian said "don't you worry about them, that's a proper race team – high level stuff. Don't you try and mark yourself against those guys." He pointed across to the driver of the Vauxhall Lotus and said "that guy there is going to be a mega. I've been watching him and he's something else."'

Mihell had no idea who this driver was.

It was Juan Pablo Montoya.

'I felt a bit jealous that he had mechanics and we only had an old Leyland truck and the boys kneeling on the floor hammering away at the back of this old car.'

What does an experience like that do for your mental processes?

'To see somebody drive away from you sideways? It makes you think *I need to do better!* Your natural reaction is to think it's because he's got a newer car but then you think *well no, because the guy's still driving away from you – and sideways*. Then I tried to watch what he was doing and I thought *I need to be able to do that by the time I get to his level of experience if I want to compete at his level. If I can't I might as well forget it.* At the point I was at – straight out of karts – nothing was going to tell me that I couldn't achieve it. I had to wait at least two years to find out I couldn't.

'I crashed at Croft driving a Formula Renault Sport at 120mph. I broke my femur in five bits and my pelvis in three. A proper crash, yes, although in comparison Mark Blundell's was an aeroplane disaster. I broke the car clean in half and you've got to work hard to do that.'

That's when you found out. What's it like when you do?

'It's like anything: the first reaction is to look for a reason, not necessarily blame but a reason. The second reaction is not anger so much as being fed up. The third reaction is acceptance.'

That does not come immediately.

'The crash was in June. I lay in hospital for a couple of months thinking about it and I had a bet with my doctor. He came in the day after he'd done the surgery and I said "right, the last race of the season is at Silverstone. I want to be able to do that." He said "Nigel, when is Silverstone?" I said September. He said "I don't think you're even going to be walking by Christmas." I said "all right, I'll bet you twenty quid." He took the bet and he was grinning. I lost dismally.'

When you were in hospital was there any doubt that you wanted to get back?

'Oh no. I wanted to do it again.'

Why?

'Because ... there is nothing like driving those cars. It's just ... awesome ... it's just ... it's a rush.'

Mihell did get better and made his return in a racing sports car, a Spyder. 'I couldn't get in and out of a single-seater, my leg didn't bend enough. I thought it would be good to drive again just to see if I was scared or not. We went to Donington Park and I had a run in Redgrave Racing's Spyder. I'd been driving for them when I got hurt.

'It was good, it was fine. I covered a couple of laps and I was a bit tentative because I was still sore. You knew about it each time you went over the rumble strips! I thought *right you've got to go for it now to see if you commit the same way you would have done before. If you can't, park the car.* I went for it and I did a time, nine or tenth quickest on the day out of 20, 30 cars so it was OK. I remember going round and feeling really chuffed that I'd done the Craner curves and McLeans flat. You get a little sideways in those corners in those cars and I didn't bottle out, it was the same rush of adrenalin. Awesome!'

But the edge had gone.

Now listen to Jacques Villeneuve, who did win a World Championship. 'Technology becomes more and more sophisticated, the cars more and more difficult to understand, the meetings with the engineers longer and longer, the contributors more and more numerous. [You're making] a daily investment which represents more time and more mental energy so that, at the least opportunity for freedom, you enclose yourself in the motorhome to stay calm and listen to a little music. You don't want to speak, you're emptied.'

Villeneuve has always been unusual among Formula 1 drivers in that, despite enormous pressures to conform, he has chosen not to.

Speaking of other drivers, he says that not a few of them are made available to the press but aren't sought after because 'they have nothing to say! If it's to play being robots and recite every day what the PR people, the marketing or the team's tyre manufacturers want said, the journalists might fall into the trap once or twice but not three times. F1 drivers completely lack personality, that's the real problem. They don't speak because they have nothing sensible to say, to reflect on.'

These comments (although vintage Villeneuve) are harsh because, while he may be able to withstand the pressures of conformity, others can't – too much at stake – or can't be bothered. In such a pressured atmosphere, the media are just one more demand before those precious moments in the motorhome with the headphones on listening to ... rock 'n' roll? So drivers mouth the phrases to the media and escape. The shortest way from one point to another is a straight line, on the track and off it.

Villeneuve's unstated premise is that drivers *ought* to have profound and interesting and enlightening things to say because mastering Grand Prix racing must involve deploying several different forms of intelligence. It's not just that they understand how to move from box to box in their minds, but that they have to have the boxes.

You *know*, listening to a footballer stumble through the clichéd wreckage of his own simple sentences, that he could not do this. Nobody expects him to. All questions to him are framed in the childlike and that's how he will respond. *He* has no pressure to conform to the nuances of PR, or explain telemetry, or cope with the fatality of a friend, and invariably do all this in a foreign language.

Yet, as this book shows, drivers do have a great deal to say. It may be that they feel freer to talk when they have retired. Some of the interviews here (except Irvine!) would certainly not have been given in mid-career.

Going in to 2003, Villeneuve turned his attention to his new team-mate at BAR, Jenson Button, and fired a barb. The problem began at the first race, Melbourne, when Villeneuve pitted a lap late and Button, due in that same lap, had to queue behind him. Villeneuve cited radio problems, and Button made murmurings about that.

Villeneuve claimed that 'when we left the track it was all smiley and everything, and we shook hands. Then he went and put a knife in my back. As a person I have lost respect for him. This was bound to blow up. Jenson joins, and everybody is telling me he is the next World Champion. And he starts blaming everyone and everything instead of trying to improve. He's lacking in intelligence.'

Button turned *his* attention to Villeneuve, calling him 'a joke'. Button pointed out that Villeneuve had always 'been outspoken about drivers, but I don't think so many have answered back. The things he said, it's just pathetic but it's Jacques, it's the way he is and he's always been outspoken. I think he thinks that's the way to go racing, but it's got nothing to do with racing.'

Ah, but it has: always dominate your team-mate because he's the enemy within, play the mind games with him, unbalance him, beat him. Button was 23, Villeneuve 33 and time beginning to run against him. More than that, Villeneuve was in the last year of his contract with the team and rumours suggested that Honda, providing BAR with engines, would be keen to have the Japanese driver Takuma Sato. Button was on a four-year contract.

It was always like this, a new generation pushing at the old: Lauda was pushed by Prost, Prost by Senna, Senna by Schumacher. But the tension between team-mates runs like a theme through our story and Villeneuve-Button was no more than the latest (and one of the loudest). Both men are asking each other the same question: *well, mentally how strong are you?*

It reminds me of a king on his death bed, his sons gathered round and one of them asks 'which of us will succeed you?' The king raises his head and says 'whoever is the strongest.'

This could be a totem for the whole of Grand Prix racing, Villeneuve-Button, Schumacher-Barrichello and all the rest.

I started this book with three rooms. I'll revisit one of them – Bentley. Blundell, Herbert and David Brabham went to Le Mans 2003 and finished second to the other Bentley after a sequence of niggling problems. I asked Blundell how changing their thought processes to become a team worked itself out.

'It is an interesting thing to look at because normally racing drivers – certainly where I came from, single-seater racing – are very much geared up to doing their own thing without having to answer to any other driver. It was the same for Johnny and for David and it does require a different outlook.

'In many respects it is quite enjoyable and more say, maybe, for Johnny and I because our careers were more in single-seaters compared to David's. He's done sports cars for a lot longer. Also Johnny and I have known each other for years because we came up through the ranks together.

'If you spend a lot of time with people in a small amount of time, like at Le Mans, a bond grows between you. We all had niggly problems in our car. You don't think about the fact that you've got to be worrying about the other two in the team – "what are *they* going to think?" You're more concerned about what the overall situation is and just trying to do the best you can. That's where your experience comes into it, after you get out of the car and you can relay your thoughts to whoever's getting into it. You can have a good chat about things and maybe ease a bit of the pressure because if you were the one in the cockpit you'd have to deal with the situation just as they will have to.

'I really did enjoy it. We had a super time.'

No cross words?

'No, no. That's the other issue. Racing drivers are quite egotistical so you've got three egos in the car, especially with people who've got credentials on their CVs. It was a question of getting a blend and a mix together. Everybody took on board that it was a big team effort. None of us said *right, I'm going to be the fastest man*. We all knew what we could do – didn't have to prove it.

'You need to change your disciplines and change your outlook slightly on how you go about things. Sports car racing, and Le Mans in particular, addresses that. Some people never crack it: they don't have the discipline, they don't want to have the patience to work with other people, they can't compromise – and that's something you must do. In certain situations you *have* to. The balance of the car, for instance, has to suit the three guys and they drive differently. The compromise word comes into a lot of areas.'

Did you find it easy to make the transition?

'Yes, to be honest, and more so now than when I first had to make it. I did sports cars in 1989 and 1990. I had a lot more of a competitive edge attached to everything and I found it more difficult then. I went in there now with a lot more confidence and experience and knowledge, and I tried to use that so it was beneficial to the way the team was going. There were certain times when you gave up your ego – you didn't say *stick a set of tyres on, I'm going for the fastest lap* – because it wasn't going to be beneficial overall. Same with Johnny, same with David. Everybody pulled their weight and that was the enjoyable part. The frustrating element was that if you took out the pit stops we had to make [battery problems] ours was the fastest car on the race circuit. If we'd had no problems we'd have *loved* to have a go at the lead car, but you got to share the down-side with the other guys in the car and then you got to share a few beers afterwards. And there's nothing better than that.'

Formula 1 regulation changes for 2003 included the introduction of single-lap qualifying, and it made the process of settling in much harder for the newcomer.

Two o'clock in the afternoon at the Goodwood Festival of Speed, the Cosworth marquee and an eddy of people flowing round the exhibits there, talking mutedly as people do in semi-museums. *Isn't that Graham Hill's Lotus over there? Let's go and have a look.*

Goodwood is a very English place, a country house of timeless elegance, vast numbers of people boiling gently in the heat as they stroll the lawns. Goodwood is also a very English compromise because a ribbon of road threads between the lawns and on this the historic cars and motor bikes come thundering up one at a time, often to genteel applause. City chaps and their gels sip champers in a tent and don't seem to mind there's a solid wall of spectators between themselves and the thunderers. The sippers recline and I wonder if a cork went off right behind them how they'd react. Like Stewart?

Goodwood is a place out of time, a place from your memory, of many thousands of people enjoying themselves and not a policeman in sight; of an open pits area where drivers and mechanics gather among the general public. *Isn't that Alan Jones over there?* Jones, heavier now than when he won the 1982 World Championship, ploughs a broad furrow through the crowd towards the car he is to drive for his, and their, pleasure.

Corporate hospitality spreads on the far side of the road, an industrial estate of temporary showrooms and hospitality units, the Cosworth marquee among them.

In the middle of it there's a circular blue curtain held by Velcro to a metal rail above it. Ralph Firman, with Jordan (running Cosworth engines) and in his first season of Grand Prix racing, is to be photographed beside the statue once the unveiling has been done. He's a tall, lean 28-year-old who seems at ease as the eddying crowd ogles him. He wields an approachable smile, and some of the crowd approach. He signs autographs, shakes hands.

At 2 o'clock, the Cosworth people start to pull the curtain down and it comes down, all right, almost all over Firman who ducks out of the way grinning broadly. Because the photographers need a backdrop, the Cosworth people now stand on chairs holding the curtain in a semi-circle as high as their arms will allow. It's like a stage, everything in front of the scenery choreographed exactly into the desired image, everything behind getting through the crisis any way you can. Just like Formula 1...

The statue, by Tim Tolkien (great nephew of *Lord of the Rings* author JRR), is a man waving the chequered flag and made entirely of automotive bits. When Firman saw it, he thought *they wore armbands in those days and I didn't know that* – sure enough, there's a metal armband.

This thought process is instructive. 'I think,' he will say in his soft voice, 'that I am more conscious of motorsport history than other people. My whole family are in it, it's in my blood.' Dad, also Ralph, set up Van Diemen, maker of superb small racing cars, in 1973 and many of the drivers we have met in this book – Irvine, Blundell, Palmer – started precisely here. Dad also signed Ayrton Senna from the obscure reaches of Brazilian karting in 1981, and we'll come to that in a moment. Mum Angie has, I suspect, been surrogate mother to a few homesick drivers in her time although she proclaims she has never talked about Senna, and won't. We'll come to *that* too, in a moment.

Ralph Junior makes all the right noises and strikes all the right poses next to the statue. Then we sit, and halfway through the first question his mobile rings. There used to be two sounds you always heard at motor racing, and in this order: the rustle of money and the howl of engines. Now there's a third: this trill-trill-trilling of mobile phones. He deals with the call quietly and quickly, and we move into the interview again.

'Cosworth,' he says, picking up unprompted where he left off, 'has been around for a long time and has had a great bearing on motorsport so this is not just another occasion to me.'

I've seen Formula 1 drivers who try to convince you they are interested, but you really were.

'Yes. I was quite happy out there. It was good. It's my first year in Formula 1 and I'm trying to put as much back in as I can whenever I get the opportunity. I'm in the lucky position where I am driving a Formula 1 car.'

It's been a most difficult season to be a rookie, purely because of the qualifying and the one-lap shoot out, no mistakes or second chances permitted.

'Qualifying is very hard ... it's very difficult. But I am getting to grips with it. The problem was that we had so little pre-season testing. All the mistakes that I have made in qualifying this year, most drivers have had the opportunity to get out of their systems.'

Firman started in karts in 1985 (British champion 1992) and moved through British Formula 3 (champion, 1996) before he went to Japan and Formula Nippon (champion 2002). He has said he didn't have the money to race in Europe. Then he came to Jordan and the new qualifying. More than that, he struggled in the races as well.

How do you cope with that?

'I knew it would come. The pressure has always impressed me in motorsport and I have always dealt with it very well but it just takes time in the car. There is no substitute for doing laps in a Formula 1 car.'

Sleepless nights?

'Always have sleepless nights before you race.'

No, I mean in terms of 'this is all going wrong' or 'I am now in a difficult situation' and the world is watching.

'I know, I know. It's a big thing and it is extremely public. I haven't been under pressure – the team has been 110% behind me. I have always done well as a racer and I knew that with more time in the car the qualifying would come. It's starting to happen. I was never really worried about it. People might have made up their minds about me too quickly but I don't think they are right. [Team-mate] Giancarlo [Fisichella] is one of the best drivers in the world and I am getting very close the last two times in qualifying.'

What has surprised you?

'It is a huge jump between anything else in motorsport and Formula 1: the Media attention, the technology that's involved. Driving a Formula 1 car was a surprise – how quick it was, how much downforce it had ... how difficult they are to drive. It takes a long time to be able to go quick in a modern Formula 1 car. They are so different from anything else, especially with all the electronics, the grooved tyres, the suspension. I think also there is a problem not knowing the circuits (Firman had only ever driven four on the way up); the second year it will be a big advantage knowing the circuits.'

Mentally how do you prepare yourself for a qualifying lap?

'You learn, first time out on a circuit, which corners you can push 100% on, but if you make a mistake it's going to cost you half a tenth. Others you make the mistake and it'll cost you three- or four-tenths, half a second. You see where you may go wide and what that will cost...'

You've a two-year contract...?

'... yes ...'

so you've got next year as well, you don't have to beat your brains out this year.

'Nothing's for sure in Formula 1, is it?'

You come across as affable.

'I am relaxed but when I put a helmet on I am aggressive. I couldn't have won all those championships if I wasn't 100% dedicated and aggressive at the same time. They meant everything to me. Being in Japan for six years from the age of 21 wasn't easy but it made me more determined, harder as a character. That should help to stay in Formula 1 and deal with it.'

And now a curious thing. These drivers are quite prepared to discuss what an ordinary person might judge to be delicate topics. For example, Firman was asked about danger[1] and replied: 'I've never honestly thought about the dangers. I don't ever feel frightened. It's all about having confidence in the car and your own driving really, isn't it?'

In the same interview he cited Senna as something of an inspiration, not least because when Senna joined Lotus – so near to Van Diemen – 'it was great to have him around the house.'

Yet now he was reluctant to mention Senna at all.

I cannot judge, and he didn't say, why and didn't pursue it because his facial expression and tone of voice were insisting *not going to do it*. The curiosity is that a driver like Firman will feel confident discussing his own mortality – 'I never think about danger' – but somehow vulnerable if asked to describe a most innocent episode of his childhood. Maybe that brings us back to the statue, the stage and the curtain: public persona this side, private persona out of sight.

By late afternoon the temperature must be at least 90 degrees, the pale-skinned English are boiled to many shades of lobster and still the cars thunder along the ribbon of roadway. A well-modulated voice on the PA gives running commentary, with all sorts of anecdotes about driver and vehicles hewn from an abstruse fund of knowledge. The boiled, milling about in such huge numbers, seem to have a great deal of the same knowledge. A St John's Ambulance crew waits patiently for the fainted and they don't wait in vain.

The boiled are of many ages: the sun-hatted elderly who all seem to know each other, the middle-aged trading a day from the office for precious pleasure, the teenagers already indoctrinated in the internal combustion engine, the plump toddlers sweating in push chairs who soon will be.

It is all like a wheel which turns, and keeps on turning. Alan Jones looks now as he looked then, not someone you'd pick a fight with, and inescapably he represents the achievements of the past, just as Firman represents the present and, surely, the future. Others will come after him, just as so many others came before Jones, and the wheel will keep turning. Like life itself, each driver brings something unique of himself.

On the way to the exit, deep among the boiled, a voice rings out in greeting – John Watson, who was in motor racing before Jones and stayed after him, this same John Watson who has been a familiar companion throughout our story. We chat – politics! – and then he says gravely and with great sincerity that he's reached the time of life when he enjoys moving about freely without being recognised any more. I nod, signifying that it must be a pleasant release after so many years of it.

At exactly this moment an autograph hunter approaches and Watson shrugs. *Sod's Law*. He tries (unconvincingly) not to look flattered, and tries even harder when two others approach in short order. A photograph of him – younger, hair suave and swept back – is proffered to be signed.

All very unremarkable, except that, reflecting much later, I began to suspect he created this example of Sod's Law to amuse himself. From the corner of his eye he saw the first autograph hunter approaching and thought at racing speed – the habit of a lifetime – *how can I get some fun out of this?* In that milli-second he worked out what he'd say, anticipated I'd have to go along with it and delighted in luring me into Sod's Law which wasn't.

It worked.

If Firman suffered as he settled in 2003, Antonio Pizzonia went straight to hell. At 22, and driving for Jaguar, things went so wrong that in a feeding frenzy the full weight of the Media insisted he was finished. Jaguar, they said, will do the deed any minute now. Jaguar didn't and by mid-season Pizzonia was qualifying respectably and finishing the races. I venture that given the circumstances – the one-shot qualifying, an unreliable car – his initial predicament was as acute as it gets.

You had to face the fact that the whole world was saying you'd be replaced.

'Exactly.'

And from that situation by mid-season you were beginning to establish yourself. So how did you take it?

'If you imagine the worst possible way to start an F1 career, this was it. I went through that: the worst situation you can imagine. I haven't seen this happen in the past with anyone else so early, so young, who had so many new things to cope with and so many problems. It's definitely not the way that I wanted to start my career, you know, but if you see the positive side of it, I learnt and it wasn't that bad because I gained a lot of experience. That only makes me stronger and stronger.'

It didn't break you.

'No, not at all.'

It must have been very difficult to cope with.

'It's not the situation … that you want. It is difficult. You just have to prove them wrong on the track. I had to prove people wrong.'

Did you ever doubt yourself?

'Not really, you know. I am still 100% confident. I know I can do the job from what I have done in the past, and I know I can do it better than a lot of drivers on the grid. I am 100% sure about *that*.

'There are problems at the moment trying to adjust the car to the way I drive, which is the biggest problem, but slowly things are getting better. Also I am finishing the races. I think that's the main thing. It's very easy to make a slow car reliable but it's very difficult to do it with a quick car – and the Jaguar is a lot quicker than last year's car.'

When you have this tremendous pressure on you, can you sleep at night?

'I guess!'

Can you eat food?

'Yesss!'

Do you go around your house kicking the doors?

'No, not really. Everyone has problems, and motor racing is a very, very tough sport. If you get the best driver, the best car and put everything together, you still lose more races than you win. It's always like that, so basically you are going to have more disappointments in a Formula 1 career than happiness. That's the way I see it. I accept that because that's the way the sport is.

'If you take say Kimi Räikkönen, he's a good driver, he's with McLaren but he lost more than he won. Ralf Schumacher, he lost more than he won. Montoya, lost more than he won, Michael [Schumacher], same thing. That's the way it is. I am sure all the drivers are alike. You are only going to be fully happy when you win a race, but of course there is a big difference between cars and teams. Maybe if I get to the podium with Jaguar that's going to feel like a win for me.'

This book began with an abbreviated quotation from Pizzonia. I'd like to give it in full now because it seems to encapsulate so much of what all of the others have been saying. That he is a rookie saying it doesn't matter a damn. A great truth is a great truth is a great truth.

Is it necessary to be hard to survive in your world?

'Well, it's difficult. Outside of the car is, I think, even tougher than inside.'

Why?

'Let's say it's a swimming pool full of sharks and you have to find a way to survive in this swimming pool. You have to be a shark? Well, you have to know how to defend yourself but that doesn't mean you always have to be a shark. Anyway, I'm too young to understand exactly what happens in Formula 1 but after all the things that *have* happened I've a lot of experience, even in my first season. The first half of it was good in teaching me how to survive. Now I have to learn how to battle in among the sharks.'

They all do, and did, and will.

When I wrote those words I had no idea that within three hours Pizzonia would have lost his battle. It was the Monday after the British Grand Prix at Silverstone, where he had outqualified team-mate Mark Webber (10th against 11th, a small but possibly significant factor in his salvation) and was running towards a finish in the points when an engine problem stopped him.

That Monday, Jaguar issued a statement saying to 'their great regret' Pizzonia 'has not been able to realise his potential with the team over the past eleven races.' It was not in his or the team's 'best interests' for him to continue as a full-time racing driver for them. However, 'in an effort to continue supporting Antonio's development, Jaguar Racing has offered him the opportunity to remain with the team as reserve and test driver.'

Just another turn of the wheel.

NOTE
1. *Independent on Sunday*, 23 February 2003.

THE RIGHT TRACK

*Bernie Shrosbree is manager of Benetton's Human Performance
Centre. Andrew Walton, of Andrew Walton & Associates,
has been a sports psychologist since 1981.*

BERNIE SHROSBREE

We're sitting in a small office in a modern building within
sight of Benetton's Oxfordshire factory. The building is
part-gymnasium. An astonishing array of machinery sits, silent
and robotic, waiting to be worked hard. The £4 million centre
was conceived as a resource for top athletes in a range of
disciplines from round-the-world yacht racing to mountain
biking and, in relation to motorsport, to provide 'a personalised,
scientific and comprehensive approach to driver and team
training.' Shrosbree is a straightforward man who comes from a
hard background in the services and cross-country skiing. He's
needed what he describes as mental toughness.

'It's been very interesting to get inside the world of the racing
driver, to find out what makes them tick. Sometimes you think
you are seeing extremely hard, tough, aggressive people, but the
best are very calm, cool-headed characters. They have
incredibly strong minds and visualisation about what they do. I
have learnt in my job that to enhance their performance you
really, really have to understand the individual. You cannot get
these guys together and say "right, you're all going to do this" –
you need to get them on their own. You can't put two guys

together who have different weaknesses because it's not like a runner or a skier. These guys are motorsport drivers and their skill is to drive that car. Some guys can be extremely fit and use a lot of physical aggression to drive, and some can be extremely calm and produce the goods too. It's all about that skill-feel factor with a car.'

Shrosbree had earlier mentioned a test with Giancarlo Fisichella, and it turned out to be another example from the Wendlinger-Coulthard school of visualisation.

'We put a full-face visor on him that was blacked out, sat him so he could do all the pedal actions, and he had to visualise the whole circuit at Monaco. You start the stopwatch, he does the lap and he's within tenths of his real times. That's how extraordinary his visualisation was but it also shows the strength of his mind: it's the concentration factor. People watch a race and say "why's so-and-so gone off into the gravel trap?" The more I get into the mind of the driver the more I come back to it being about pure concentration. There is so much going on in that mind. I know a lot of people feel it happens by habit from repetitive training but the drivers have to keep that focus for close to an hour and 45 minutes and are not allowed to lose concentration for one tenth of a second. You can switch into robotic mode just following the car in front but, most of the time, the best drivers will be pushing, looking for that edge. It's that continuous focus, that continuous discipline to stay on the pace and keep the sharpness, the alertness of reaction.'

Does a driver need psychological protection to survive in the F1 hunting ground?

'They need guidance from someone who's competed at the top and knows what it's like to be beaten and keep being beaten, but who also knows about the euphoria of winning.

Sometimes you might just need to nod your head, wink an eye, thumbs up, pat on the back. There won't be a lot of verbal communication.

'Away from that environment, in the two days leading up to a race, there's so much going on with the media and looking after sponsors and the qualifying, that it's too late. The preparation on a quiet Tuesday afternoon here is the important part. I've just done three days in Monaco sticking the guys [Jenson Button and upcoming driver Mark Webber] in an environment where they are riding bikes on their own for two hours continuously. They're away from people and it gives them time to think. Physically it's tough but what it does do is give them time to look where they're at.

'We talk about it afterwards, because people will go to the gym to work out for the hell of it whereas the training we do here is to try and enhance their well-being and their self-confidence. If you make a driver fitter and stronger, and he sees himself getting quicker on the reaction times, it builds and builds more confidence. We're trying to build all this further, so when you put them in the car and they're waiting for the lights to go off they're not intimidated that Michael Schumacher's coming through on the inside or somebody else's coming through on the outside. The idea of getting a driver's mind right about that is just part of it. *Don't get paranoid. You have to respond, you have to grind the opposition down.* That's what makes these guys so special: there's no let up, no forgiveness, no way I'm going to give in to you. I will be back and I will be in your face. That's the key.'

Is the driving a male thing, a jockeying for dominance?

'It's like rugby. Someone asked me about the fitness of a driver and I said it was like the neck of a prop forward and the endurance of a marathon runner. I prefer to liken it to gladiators rather than rugby – in the last five minutes of a qualifying session the drivers are true gladiators. You can have three or four drivers outwitting each other and that for me shows the cutting edge of this sport, the knife-edge. Now imagine winning Monaco. It's like all the great emperors come along to watch which gladiator will survive. It's a modern version of that – and Monaco is the great emperor race.'

In the whole of this book, only Jonathan Palmer admits a team-mate was better.

'When you're at the peak of form you've got the psychological warfare and it's no surrender. Even if you know in your heart that a driver may be better, you'll say it's because his car is better. That keeps the wick alight!

'I'm here and Flavio Briatore will send me [young] drivers and ask me about them, how fit they are, their attitude. It's like little schoolboys coming for their first interview for a job – knowing they can walk into a job where they won't be stacking shelves in a shop but in two years could be a very, very rich and famous person; it's like wonderland. That is a very short-lived phase in a driver's career and you do need guidance. If a kid at 21 becomes a multi-millionaire, like Jenson, it's extremely hard not to run with it, but in his defence I have to say I've just been with him in Monaco working hard and he said "this is really, really good for me." The natural human way of life is to be very proud of what you've got' – a big yacht in Monaco harbour – 'and your life becomes a high-flying social life. That is where some of the drivers – not all – can go down the wrong track.'

So what did you do with him for the three days?

'We popped up into the mountains. He'll tell you himself: "When Bernie comes over, I eat, I train and I sleep." They know what I'm like. I take away the girlfriend-wife scenario although they may meet up with them in the evenings. My job is to keep the vision, to keep them on the right track. Drivers do have a crowded schedule, racing and testing, and when they have a few days off they want to pack a celebrity lifestyle into it.'

One of the most revealing stories in the book is that Eddie Irvine says he would be unaffected by running over a mechanic if a pit stop went wrong.

'I can sort of agree with that. You are only as good as your team. I come from a background in the services where if you foul up, someone gets killed. If someone makes a mistake and gets shot – it's the same sort of thing, or rather an extreme version of it – you've got to carry on. Deep down, if Irvine has fouled up it would live with him, but if it wasn't his fault and the mechanic had fouled up he should not let it affect what's going on although he should be aware of it.

'If at the pit stop you got out of the car to see how the mechanic was and somebody said "oh, he's all right" you'd get slated because you've failed in your job. And we are all given a job role. If you finished the race and said "I couldn't concentrate" then you've failed. There are 300-odd people in the team all wanting you to win, and you're worrying about someone who's been run over ... it's the same thing as the marshal who died when the wheel came off [Villeneuve in Australia, 2001]. I'm sorry to say that it is the sport. If Jacques worries about that he shouldn't be there. If it had been a member of Eddie's family then yes, it would have knocked him for six, but he is relying on people who are in their jobs knowing it's dangerous. The bottom line is "if you don't want to drive it we have to put somebody else in who does." It's a top-end sport ...'

Several drivers have called winning a drug.

'I know what they mean. It's what it does to you – it releases all the adrenalin and it is better than sex. Well, it's the euphoria of having the best lay of your life. That's a quite tacky way to put it, but true. That incredible euphoria can only be likened to good sex.'

How do they survive without the drug when the career ends?

'People asked me [towards the end of Damon Hill's career] "d'you think Damon's lost it?" I didn't believe that, I just thought he started to accept that it was enough. You know, the wick starts to go out a little bit. It's a sport where a youngster like Montoya comes into it with fire in his eyes. He is so hungry. But think what the driver faces: year-in year-out the testing, maybe a bit of an under-performing car, the discipline, the sacrifices.'

What are the differences between Grand Prix drivers and ordinary people?

'The passion for achievement that has been there from a very young age. They have been given an opportunity which most people don't get, because you need so much money and there are so few drives. Looking at it the other way, though, your dad might have been the greatest driver but if you get on a kart for the first time and you're scared, and you don't like it, you're not going to make it. But if you aren't like that, and you are a guy who has been given this opportunity to excel, you *need* to see it through. It's a fantastic fantasy world that you can live. To reach that, however, you need to be disciplined and very mentally tough. The weak ones will flake very quickly.'

Jenson Button is quoted in the book about how he understands Schumacher's controversies because this is a hard sport played by hard men. Jenson gives the impression of being polite, well-

bred – the kind to help old ladies across the street.

'He is that guy, but once the helmet goes on he is there to do what he is capable of doing, which is to take no prisoners. It's me or you.

'At Monaco we were descending from the mountain on the bikes – we're reaching speeds of nearly 60mph, and there are switchback bends with 2ft high blocks on the edge and then a 350ft drop. Mark Webber was there and he had a bit of a slippy moment. Jenson said "we shouldn't ride down together, Bernie, because you're a competitive person and we're racing drivers. We'll be competing and nobody will give up until someone crashes."'

ANDREW WALTON

We're sitting in a conservatory which is part of a small country house in the Midlands: it's a hotel cum restaurant now, and quietly dignified. Andrew Walton has spent a couple of decades as a consulting psychologist (www.andrewwalton.co.uk) working in sport and he interprets what, why and how sportspeople do what they do. The conservatory is a very quiet place and ideal for contemplation. You can't even hear passing cars.

'Anonymity is like virginity,' he says. 'When you've lost it, you've lost it for ever.'

This amuses me because, after all these years of writing about Grand Prix I can assure you that every driver I've ever met had lost his virginity and anonymity, but you take the point he is making: the mental world of the driver involves a lot more than driving. He must accommodate becoming a very visible symbol of money, power, bravery and sex – and risk public failure too.

'Every competitive sportsperson benefits from understanding

the psychology of their own capabilities. The truth is that sportspeople have certain things in common but it's difficult to quantify this. They all have a competitive urge and an urge to enjoy physical effort – most sports tend to be physical in nature. Because professional sport is so competitive they are required to master the mental needs which go hand in hand with the physical needs. Every sport where there is a table of achievements – a league, a championship – exerts extreme mental pressures, and coping requires significant mental input.'

How does motor racing compare with other sports?

'The most obvious factor is the complexity of the relationship between machine and man. Most sports are played with non-mechanical implements – rackets, cricket bats, golf clubs and so on. There are increasingly clever designs to enhance the performance of rowing boats in the water but the rowers don't have to constantly adjust the boat during a race in the way that racing drivers do with their cars. They more or less just row! That, I believe, highlights not just the complexity of the man-machine relationship in Grand Prix racing but the complexity of the racing car itself.'

There is a further aspect to motor racing: you can get killed doing it. Most sports simply don't have that.

'The most obvious ones which might seem to offer a comparison are downhill skiing and bob-sleighing but an experienced competitor in either can anticipate the type of "encounter" that's likely to be dangerous because the range is so small. In motor racing the encounters are many, varied, can happen in bewildering combinations and at much faster speeds. This makes further mental demands on the driver.'

Does this mindset separate the racing driver from the rest of us?

'The key difference is the level of danger and the limited amount of time to respond in. The FIA have a set of rules regarding etiquette – I was going to say courtesy – on the track. There has to be a framework of appreciation so that drivers have an idea what other drivers are supposed to be doing – not what they will do, but what they are supposed to do.'

The time to respond in: that's a crucial phrase.

'With racing drivers, it is very much the instant of decision that counts, and the decision has to be right because otherwise the consequences might be catastrophic. That is without question a fundamental difference between them and others. It's not just the time, either, or the swiftness of reaction but the ability of the driver to multi-task. That means to be aware of a number of things simultaneously, or as near simultaneously as it is possible to be. The key difference between the winners and the also-rans is this ability to keep an eye open on every situation and monitor it on a regular basis. That means you're able to maintain a complete mental overview of everything relevant.'

(In an interview with *Autosport* in 2001, Ferrari Technical Director Ross Brawn broadened this theme when he explained that 'there was neither the level of information nor the complexity of strategy ten years ago, and every year it is getting more and more intense – but Michael [Schumacher] is keeping up with it, constantly adapting. He is fascinated by every aspect of it and just completely immerses himself in the job at all levels.')

'In a crisis, the amount of time that the driver can spend on multi-tasking is very, very limited, which is why the interior of the cockpit is ergonomic. That means the dials and controls are simplified as much as they can be. The key point is that if something serious is going wrong the driver will probably sense it from the vehicle, it won't be revealed by the dashboard.'

Are Grand Prix drivers different from the rest of us?

'Their skills have been honed so that they have specific capabilities much greater than the average person. Man is a mixture of his genetic make-up, his physical qualities and his experiences and how he has construed those experiences to be relevant to his future. Man is at the cutting edge of time: he can only anticipate, and base that on experience.

'The first psychologist to really understand this process was George Kelly who, in 1955, as professor at the Ohio State University, published a work called *The Psychology of Personal Constructs*. The cornerstone is prediction, anticipation, having a shrewd idea of what is going to happen. It must be as accurate as possible so he can control events as they come. To function where circumstances change so quickly – the speed Grand Prix racers drive at – everything needs to be at its optimum level.'

Are some people born competitive?

'You can inherit advantages and disadvantages from your parents and grandparents and their parents. There are undoubtedly genetic factors in the ability to achieve. Eyesight, hearing, reaction time and physical strength are all qualities which effectively are in your genetic make-up (although intriguingly some recent research, shown on the television programme *Speed*, demonstrated that we all have rapid reactions of much the same calibre).

'The advantages can be developed but the potential will have already been there. Look at Michael and Ralf Schumacher, brothers among the very small number of Formula 1 drivers and both capable of winning in different cars. As brothers, they must have inherited a great deal in common.'

But you might have totally uncompetitive parents. Jonathan Palmer's mother ran a nursing home and his father was a doctor.

'He would have inherited certain attributes which gave him the push and edge to go forward and they are reinforced by a dimension which isn't inherited: the pleasure factor that comes with winning. It's what can be called rather grandly an intermittent reinforcement schedule. There is a region of the brain responsible for pleasure and if it gets stimulated from time to time you develop the urge to receive that pleasure over and over again. Grand Prix racing seems the perfect example of that. If a driver wins all the time he could become complacent, but drivers don't win all the time so by definition the winning is something the driver finds very desirable to repeat.

'It is true of all competitive sportspeople. The pleasure of winning – not the money – requires them to carry on doing it. Of course the nice fat cheque which comes with winning, say, the British Grand Prix will please the region of your bank manager's brain responsible for pleasure, but that misses the point. By the time the driver has reached that level, he is making large amounts of money and finance is no longer a primary motivation. Michael Schumacher may get $30 million a year from Ferrari and, perhaps, another $20 million in endorsements. After a year or two of that the money loses relevance.

'The point lies in the moments of success: being able to raise your fist as you go past the chequered flag because, at that moment, you are number one and you know that however good the other drivers in the race were, however hard they worked, however fast they drove, they are all behind you. Then there's being up there on the podium and up there on the top rung above second and third, there's your national anthem, there's breaking open the champagne bottle, there's the television interview to the world where they always speak to you first because you're the winner. This is what you want – again and again. It is not purely self-indulgent and selfish adulation. Let me apply that to Schumacher, who does win a lot but isn't starting to think of himself like an Ayrton Senna, as a sort of deity. In a scientific and secular society, most drivers realise they are there by the efforts of themselves and their team, so when Schumacher crosses the line and raises his fist it's for Ferrari as much as himself.'

Is that a very basic human condition?

'To want to be recognised by your peers, yes. It's nice to be acknowledged by outsiders who are aware of what you've done, but to be acknowledged by your peers is a necessary urge – it happens in every walk of life.'

When you look at Schumacher what do you see?

'The quintessential, calculating, orderly, authoritarian, emotionally-controlled Prussian officer – in comparison to the Irvine stereotype who is the tousle-haired, cravat-wearing, button-opened Spitfire pilot who basically likes to live but can control a machine too. Irvine seems to feel that life is all about having instant gratification. Let's grab that girl, she looks sweet. Irvine's attitude is one which attracts the media as desirable: the fun-loving character who won't simply become a one-dimensional, mechanical man. That's a useful compensation for the fact that the racing driver needs to be so one-sided, dedicated and devoted in his career.

'Senna, as it seemed, possessed a God-like dismissal of danger. He'd probably have had a different attitude if he'd grown up in a different country and a different social environment, but he grew up a Catholic and in Brazil and was shaped by that. What your belief structure is – what you hold to be true, whether you feel you'll meet your ancestors when you reach the hereafter – has particular relevance in the case of someone like Senna. It will determine whether you want to protect your life as much as possible or whether you are prepared to take dangerous risks. Senna probably felt God was on his shoulder. What Senna believed was the equivalent of a dogma, and because he had no evidence to refute it he believed it wholeheartedly. That enabled him to act on it.

'I'm quite sure Schumacher is not like that. He's at the other end of the spectrum: far more calculating, far less temperamental. He is able to discipline his mind to attend to the priorities which come along in a race and, I suspect, he must have an almost formulaic approach to this prioritising.'

How do drivers cope when their own particular philosophy is tested, perhaps by having a serious accident?

'About 15 years ago a Cambridge psychologist, John Teasdale, came up with something called the attributional style. It's about coping with loss: every loss has to be explained away. This is a natural human requirement and it doesn't have to be a person, it could be loss of face, income, liberty, health. It has obvious relevance to Grand Prix drivers and is done in three ways.

'Is it internal or external? Internal means: does the driver blame himself if the car crashes? Does he say it's his fault? External means: Is it the track conditions? Did the car fail? A puncture? It could be a number of reasons, perhaps in combination, but none his fault.

'Is this a short- or long-term difficulty? Am I going to learn from the accident, modify my driving and overcome what caused it? Do I allow the problem to dominate me? If I do, that disqualifies me from dealing with it – but if I can keep it in a compartment and say "well, it doesn't stop me having other qualities" I won't be allowing it to dominate me.

'The attributional style certainly seemed to be apparent in the way Senna viewed himself and God's protection. Rudolf Ratzenberger's explanation that Roland lived his life twice as fully as a normal person is an attribution which defies the rational but consoles the bereaved.'

And there is the matter of a family.

'When drivers marry and start a family the temptation is to be less cavalier and more responsible, perhaps more thoughtful in a general way. It's fascinating to look at Schumacher's methods which have served him extremely well, so well that despite the extra responsibility of a family he is still capable of winning Grand Prix races on a regular basis.'

Martin Donnelly's car suffered a mechanical failure and nobody can ever guarantee that won't happen again – but Donnelly lived to get back in the car. How do they do that?

'They overestimate their ability and their sixth sense to anticipate any mechanical failure. When we sit in our cars and we hear a funny noise we don't necessarily know what it is but we know it's not right. A racing driver is intimately familiar with his car and has a feel – which is not really quantifiable – for that car's overall performance. He puts a great deal of store by that and consequently is prepared to extend a leap of faith into a presumption: that the car will continue travelling in a stable manner. Therefore he simply does not dwell on the possibility that there might be a mechanical failure, and even if he does think of it he's sure the sixth sense will give him advance warning.'

But he has almost certainly had mechanical failures before which have led to crashes. Is it possible to find a credo to exclude that?

'Without realising it, he is introducing a way of overcoming what's called globalisation, which is picking on one small event and magnifying it out of proportion. A professional driver, knowing as much as he does about the construction of the car, its capabilities and its engineering standards, will make an informed judgement about the probable likelihood of mechanical failure and will be able to cope with that notion by balancing the probabilities. He has a pie chart in his mind, as Perry McCarthy points out, and on it the prospect of that failure is a thin sliver. Pictorially he will have a sense that 99.9% of the pie is not the sliver. A driver's philosophy of life makes a difference in areas where he has no control. He is a realist. At the end of the day the realist reaches for a perspective and concludes that the likelihood of anything going wrong is so small that it can be considered as being as close to zero as possible.

'Niki Lauda survived his fiery crash at the Nürburgring and then the lesser one at Hockenheim. No ordinary person who'd just crashed at Hockenheim would think 'I have got time to get into another car' but that is exactly how racing drivers do think. At such moments that is all they think.'

Didier Pironi couldn't drive a Grand Prix car again after his injuries at Hockenheim but he restored his level of confidence enough to race a powerboat.

'You might say that he perceived the risks of powerboat racing as lower than those of car racing and he needed the thrill of something glamorous, something fast. I sense his whole lifestyle necessitated him being involved in that type of environment, the need for something that enabled him to maintain his identity amongst his friends, and to himself, because that was who he was. They may be idols and role models, and it goes back a long way into the human psyche. I am sure chariot drivers were idolised in the Coliseum.'

Which makes me wonder if every sportsperson has to be selfish.

'Yes. However I didn't see any evidence in the book of what we call antisocial personality.'

Walton sums up with a question. 'How much effort is really required for the racing driver to acquire what he needs to succeed? A famous American psychologist, Abraham Maslow, created what he called the Hierarchy of Needs. He said there were fundamental needs we all have to satisfy – eat, sleep, be warm – but considered there were higher needs, community needs, and at the pinnacle was the fulfilment of your own potential, known as self-actualisation (you become the person you have the potential to be). Not everybody is going to reach that but you can say that a Grand Prix driver, any Grand Prix driver, has done.

'Maslow argued that to have any chance of fulfilment those basic needs must be satisfied. The relevance here is that the next stage, the community needs, are represented by the driver's team. He delegates things to them so he has enough time to reach the pinnacle. The stage after that becomes an indication of the depth of his desire, and it is almost a sacrifice. The amount of time spent practising on race tracks in his youth, the hours of travel, the nights learning about the mechanical side of the car, must – at the exclusion of everything else – display the depth. That will tell every driver whether the pinnacle is too far away or can be reached.'

The pinnacle may be too far away but that doesn't mean the end. Brian Hart drove in a Grand Prix in Germany in 1967 and subsequently became a celebrated engine manufacturer. Bernie

Ecclestone tried to qualify twice, in Monaco and Britain in 1958. In fact, Hart gave me the perfect end to any study of the racing driver's mind. We were discussing the on-going to-and-fro between Ecclestone and the European Union over television rights and tobacco advertising.

Hart said: 'It's simple. Bernie will win – he'll out-think them.'

INDEX

Figures in italics refer to illustrations in plate sections, unfolioed pages *P1–P16*

100cc European Championships 57
3001 International team 89

Adelaide 136, 158, 207, 223, 234, 250,
    283, 294, 313
AGS 189, 295–296
Aiello, Laurent 48
Alboreto, Michele 23, 75, 158, 189, 206,
    214–215, 219, 223, 225, 229, 239,
    312, 314, 327, *P12*
Alesi, Jean 75, 104, 130, 144, 189–190,
    206–207, 212, 214, 222, 311, 329,
    331–333, 337, *P11*
Alliot, Philippe 156, 184, 187, 206,
    244–246
Allsop, Derick 96–97, *P2*
Allsop, Kate 96, *P2*
Allsop, Sue 96
Alzen, Uwe 48
Amon, Chris 313
Anderson, Gary 152
Anderson, Ove 316
Andrea Moda 22, 41, 85, 91, 173, 175, 220,
    P4
Andretti, Mario 55, 126, 155, 195, 213,
    240, 278, 313
Andretti, Michael 136
Apicella, Marco 89
Arai helmets 82
Argentina *P11*
Arnoux, René 164, 184, 228, 233, 273
Arrows Grand Prix 75, 79–80, 93, 180,
    207, 221, 265, 273, 326, 331, 337
ATS 81, 93, 144
Attributional style 371
Audi 66, 176, 312, 327
  R8 312
Austin-Healey Sprite 63
Australian Grand Prix 169, 226, 245
    1987 214
    1994 92

1995 313
1997 197
1999 212
2001 71, 300, 363
Austrian Airlines 315
Austrian Grand Prix 123, 214
    1976 159
    2000 124
    2002 13
Auto Union 66
Autocar magazine 62
Autocourse magazine 220, 232
Autosport magazine 92, 232, 273, 367
Ayrton Senna: As Time Goes By book 225

Badoer, Luca 97, 188
Bailey, Julian 22, 60, 67, 83, 85, 93,
    126–128, 130, 145, 167, 172–173,
    180–181, 191, 194, 246, 260, 317
Balestre, Jean-Marie 242, 274
BAR 201, 300, 346
Barcelona 19, 140, 146, 171, 188, 235,
    292–292, 294
Barclay, Jack 14
Barnard, John 79, 240–241
Barrichello, Rubens 10, 12–13, 97, 101,
    107, 115, 122–123, 135, 152, 188,
    216, 271, 299, 347, *P11*
Bayern Munich football team 32
BBC 154, 184
Beggio, 57
Belgian Grand Prix 169, 190, 207, 271
    1987 243–244
    1995 22, 108
Bell, Derek 134–135, 148
Bellof, Stefan 134–135, 147, 156–157, 280,
    313
Belmondo, Jean-Paul 143
Benetton 68, 92, 108, 121, 128, 135,
    147–148, 183, 274
    Human Performance Centre 359

Benson, David 8–9
Bentley 14–16, 347, *P3*
Beretta, Olivier 287
Berger, Gerhard 93, 129–130, 138, 144, 147,
    168, 181–182, 197, 209, 214, 222–224,
    228, 257, 286, 292, 326, 328, *P14/15*
Bernard, Eric 64–65, 183–184, 327–328, 330
Beveridge, Graham 300
Birmingham Superprix 214
Blundell, Mark 15, 18, 42, 125, 137–138,
    163, 172–173, 180–183, 191, 196, 217,
    223, 251, 266, 281, 284, 313, 317–318,
    343, 347, 351, *P3, P10*
BMW 326
Boesel, Raul 92
Boutsen, Thierry 68, 92, 137, 212, 214
Brabham 131, 134, 137–138, 147–148, 165,
    173, 182, 194–195, 213, 223, 238,
    313
Brabham, David 15–16, 178–179, 347, *P3*
Brabham, Jack 196
Brands Hatch 37–38, 53, 63, 68, 83, 92–93,
    144, 154, 179, 185, 228, 234, 248, 250
Brawn, Ross 10, 105, 116, 367
Brazilian Grand Prix 85, 127, 164, 189, 192
    1983 146–147
    1988 230
    1994 152, 183, 287
    2001 272
Briatore, Flavio 362
Bridgestone 80
British Formula 3 Championship 92, 352
British Grand Prix 93, 259–260, 337, 369
    1958 375
    1981 78
    1993 283
    1995 322
    2003 358, *P11*
Brittan, Nick 209, 214
BRM 313
Broadley, Eric 169
Brundle, Martin 81, 156, 158, 181–183, 197,
    208, 229, 328, 330
Buckmore Park karting circuit 49–50
Budapest 141, 143
Burti, Luciano 115, 124
Button, Jenson 35, 42, 49, 68, 73–74, 78,
    209, 271, 346–347, 361–362, 364–365
Byrne, Rory 116
Caesars Palace, Las Vegas 210
Caffi, Alex 244–245

Camel 128, 130
Canadian Grand Prix 101, 123, 189, 194, 228
    1982 274, 281
    1988 *P12*
    1989 206
    1993 140
    1995 332
    1997 *P13*
Capelli, Ivan 184, 187–191, *P6*
Capello, Rinaldo 15
Caracciola, Rudolf 54, 66
Carlier, Agnes 70
Catalunya 32
Cavendish Finance 83–84
Cevert, François 303, 313
Champ cars 251
Channel 4 TV 184
Chapman, Colin 148, 240–241, 274
Cheever, Eddie 43, 165, 184
CIK Junior Cup 57
Citroën 254
Clark, Jim 178, 236, 240, 302
Cobra, Nuno 20
Cockings, Jerome 313
Collins, Peter 128, 140, 148, 191, 193, 249,
    274
Comas, Erik 299
Constanduros, Bob 172
Cosworth 349–351, *P13*
    DFV engine 144
Coton, Didier 209
Coulthard, David 20, 23, 32, 123, 204, 214,
    216, 231, 235, 275, 360, *P14/15, P16*
Croft 343
CSS promotions 157

Daily Express newspaper 8, 300
Daily Telegraph newspaper 29
Daly, Derek 80
DAMS 88–89
Danner, Christian 157
de Angelis, Elio 56, 281, 309, 335
de Cesaris, Andrea 96, 164, 180, 184, 195,
    241
de Chaunac, Hughes 66
de Laborderie, Renaud 313
de Savary, Peter 82, 93
Dennis, Ron 37–38, 65, 78, 89, 167, 210,
    240
Depailler, Patrick 213
Detroit 165, 184

Devlin, Ed 153, 253–254, 256–258
di Montezemolo, Luca 36, 190–191
Dodgins, Tony 174
Donaldson, Gerald 232
Donington Park 54, 90, 132, 137, 140, 239,
    305–306, 344
Donnelly, Diane 255, 257, 263
Donnelly, Martin 22, 75, 92, 117, 130,
    153–154, 222, 233, 251, 253–263, 275,
    310–311, 331, 337, 372, *P6*
Drapeau Rouge book 313
Duke Video 275
Dumfries, Johnny 227–228, 330
Dungl, Willy 166, 184, 255, 257–258,
    260–261, 293
Dutch Grand Prix 1976 159

Earle, Mike 89–90
Ebel, Kai 32
Ecclestone, Bernie 25, 104, 131, 134,
    194–195, 299, 303–304, 313, 315, 362,
    365, 375
Eddie Irvine: The Inside Track film 48, 118
Einstein, Albert 222
Elf 64, 298
Ensign 274
Equinox TV programme 184, 301
Estoril 136, 157, 325
Euro Brun 146, 254
European Grand Prix
    1983 81, 144, 148
    1984 148
    1997 92
    1999 322
European Union 375
Evans, David 82

F1 Racing magazine 29, 48, 124
FA Cup 48
Fabi, Teo 68, 92
Fangio, Juan Manuel 11
Ferrari 10, 12–14, 36, 40, 50, 55, 95, 97, 99,
    104–105, 108, 110, 115–116, 121–123,
    142, 146, 168, 188–191, 203, 206, 209,
    214, 222, 226–227, 231–232, 271,
    273–274, 311, 325, 332, 367, 369–370
Ferrari, Enzo 97, 123, 227
FIA 25, 71, 152, 232, 242, 248, 274, 295,
    298, 367
FIA GT Championship 287
FIA Review Board 183–184

FISA 274
Financial Times newspaper 111
Fiorano 10, 97, 188
Firman, Angie 351
Firman, Ralph 351
Firman, Ralph Jnr 339, 350–355, *P13*
Fisichella, Giancarlo 102, 124, 324, 352, 360
Fittipaldi, Christian 89
Fittipaldi, Emerson 270
Fittipaldi, Wilson 313
FOCA 25, 223
Focus magazine 97
Foitek, Gregor 178, 185, 248
Fondmetal 220
Footwork 221, 225
Ford Motor Co. 24
    engines 266
Formula Ford 60, 87, 223
Formula Ford 1600 56, 182, 314
Formula Ford Zetec Euro Cup 71
Formula Nippon 352
Formula One Administration Ltd 48
Formula Palmer Audi 62, 66, 328
Formula Renault 71, 75, 331
Formula Renault Sport 343
Formula Renault 2000 71
Formula Vauxhall-Lotus 87–88
Formula 2 70, 77–78, 80, 92–93, 145, 156,
    196
Formula 3 38, 55–56, 64–66, 71, 75, 77–79,
    82, 87, 92, 96, 141, 145, 160, 168, 178,
    260, 331, 352
Formula 3000 17, 37, 56, 64–65, 68, 75,
    83–85, 87–89, 93, 128, 130, 146, 149,
    152, 178, 180, 207–208, 214, 223, 248,
    252, 294, 305, 309, 341
French Grand Prix 123, 194, 206, 312, 316,
    337
    1989 75, 222, 331
Frentzen, Heinz-Harald 19, 32, 96, 123,
    141–143, 155, 176, 197–199, 201, 212,
    214, 218, 271, 287–288, 293–294
Full Throttle: the technology of speed TV
    programme 160

Gaignault, Gilles 313
Gartner, Jo 280, 313
German Grand Prix 123–124, 158, 190
    1967 374
    1987 93
    1995 108

1999 122
2000 97
Giacomelli, Bruno 80
Gilardi, Andrea 57
Giovanardi, Fabrizio 188
Goodwood Festival of Speed 349, *P13*
Goodyear 75
Goon Show, The radio series 184
Gothenburg 57
Grand Prix Data Book 212
Grand Prix Drivers' Association (GPDA) 302, 313
Grand Prix Medical Service 313
Grand Prix People book 232
Gugelmin, Mauricio 93, 187, 267–269
Gugelmin, Stella 187

Häkkinen, Erja 243
Häkkinen, Mika 14, 32, 36, 64, 88, 136, 181, 191–194, 198, 203–204, 209–212, 214, 216, 231, 234, 243, 245, 250, 260, 272, 283–284, 313, *P8*
Hamilton, Maurice 232, 255, 275, 311
Hard Rock Club, Tokyo 152
Hart engines 152
Hart, Brian 152, 233, 242, 261, 311, 374–375
Hawkridge, Alex 65, 128, 147
Hayhoe, David 212
Heidfeld, Nick 73, 170, 176–177, 183
Hemingway, Ernest 126
Henman, Tim 26
Henry, Alan 220
Henton, Brian 80, 156
Herbert, Becky 185
Herbert, Johnny 15–16, 22, 37–38, 49, 67, 92, 109, 115, 121, 127, 130, 135, 140, 147, 164, 178, 180, 185, 191–192, 194, 212, 214, 234, 248, 251, 274, 286, 311, 322, 325–326, 347, 349, *P3*
Hercules Corporation 242, 274
Hesketh, Lord Alexander 129, 147
Hethel 191, 213
Hierarchy of Needs 374
Hill, Damon 42, 68, 89, 92, 130, 150–151, 153, 179–180, 311, 364, *P14/15*
Hill, Graham 70, 196, 349
Hockenheim 27, 100–101, 141, 172–173, 207, 210, 215, 222, 224, 226, 261, 266, 373
Hofer, Heinz 159

Holland, 212
Honda engines 56, 198, 346
Hulme, Denny 196
Human Face of Formula, The book 228
Hungarian Grand Prix 168, 190, 226
1987 93
1991 210
1992 220
1998 108
2000 97
Hungaroring 221
Hunt, James 36, 55, 70, 118, 147

Ickx, Jackie 70, 148
Imola 19–20, 137, 140, 153, 157–158, 182, 189, 192, 197, 230, 257, 269, 278, 281, 286–288, 295, 298, 305, 312–313, 318
Independent newspaper 96, 358
Indianapolis 270–271, 275
IndyCar 37, 261, 267, 284, 317, *P10*
Innsbruck Winter Olympics 313
Interlagos 272
International Management Group (IMG) 69, 92
Irvine, Eddie 21–22, 24, 36, 39–40, 69, 87, 95, 109–112, 120, 122–124, 135, 149–154, 183–184, 211, 214, 231, 243, 298, 345, 351, 363, 370, *P8*
Italian Grand Prix 169, 190
1978 147, 278
1981 235
1984 148
1993 298
1990 264
1994 *P11*
1995 322
2000 40, 300, 306
ITV 182

Jacarepagua 295–297, 336
Jaguar 37, 111, 118
Jaguar Racing 112, 116, 120, 124, 212, 319, 325–326, 355, 357–358, *P5*
Japanese Grand Prix 55, 151, 169, 194
1993 136
1994 287
1999 40, 110, 198, 211
Jerez 71, 128, 253, 261, *P6*
Jim Clark Trophy 158, 184
Johansson, Stefan 31, 134, 148, 227–229, 339

Jones, Alan 43, 238, 273–274, 350, 354–355

Jordan 34, 54, 96, 115, 122, 144, 149–150, 152, 198–200, 214, 254, 270, 274, 310–311, 350, 352, *P6, P13*

Jordan, Eddie 75, 128, 190, 198, 200, 271, 311, 331

Jordan-Peugeot 22

Karting magazine 57

Katayama, Ukyo 220, 222

Kehm, Sabine 96–97

Kelly, George 368

Klammer, Franz 287, 313

Kopczyk, Peter 96, *P2*

Kray, Reggie 303

Ktistensen, Tom 15

Kyalami 322

Laffite, Jacques 144, 148, 213

Land, Prof Mike 160

Larrauri, Oscar 146

Larrousse 299

Larrousse, Gerard 299

Lauda Air 315

Lauda, Niki 27, 55, 70, 79–80, 129, 131–134, 165, 184, 194–195, 208–210, 213, 229, 234, 239, 257, 315, 325–326, 340, 346, 373, *P5, P11*

Lausitzring 312

Le Mans 24hr race 18, 45–46, 148, 204, 225, 280, 312, 339
  1986 313
  1998 48
  2003 15–17, 347–348, *P3*

Leberer, Josef 138–139

Lehto, JJ 141, 143, 172–173

Lewis, Stephen 313

Leyton House 189

Ligier 183–184, 282, 295

Log Cabin, Suzuka 36

Lola 89, 169, 244

Lombard RAC Rally 214

Lombardi, Claudio 189

Long Beach 241

Lotus 75, 79, 127, 130, 140, 148, 153, 181, 191, 193, 195, 213, 222, 226, 230, 240, 251, 253–254, 260–261, 264, 278, 286, 349, 354, *P6, P9*

Lotus Cortina 62

Luton Airport 111

Luton Football Club 82

Macau Grand Prix 56, 66

Magny, François-Xavier 313

Magny-Cours 140, 205

Malaysian Grand Prix 55
  1999 110, 231
  2000 159, 216
  2001 300

Mallory Park 341

Manchester United football team 32, 48, 116

Mansell, Nigel 39, 64, 163, 166, 168–169, 176, 210–211, 220, 222, 229, 233, 273, 284, 330, 333

Maranello 10, 20, 104, 188, 190–191, *P2*

March 78, 80, 143, 189, 322

Marlboro 64, 89, 92, 97, 130, 185, 235

Marlboro Grand Prix Guide 212

Marriott, Andrew 157

Maslow, Abraham 374

Matra people-carrier 334–336

Mayer, Teddy 195, 214

McCarthy, Perry 22, 41, 44, 85, 87, 91, 130, 143, 162, 171–175, 180, 220–222, 232, 320, 373, *P4*

McCormack, Mark 92

McDonald, John 78, 82, 93, 156

McKenzie, Bob 300

McLaren 25, 38, 65, 78–80, 88–89, 92, 105, 131, 134, 136–138, 153, 166, 180, 183–184, 197, 201, 203, 209, 211, 214, 229–231, 235, 239–240, 259, 274, 284, 298, 327, 340–341, 357, *P12*

McNish, Allan 33, 45, 48, 50, 56–58, 60, 64, 89–92, 140, 178, 202, 204, 206, 305–306, 316–317

McNish, Bert 60, 87

Melbourne 71, 346

Mercedes 54, 64, 66, 246

Mexican Grand Prix 189
  1986 157
  1988 246–247

MGB 302

Michelin 46, 81

Michigan speedway 270

Mihell, Nigel 341–343, *P4*

Millwall football team 116

Millward, Peter 82, 155

Minardi 34, 45, 74, 91, 122, 205

Miyakawa, 337

Monaco 18, 25, 72, 117, 123, 129, 140,
    157–158, 167–168, 184, 189–190,
    193–194, 200, 204, 209, 230, 289,
    322, 325, 327, 360–362, 365, 375, P6
Monte Carlo 190, 239, 321–322
Montoya, Juan Pablo 107, 272, 342, 357,
    364
Montreal 206, 245
Monza 10, 40, 118, 138, 141, 147, 235,
    237, 242, 263, 266, 271, 274, 278,
    298, 306, 332–333, P9
Moreno, Roberto 22, 79, 93, 184, 220–222,
    254
Mosley, Max 71, 315
Mosport 313
Motor magazine 62
Mugello 19–20, 71, 108, 294
Müller, Jörg 48, 57
Murray, Gordon 133, 147, 213

Nannini Alessandro 169
Naspetti, Emanuele 306, 308
Nichols, Steve 229–230
Nilsson, Gunnar 55
Nissan 169
Nogaro 294
Nürburgring 108, 148, 234, 257, 322, 324,
    373
Nye, Doug 184

Ohio State University 368
Ojjeh, Akram 184
Ojjeh, Mansour 166–167, 184
Oliver, Jackie 79–80, 93, 221
Olivetti-Longines timing 232
Oreca 64, 66
Orsini, 57
Ortelli, Stéphane 48
Osella 244, 274
Oulton Park 304, 309

Pace, Carlos 36, 48, 195, 213
Pacific Grand Prix 1994 184, 305
PacWest 266, 281, 317–318
Paletti, Riccardo 245, 274, 281
Palmer, Jonathan 60–61, 66, 76, 79–82, 85,
    87, 92, 140, 144–145, 147–148, 155,
    157, 167, 184, 206–209, 214, 218,
    229, 243–245, 280, 315, 330, 351,
    362, 369, P10, P14/15
Panis, Oliver 138

Parmalat 132
Patrese, Riccardo 56, 137
Paul Ricard 66, 75, 79, 176, 194, 203, 208,
    281, 288–289, 292, 315, 335
Paul Stewart Racing 341
Penske 158
Penske, Roger 158–159
Perkins, Larry 195 213
Peterson, Ronnie 55, 134, 147, 195, 213,
    239, 274, 278
Peugeot 22, 319
Phoenix 192
Piccinini, Marco 226
Piecha, Stan 92
Piquet, Nelson 56, 134, 147–148, 238, 262,
    273–274, 333
Pirelli 82, 223
Pironi, Didier 165, 210, 261, 273–274, 373
Pizzonia, Antonio 8, 355, 357–358, P5
Porsche 45–46, 48, 157, 225, 313
Portuguese Grand Prix 169, 190
    1984 148, 184
    1989 207
    1993 136, 141
Postlethwaite, Harvey 168, 190, 209, 316
PPG IndyCar World Series 266
Professor Watkins' Brain and Spine
    Foundation 111
Prost 34, 124, 170, 199–200, 333
Prost, Alain 34, 56, 92, 122, 131, 133, 147,
    149, 153, 164, 166–167, 184,
    195–196, 208, 210, 229–231, 242,
    250, 262, 298, 346, P12, P14/15
Psychology of Personal Constructs, The 368

Quero, Michel 22
Quest 127

Radio Times magazine 109
Rahal, Bobby 37
RAI television 191
Räikkönen, Kimi 49–50, 70–71, 74–75, 87,
    154–155, 203, 218, 357
Ralph, Mick 93
Ralt 81, 92
Ralt-Toyota 92
RAM 81, 93, 156, 206
Rambo magazine 255
Ramirez, Jo 136, 274
Ratzenberger, Roland 19, 277–278, 286,
    288, 304–305, 313, 372

Ratzenberger, Rudolf 277–278, 372
Red Lion, The Caston 253
Redgrave Racing 344
Rees, Alan 79, 93
Regazzoni, Clay 241, 274
Reitzle, Dr Wolfgang 24
Renaissance Centre Hotel, Detroit 44
Renault 64, 295, 310, 315, 319
Reutemann, Carlos 80, 194, 213, 313, *P11*
Reuter, Wolfgang 97, 100–102, 107–108
Revson, Peter 303
Reynard 128, 248, 266
Rindt, Jochen 10, 70, 196, 240
Rio 251, *P7*
Roebuck, Nigel 273
Roley, Ian 341–342
Rosberg, Keke 79–80, 144, 148, 165, 210,
    242
Rosemeyer, Bernd 54, 66
Rothengatter, Huub 157, 206
Royal Albert Hall 111, 120
RTL television 32

Salazar, Eliseo 79
Salo, Mika 122, 202–203, 214, 216, 316
San Marino Grand Prix
    1984 229
    1994 184, 280
    2001 20
    2003 14
Sassetti, Andrea 221
⬛o, Takuma 346
⬛uber 19, 25, 71, 73, 87, 140–141,
    ⬛ 170–171, 197, 202, 216, 286, 292,
    ⬛5, *P6*
⬛il factory 70
⬛er, Jody 160, 194, 303
Scheckter, Tomas 160–162
Schumacher, Gina-Maria 98
Schumacher, Michael 8, 10–11, 13–14, 21,
    36, 38, 40, 50, 57–58, 64, 68–69, 92,
    95–96, 98, 107, 110, 115, 121–124,
    130, 133–135, 142–143, 150, 159,
    166, 176–177, 188, 209, 212–214,
    216, 229, 231–232, 250, 262, 272,
    287, 306, 332–333, 346–347, 357,
    361, 364, 367–372, P2, *P13*, *P14/15*
Schumacher, Miki 98
Schumacher, Ralf 14, 50, 67, 107, 176, 300,
    324, 357, 368, *P13*
Scott, Dave 79

Scuderia Italia 189, 213
Seaman, Richard 54, 66
Seneca Lodge, Watkins Glen 35
Senna, Ayrton 19–20, 23, 32, 38–39, 65–66,
    77–78, 87–88, 97, 108, 118, 121, 124,
    129–131, 133, 135–138, 143,
    147–151, 153–154, 156, 158, 163,
    166–168, 170, 182, 184–185, 197,
    208–209, 214, 224, 225, 229–232,
    235–236, 242, 247, 250, 254,
    258–259, 262–263, 274, 281, 286,
    296, 298–299, 304–305, 310, 312,
    328, 333, 337, 341, 346, 351, 354,
    370–372, *P2*, *P12*
Sepang 55, 231
Shanahan, Neil 314
Shrosbee, Bernie 359
Silverstone 75, 78, 80–81, 92, 107, 110,
    137, 140, 164, 171, 207, 214, 231,
    250, 259, 282, 310, 319, 322, 343, 358
Simtek 278, 305, 313
Sisley, Bill 49, 54, 128
Smith, Guy 15
Snetterton 153, 184, 253–254
South African Grand Prix 189, 341
    1983 273
    1993 190, *P6*
Spa 96, 108, 148, 157, 170, 173, 175, 207,
    214, 217, 229, 233, 246, 266, 281, 300
Spanish Grand Prix 23, 108, 124, 169, 189,
    235, 253
    1986 157
    1990 251
    1995 284
    1999 32
Speed TV programme 368
Stanley, Louis T. 301–302, 313
Stepney, Nigel 113, 124
Stevens, John 26, 28–29
Stewart 122, 160
Stewart, Sir Jackie 8–10, 14, 44, 48, 69,
    159, 196, 300–302, 313–314,
    339–341, 349
Streiff, Philippe 64, 184, 206, 228,
    243–244, 246, 295–299, 334–337,
    339, *P7*
Streiff, Renée 297
Stuck, Hans 195, 213
Sun, The newspaper 92
Surer, Marc 80
Surtees, Edwina 50

Surtees, Henry 50–53
Surtees, John 49–50, *P8*
Suzuka 36, 48, 113, 124, 136, 149,
     152–153, 198, 212, 214, 242, 294
Swedish Grand Prix 195

TAG 184, 232
Tambay, Patrick 195
Tarquini, Gabriele 220–221
Tassin, Thierry 92
Tauranac, Ron 77, 79–80, 82, 92
Teasdale, John 371
Thomas, James 112
Thruxton 63, 79–80
Todt, Jean 10, 99, 116
Tokyo 152
Toleman 65, 147–148, 156, 158, 182, 184,
     319
Tolkien, JRR 350
Tolkien, Tim 350, *P13*
Toyota Formula 45, 202–203, 315–316
Toyota Motorsport 316
Triumph and Tragedy in Formula One book
     275
Trulli, Jarno 34, 54–55, 74, 199, 270–271
Tyrrell 63, 75, 81, 93, 126–127, 130, 145,
     147, 156, 158, 167, 182, 189,
     206–207, 209, 219, 222, 239,
     243–244, 247, 281, 284, 295–296,
     313, 329, 331
Tyrrell, Ken 67, 83–84, 146, 164, 169, 207,
     222, 245

Uden Associates 184
United States Grand Prix 55, 192, 270
     1973 303
United States (East) Grand Prix 44
     1982 184
United States (West) Grand Prix
     1980 274
Universal Studios 119
University of Sussex 160

Vairano 188
Valencia 124

van de Poele, Eric 220–221
Van Diemen 184, 259, 351
Vauxhall Lotus 341–342
Venturi 220
Verstappen, Jos 183
Villeneuve, Gilles 33, 309
Villeneuve, Jacques 32, 69, 92, 100, 123,
     210, 300, 344–347, 363, *P14/15*

Walker, Murray 273
Walton, Andrew 359, 365
Warwick, Derek 75, 156, 158, 254, 257,
     261, 264, 309, 319, 330, 337, *P9*
Warwick, Paul 309
Warwick, Stan 309
Watkins Glen 35, 48
Watkins, Prof Sid 90, 256–259, 262–263,
     275, 308
Watson, John 23, 31, 35, 39–40, 47, 55, 70,
     87, 131–132, 135, 137, 158, 161, 164,
     184, 194, 209–211, 213–214, 231,
     235–238, 241, 273–274, 301, 304,
     313–314, 320, 355
Webb, John 83, 93
Webber, Mark 358, 361, 365
Weber, Willi 209
Wendlinger, Karl 18–19, 140, 142, 277, 286,
     295, 322, 360, *P6*
West Ham football team
Wickham, John 176, 221
Williams 15, 39, 68, 79–81, 137, 144, 148,
     150, 196–197, 199, 224, 229, 238,
     272, 298–300, 327
Williams, Sir Frank 43, *P11*
Winkelhock, Manfred 184, 280, 313
Wollek, Bob 48
Woods, Tiger 26
Wurz, Alexander 160

Zakowski, Erich 157, 184
Zakspeed 157–158, 184, 206
Zanardi, Sandro 89
Zeltweg 101, 215, 226
Zolder 43
Zonta, Ricardo 201–202, 205–206